The BP book of
Festivals
and events
in Britain

Made in Great Britain at the
Aldine Press Letchworth Herts for
J. M. DENT AND SONS LIMITED
Aldine House Bedford Street London
A Phoenix House publication
First published in this edition 1966
Designed by George Ayers

Colour Plates

* Colour sketches used in endpaper design

Acknowledgments

The author gratefully acknowledges his indebtedness to all who have helped with information, the loan of books and old programmes, or by providing photographs for reproduction, many from their private albums, and in particular to the following

Charles Abdy, Hon. Secretary,
Southern Cathedrals Festival, Salisbury.
Alison E. Adair,
Publicity Director, Festival '65.
Jack C. Adams, A.I.I.P., A.R.P.S.,
Photographer of Hythe Venetian Fête.
P. H. Bartlett, L.A.M.T.P.I.,
Town Clerk, City of Rochester.
Leslie Beak,
Entertainments Manager, Broadstairs.
J. A. Berry, Town Clerk,
City of Ripon.
Clifford Beswick, F.I.M.E.M., F.R.S.A.,
Manager of Civic and Wulfrun Halls, Wolverhampton.
R. B. Blair,
Northern Ireland Tourist Board.
Miss M. Boyd, Photographic Section,
Bord Fáilte Eireann.
John Boyle, LL.B., Town Clerk,
City of Canterbury.
Mrs G. B. Le Brocq, Secretary,
Jersey Battle of Flowers Association.
Michael Burrell, Administrator,
King's Lynn Festival.
John Cabourn,
Photographic Research Consultant.
Iain C. Cameron, Vice-Chairman and Convenor,
Hertfordshire Highland Games Society.
Roy G. Capel, Photographer,
Broadstairs Dickens Festival.
N. Catchpole, M.A.,
Town Clerk, Colchester.
Albert Cook, Hon. Publicity Chairman,
Stroud Festival Committee.
The Lady Crathorne.
W. G. Davies, Clerk,
Bourton-on-the-Water Parish Council.
Philip Drackett,
Royal Automobile Club.
George Dracup, Hon. Secretary,
Stour Festival of Music and Painting.
The Rev. Ralph E. H. Dudley,
Vicar of Edington.
Mrs A. H. Evans, Secretary,
The Dolmetsch Foundation.
Arthur J. Evans, Clerk,
Llangefni Urban District Council.
David and Virginia Fairweather,
National Theatre.
Peter Fletcher, Director,
St John of Beverley Festival.
F. E. Fright, Hon. Programme Secretary,
Hythe Venetian Fête Society.
H. W. Goodinge, Deputy Director,
British Aerospace Society.
Mrs W. E. M. Gough, Hon. Secretary,
Llandaff Festival.
Mrs M. Hargreaves, Hon. Publicity Secretary,
Lake District Festival Society.
Miss B. E. Gregory, Hon. Secretary,
Tilford Bach Society.
Mrs G. Harrison, Hon. Organizer,
Little Missenden Festival.
Mrs Dagmar Hayes, Steward,
The Friends of Canterbury Cathedral.
S. P. Harrold, Hon. Secretary,
Hexham Abbey Festival.

John Healy, F.C.C.S., Town Clerk,
Berwick-upon-Tweed.
Hans Hess, O.B.E., Artistic Director,
York Festival Society.
W. J. Holman, Hon. Secretary,
Dawlish Arts Festival.
J. Owen Hunt, Clerk,
Matlock Urban District Council.
Allan Wynne Jones and E. T. Lewis,
Wales Tourist and Holidays Association.
L. A. W. Jones,
Publicity Officer, Southend-on-Sea.
Morris Jones, Chairman,
Chwaraedy Garthewin.
Miss E. M. Kelly,
Isle of Man Tourist Board.
R. W. Lavenbein, Chief Librarian, and Miss Sweeney,
British Travel Association Photographic Library.
John A. Lister,
Scottish Tourist Board.
Rupert A. Lockwood, M.I.M.ENT., Administrator,
Bexhill-on-Sea Festival of Music.
J. McGuinness,
Entertainments Officer for Bolton.
L. A. Marcus, A.S.A., formerly Chief Librarian,
Metropolitan Borough of St Pancras.
Roger Milner, Hon. Secretary,
Ludlow Festival Society.
Mrs S. M. Musgrave, Hon. Secretary,
Lake District Festival Society.
J. W. Nunn, A.C.C.S.,
Spa Director, City of Bath.
Major J. O'Neill, Agent,
Blithfield Hall.
Miss Jean Pamley,
Spalding Farmers' Union.
Michael Peto, Photographer,
Richmondshire Festival.
L. G. A. Pinn, J.P., Hon. Secretary,
Swansea Festival of Music and Arts.
N. G. E. Pugsley, Chief Librarian,
City of Exeter.
Michael Rayward,
Buxton Corporation Entertainments Department.
Irish Tourist Board
Miss F. C. Redmond,
Arthur Guinness, Son and Co. (Dublin) Ltd.
A. G. Robinson, Chairman,
Saffron Walden Festival Organization.
Philip Sawyer, Festival Secretary,
Three Choirs Festival, Worcester.
Robin Stayt, Festival Secretary,
Three Choirs Festival, Gloucester.
George Stringer,
Cambridge Festival Association.
Benjamin Summerton, Secretary,
York Minster Diocesan Musical Festival.
G. V. Tansley, Hon. Secretary,
Matlock Bath Venetian Nights Committee.
Alan Thomas, Public Relations Officer,
Caerphilly Urban District Council.
Gordon Tilsley, Town Clerk, City of Norwich,
and Chairman of Triennial Festival Management Committee.
J. A. Weston, LL.B., Town Clerk,
City of Hereford.
G. A. M. Wilkinson, M.B.E.,
Organizer of Cheltenham Festival.
A. Wilson, Hon. Secretary,
Selby Festival.
Clive Wilson, Adminstrator,
Harrogate Festival of Arts and Sciences.
Miss Gladys Waterer, Hon. Secretary,
Broadstairs Branch of Dickens Fellowship.
R. O. F. Wynne, President,
Garthewin Players and Denbighshire Drama Association.

Glass etchings by New Zealander John Hutton, who has also designed glass panels for the Coventry and Guildford Cathedrals.

Stratford

'The Shakespeare Festival' by John Hutton, whose glass etching was photographed with coloured silks draped behind. The effect here was achieved by painting black the unetched areas of glass in the print

The BP book of
Festivals
and events
in Britain

by Christopher Trent

Phoenix House, London

Contents

Foreword

A festival is a great occasion. Christmas and Easter are festivals in the true sense of the term, which derives its meaning from the anniversaries in the religious calendar, the feast days which underline the continuity of important things in people's lives. The Shakespeare Festival at Stratford-on-Avon is equally a festival, the longest festival in the world. It brings together hundreds of thousands of people every year, all fired by enthusiasm for the works of dramatic genius bequeathed by Britain's greatest poet.

There is nothing archaic, nothing self-consciously revivalist in the idea of a festival. It is not even necessarily a celebration of past glories. It can be very, very modern. You can have a festival of contemporary music as appropriately as a festival of Bach or Beethoven. You can have a festival of art or of films as compelling in its own way as a festival of music. The aim is identical – to present the best of some medium of expression for the pleasure of people who express themselves in that medium. The legacy of the past is priceless, but the present has its own ways of creating beauty in music, in the arts and in hundreds of other ways, and this will become the legacy of the future.

This book is catholic in its interpretation of festivals and includes a number of special events which are not strictly speaking festivals. You will find information about the Shakespeare Festival, about Glyndebourne, about the Aldeburgh Festival and the Haslemere Festival. You will be reminded of many fascinating customs and traditions which have been handed down to the present, in a less formal setting. You will read how you can watch the sun rise on midsummer morning at Stonehenge in company with an order which traces its history back two thousand years. You will find how you can join in the May Day celebrations which have been a part of British life for five hundred years and had their origin in far more ancient rites.

Every day in this calendar of festivals is a red-letter day. It has a special place in the community of ideas. It is, in effect, a fragment of social history, a mirror of the British way of life. Over two hundred and fifty festivals and events are included in this book. The number would be doubled if the festivals of chiefly local interest, the annual carnivals, the fairs and the agricultural shows which make a great impact on the countryside, were included.

'Bath Festival' by Julian Trevelyan,
an eminent painter and etcher, and
tutor in the print-making department
of the Royal College of Art

Carnivals are of two kinds. Both kinds are almost always good fun. One variety is the country town carnival in aid of local charities, staged by enormous voluntary effort with a special eye on the entertainment of the children. There is a procession led by the town band, often competitive games in the recreation ground and sometimes a display of fireworks and a torchlight parade to end the day.

The other kind is the 'carnival week' organized by civic authorities (often with the help of voluntary effort) at the seaside resorts. Angling competitions, aquatic sports, special dances and band performances are common features. Sometimes there is a bathing beauty competition or the like, and a carnival parade with decorated floats and amusing or attractive tableaux. Every holiday town aims to provide varied entertainment for its visitors. Carnival week is a time when its efforts are redoubled. If you like a place where something is always happening, carnival time is the time for you to go there.

The Royal Show, which has a different venue each year, is the most important of Britain's agricultural events, with real fascination for everyone who has even a slight interest in farming and the life of the countryside. The show ground is like a small town, with interest in every 'street' and enclosure and especially in the inhabitants of the 'town', animal and human. The Bath and West is the oldest established of the rural shows, but all county or district shows – the Royal Norfolk, the Great Yorkshire, the Royal Lancashire, the Royal Counties and dozens of others – are meeting places for farmers and many others interested in the land from a much wider area than the actual county of the show. Most are held in June or July.

The sources from which the information relating to the festivals and special events described in the following chapters has been derived are many and various. The accounts given of most of the major festivals are from personal experience. I have visited every one of the places mentioned except the Shetland Islands; but I could not have completed this uncommonly rewarding task without the generous help of the many festival organizers, secretaries of festival committees, local government officers and librarians who have put a mass of background material at my disposal – old programmes, books long since out of print, press accounts of festivals past and present, photographs and prints and, in the case of festivals of comparatively recent foundation, personal recollections of the origin and progress of the events.

I am deeply grateful for their help, which is acknowledged in more detail elsewhere. My sincere hope is that readers will find in these pages festivals and special events which arouse their interest whatever their tastes. The regular festival goer is rarely disappointed.

Dancing round the maypole
at Ickwell Bedfordshire

Midland England

1

Midland England is the Anglo-Saxon England of tradition, just as the south-western counties are coloured by the Celtic tradition and the eastern counties by the Scandinavian. Almost entirely rural before the industrial revolution, midland England is still chiefly a land of smiling fields and rich arable land mingled with sheep pastures. Less than two hundred years ago Birmingham was a small village, Lichfield of far greater importance economically. Today, although the greater part of the Black Country lies within it, more than four-fifths of Staffordshire is rural in character, some of it seemingly as remote as any of the lowland counties of England.

All the counties are peculiarly English in appearance. The green-fringed lanes of Warwickshire with their long lines of generous hedgerow timber are typical of the English scenic heritage. Green-fringed lanes, though not always with hedgerow timber, can be found in all these counties. They reflect the late change-over from the traditional English agriculture of the open field system in the eighteenth century, when the Georgian enclosure commissioners redistributed the open fields among individual farmers and cut new straight roads across the fields, their width determined by the need to avoid rutting by heavy farm wagons in winter. Country roads were not surfaced then, and many farming communities had been isolated for months on end when deep mud on the tracks made the passage of vehicles impossible.

So this sweeping change in agricultural method changed the face of the midland counties out of all recognition. But there has been no further change. Hundreds of miles of these commissioners' highways survive, now well surfaced byways which show the country as it really is. Many of the farmhouses are still the same as when the village farmers left their village homes and built farmhouses 'in the fields'.

It is not surprising that this region, which was so retentive of its traditional way of life, should have retained many old customs and ceremonies, and a number of the great fairs which originated in the Middle Ages. The Mop Fairs at Stratford, Warwick and Chipping Norton, St Giles Fair at Oxford, Nottingham's Goose Fair and many others perpetuate the memory of the past. Though they are now fairs for pleasure, in many cases they are held in the same streets and squares that were their venues hundreds of years ago. The crowning of the May Queen at Elstow, the May Day dances round the maypole of Welford-on-Avon, the Horn Dance of Abbots Bromley, the survivals of old customs at Hallaton and Dunstable (all of which are mentioned later) are characteristic. The Sheriff's Ride, the Greenhill Bower and Court of Arraye at Lichfield are medieval in origin. They are still carried out with the enthusiasm for the traditional which is common to the whole area.

The growth of industry round Birmingham and Coventry, and to a lesser extent in all the midland counties, has superimposed a new way of life on the old. This new cultural pattern has brought in its train a modern type of festival with the accent on drama or music. Even here, however, the traditional element is never far away. That is particularly true of the Shakespeare Festival at Stratford-on-Avon, the best known and one of the most important festivals in Britain, perpetuating an interest in the town in which the poet-dramatist was born and died, as well as in his plays. Equally the concerts in the blatantly modern Coventry Cathedral perpetuate the medieval idea of a church as a centre of communal life and culture.

Bedfordshire

ELSTOW – May Day Celebrations

Unspoilt in spite of lying astride a main road, Elstow is a place well worth visiting quite apart from its May Day festivities. It is best known, perhaps, as Bunyan's birth-place, though that great preacher was born a mile away from the village green. He did, however, live in a cottage by the green after his marriage. But the green itself is the most vivid link with Bunyan – the green on which, accord-ing to his own account, he had a vision which 'put him into a maze' while he was playing tip-cat on Sunday afternoon. The sixteenth-century moot hall was the meeting place of the Bunyan Congregation until the present century, while it was in the detached bell-tower of the medieval church that Bunyan practised bell-ringing. In the church itself are the font in which Bunyan was baptized and modern windows celebrating *Pilgrim's Progress* and the Holy War. Here, as at Welford-on-Avon, there is dancing on the green and a May Queen is crowned and there is a colourful procession. These May Day festivities are not necessarily on the first day of the month. Exact dates and further details can be obtained from the British Travel Association.

ICKWELL – May Day Celebrations

Another village in Bedfordshire which has a long history of dancing round the maypole each year, where a colourful ceremony is staged and the May Queen is crowned.

DUNSTABLE – Orange Rolling

This ceremony, the only one of its kind in the south of England, is held on Good Friday, when hundreds of oranges are rolled down Pascombe Pit on the Dunstable Downs by local children. The custom is almost certainly connected with the far better known one of pace egging carried on at Eastertide in several places in the north of England. The rolling of the eggs or oranges is said to recall the rolling away of the stone from the tomb of Jesus Christ.

Leicestershire

HALLATON – Easter Festival

Hallaton, a pleasant village or small town with a magnifi-cent medieval church, has a quaint conical 'cross' on the green, and an old conduit house. It is the scene of a unique Easter custom – the Hare Pie Scramble. The extraordinary nature of this custom, which is certainly very old, always attracts a number of strangers as well as most of Hallaton's population. Two hare pies specially baked for the occasion are cut up in the rectory and then scattered in small pieces among a crowd gathered on Hare Pie Bank. In the scramble which follows it is considered exceptional good luck to capture a piece of the pie.

The scramble is followed by the bottle-kicking. In this case 'bottle' has its ancient significance of cask or barrel. Three casks are involved, two filled with beer. In the kicking game the young men of Hallaton are opposed by the young men of neighbouring Medbourne, and the game is won when one side or the other has kicked two casks across the opponents' goal, the goals in this case being streams nearly a mile apart. There is no real agreement on the origin of these customs, although one account relates the hare of the pie to a symbol of the animal sacrifice which was often made in pagan times about this time of year to propitiate the gods to ensure a good harvest in the coming summer. One doubts whether the lusty people who take part in and thoroughly enjoy this interesting spectacle have any idea of its symbolization.

Northamptonshire

PETERBOROUGH – The Ponies of Britain

This is an annual summer show held at the show ground in Peterborough, on two days late in August. It is one of the most colourful pony shows in the country, and in-cludes a children's riding pony championship and driving competitions. Fifty championship cups are awarded for every class of pony. There is also a gymkhana champion-ship, with dog shows thrown in for good measure. Full details can be obtained from the Secretary, 'Ponies of Britain', Brookside Farm, Ascot, Berkshire.

Nottinghamshire

NOTTINGHAM – The Goose Fair

In history and in the calendar of modern festivals the Goose Fair is to Nottingham what the Mop Fair is to Stratford-on-Avon. And it is in the same month, the first Thursday in October and the two following days, just around the time of Michaelmas, when 'geese are obtained to bleed at Michael's shrine'.

You will not find a single goose at Nottingham Fair in this year of grace, though at one time twenty thousand geese a year were brought to the market place and sold by the gooseherds, who drove them from farms many miles away. Mostly it would seem they came from the Lincoln-shire pastures, because there is a street on the Lincolnshire side of the town still called Goose Gate.

Then the fair lasted three weeks. In 1284 leave was granted by charter to hold a fortnight's fair in addition to the already established week-long Goose Fair. Both were held in the great market place, a noble square of $5\frac{1}{2}$ acres, the largest of its kind in Britain, the selfsame square which was laid out in 1927 as a dignified foreground for the modern Council House.

St Giles Fair at Oxford

Long before that the fair had become a carnival of much pleasure, a gigantic fun fair, but it was still held in the great square. Now it is held on a new site in the Forest recreation ground.

That 'Forest' is another link with tradition, for it is named after (was once on the edge of) the Forest of Sherwood, the happy hunting-ground of the legendary hero Robin Hood, the cheerful outlaw who held court in the woodland thickets and robbed travellers on their way to Nottingham. He took from the rich in order to give to the poor. At least, that is the story.

You will find the statue of Robin Hood outside the walls of Nottingham Castle only a few minutes' walk from the Goose Fair; it is clad in the traditional garments of the Forest and armed with bow and arrow. So real has Robin Hood become to ordinary people that when episodes in his life were shown on the television screen the present Sheriff of Nottingham received threatening letters from viewers!

Oxfordshire

OXFORD – St Giles Fair

One of the oldest and most famous of the midland trade fairs, St Giles Fair, is particularly interesting because, although it has changed its purpose, it continues to be held at or near the place where it has been held since before the Reformation, in Magdalen Street and St Giles. There is a legend that a charter was granted for the fair in the thirteenth century, with the proviso that it should be available to cripples, who were not normally admitted inside the city walls. Certainly the place selected for it is just outside the old town walls of Oxford in the manor of Walton, and St Giles is the patron saint of cripples. When the need for such a fair no longer existed, it continued as an important trade fair comparable in relation to Oxford with St Bartholomew's in relation to the City of London.

Like all the other great medieval fairs, however, it ceased to exist as a genuine trade fair when trade was modernized and shops and offices took the place of markets and fairs.

It is held early in September. Visiting it gives an opportunity to see Oxford when the university is 'down' and the medieval college buildings can be seen by visitors more easily than during term. It is an intriguing thought that St Giles Fair symbolizes the centuries-long struggle between Town and Gown which began when the university was granted immunity from lay jurisdiction by the papal legate, provoking immediate riots and rivalry which persisted until the Reformation. Even now, when Oxford has become industrialized, one can sense something of the age-old rivalry.

May Morning at Magdalen College

From time immemorial choristers have sung on May Day from the tower of Magdalen College to greet the sunrise.

There have been a few breaks in the tradition, but it is now as firmly entrenched as ever. The choirboys sing the May song, a Latin hymn *Te deum patrem colimus*. Immediately the singing is over the fine peal of college bells rings out in joyful welcome to the summer.

HENLEY – The Royal Regatta

Henley is a riverside town near the point where Oxfordshire, Buckinghamshire and Berkshire meet. It is a picturesque place retaining a number of half-timbered houses, a fine medieval parish church by the bridge, and several coaching inns which are a reminder of one of Henley's most notable periods of prosperity, when it was on the road generally used by coaches from London to Oxford. The river is spanned by a bridge built in 1786, a singularly graceful structure typical of the latter part of the eighteenth century.

The regatta, which has done much to establish Henley's modern fame, takes place on a course a little below the bridge – a broad straight reach more than a mile in length lined by poplars and extending as far as the mock temple on Regatta Island, with the wooded Chiltern Hills forming the backcloth of the scene, as attractive a setting for a river event as any in England.

Despite its twentieth-century reputation as England's premier river event, Henley Regatta is of comparatively recent origin. The first important race on the regatta course of which there are records was the University Boat Race, transferred there in 1829. An annual regatta was founded in 1839, when the Grand Challenge Cup for eight oars was offered for the first time and won by First Trinity, Cambridge. Today the Grand Challenge Cup is still one of the most coveted trophies for eights, while the Diamond Sculls has become an event of equal importance.

Henley had little real significance until 1851, when the Prince Consort gave it his patronage and the title Royal. Like Royal Ascot and a number of other sporting events, it has become one of the festivals of the London Season, immensely popular with many who have no practical interest in rowing. The houseboats, which only thirty years ago brought an added splash of colour to the scene, and incidentally were so numerous that with the vast number of other craft it was often difficult to clear the course, are no more, but there are still hundreds of craft on the river above and below the course, and thousands of spectators cheering their favourite crews from the bank. The regatta is held for four days at the beginning of July from Wednesday to Saturday. Further details may be obtained from the Secretary, Henley Royal Regatta, Secretary's Office, Henley-on-Thames, Oxfordshire.

The choir of Magdalen College Chapel singing the May Hymn on the summit of the tower, and May morning at Magdalen Bridge, Oxford

Eights approaching the finishing point at Henley Regatta

Staffordshire

LICHFIELD

This cathedral city, its many ancient houses and narrow streets dominated by the three spires of the cathedral (traditionally known as the Ladies of the Vale), is associated with several survivals of ancient pageantry. The two most interesting of these, which give thousands of visitors a chance to see the city and visit Dr Johnson's birthplace and the Johnson Museum, as well as the cathedral, are the Greenhill Bower and the Sheriff's Ride.

The Greenhill Bower

This is a most curious but genuine survival of the ancient Court of Arraye, which probably dates from the twelfth century when the city was growing around the rebuilt Norman cathedral, completed in 1150 (nothing survives of this Norman building). It is probable that in return for trading privileges the people of the growing town were required by the Crown to provide a stated weight of armour. Once every year the citizens carried the armour to the Court of Arraye for inspection and approval. The armour was to be used in the defence of the cathedral walls. The survival of this custom takes place on Whit Monday, when a number of the citizens parade in coats of mail, many of them ancient. This traditional ceremony has become part and parcel of what was originally a quite separate observance, the Greenhill Bower, a pleasure fair which also has a medieval origin.

The Sheriff's Ride

This old custom arises from a royal charter granted in 1553, one condition of which was that the sheriff should re-define the boundaries of the city once every year on the Feast of the Nativity of the Virgin Mary, 8th September. Lichfield is proud that this obligation placed on the sheriff by royal charter more than four hundred years ago has been carried out with few, if any, breaks. The ceremony is not now necessarily on the Feast of the Virgin Mary, but usually on the Saturday nearest to 8th September. The event is advertised in the local press and details can be obtained from the sheriff at the guildhall. Essentially it consists of the sheriff and a number of others on horseback riding round the boundaries of Lichfield, which extend for almost twenty-four miles. When the ride has been completed there is a formal parade through the streets with the city sword-bearer and mace-bearer escorting the sheriff to the guildhall.

ABBOTS BROMLEY – The Horn Dance

A dance pageant of very great antiquity, the Abbots Bromley Horn Dance is one which is also most interesting to watch, as many thousands of visitors to the Commonwealth Dance Gala in 1965 realized. There are twelve dancers, six of whom carry the horns of reindeer fixed in wooden heads. The six wear a traditional costume which is clearly of Tudor origin. Of the other six one is dressed as Robin Hood and rides a hobby-horse, another as Maid Marian. One is a boy with a crossbow and arrow, one represents a medieval entertainer, two others are musicians, traditionally 'armed' with concertina and triangle.

The Horn Dance has been formalized, but the horns are the same as those which have been used for hundreds of years, and the accompaniment is provided by the same kind of instruments as the traditional ones, assisted by the scraping of the arrow upon the bow and the clicking of the wooden jaw of the hobby-horse.

At one time the Horn Dance Festival was celebrated at Christmas, New Year and Twelfth Day, but now takes place only on the Monday following the first Sunday after 4th September (5th September in 1966). Performances are given at frequent intervals throughout the day, some in farmhouses and nearby mansions, and a special one on the village green. The two most interesting things about the Abbots Bromley Horn Dance are that the horns were kept for hundreds of years in the village church (Abbots Bromley was formerly a large and prosperous market town) and that they are undeniably of reindeer. The reindeer is known for certain to have been extinct in Britain before the Norman Conquest. One might think plausibly that the horns had been imported, but the suggestion carries far less weight when one bears in mind that there are written records of the dance, specially mentioning reindeer horns, in the seventeenth century; in fact the dance has scarcely altered at all since Plot wrote an account of it in 1680. Abbots Bromley is in the centre of what was medieval hunting country, Needwood Forest, where reindeer as well as wild boar and other animals would have roamed. It is likely that these horns date back to this time, that is, to the Anglo-Saxon period. In that case the dance originated as a symbol of the rights of the people of Abbots Bromley to hunt deer in Needwood Forest. According to

one account, the first performance of the dance in its present form was during the reign of Henry III, to commemorate the restitution of the people's rights in the forest and the reversal of the policy of the early Norman kings of depriving the Saxons of these rights.

WOLVERHAMPTON – The Music Festival
This competitive festival of music and dancing is held for ten days in the second half of June (15th–25th June in 1966, the twenty-third festival), in the Wulfrun and Civic halls. There are sessions every evening and on several mornings and afternoons. The main events are concerned with ballet, stage and folk dancing, pianoforte, strings, recorders, voice and organ. There are also verse-speaking events. In all classes there are competitions for age groups between under nine years and eighteen years. Further details may be obtained from the Festival Secretary, Civic Hall, Wolverhampton, Staffordshire.

BLITHFIELD HALL – Shakespeare Festival
This magnificent Elizabethan house near Rugeley, with Georgian and Regency additions, famous also for its landscape garden and orangery, is the scene of a Shakespeare Festival held for three days towards the end of July (28th–30th July in 1966). One of the plays (*The Merchant of Venice* in 1966) is performed in the inner courtyard. The beautiful setting of the performance and the opportunity to see parts of the house and the gardens, which are also

The Abbots Bromley Horn Dancers at Blithfield Hall

Floral tributes carried in procession to Holy Trinity Church during the Shakespeare Birthday Celebrations

occasionally open to the public at other times, make a visit to the Shakespeare Festival a specially memorable event.

Blithfield Hall is also one of the mansions at which, by tradition, the Abbots Bromley Horn Dancers carry out their ritual on the front lawn on the Monday of the Horn Dance Festival (5th September in 1966).

Warwickshire

STRATFORD-ON-AVON – Shakespeare Festival
This is centred on the Royal Shakespeare Theatre and is the longest festival in the world, lasting from April to December, and presenting a selection of Shakespeare's plays each year performed by a rota of the finest actors in the country. In nearly eighty seasons performances have ranged over the whole canvas of Shakespeare's dramatic works, including *Pericles*, which does not appear in the First Folio.

The eighteenth-century actor-manager David Garrick established a short-lived festival of Shakespeare's plays, but the first festival in its present form at Stratford, where the poet-dramatist was born on 23rd April 1564 and died the same day in 1616, was inspired by Charles Flower in 1864. His dream came true, and a Flower is still chairman of the Festival Theatre – Sir Fordham Flower, O.B.E., D.L.

The first memorial theatre was opened in 1879. Contemporary drawings show it to have been a far from beautiful building in a bizarre Victorian style of Gothic,

so unlovely that when it was destroyed by fire in 1926 few regretted its disappearance. George Bernard Shaw characteristically sent a telegram of congratulation to the governors. While funds were raised to build a new and finer theatre the festival went on, against all probability, in the auditorium of a local cinema.

When the new theatre was opened on Shakespeare's birthday in 1932 there was great rejoicing, marred slightly by the comments of some observers that it was hard to distinguish its design from that of a factory. But taste has changed; today it is regarded if not as a thing of beauty, at least as an institution hallowed in those few years since it was opened and takes an honoured place in Stratford's river landscape.

Birthday Celebrations
Although the Shakespeare Festival goes on for more than half the year, the poet's birthday is a special day of pageantry. On the morning of 23rd April you can hear the bells of Holy Trinity Church, where Shakespeare was baptized and buried, ring out a long paean of thanksgiving, the sound drowning the everyday noises of the streets and flowing along the waterway of the Avon past the theatre, a clarion call for a memorable day heard by people as they cross the ancient Clopton Bridge.

Then there is a public birthday luncheon organized by the Shakespeare Club and held in the conference hall. In

Anne Hathaway's cottage at Shottery, not far from Stratford

Shakespeare's Birthday Trust

Attending one of the performances of the Shakespeare Festival provides an opportunity to visit five other links with the poet, which are administered as a memorial by the trustees and guardians of Shakespeare's birthplace. The first is the birthplace in Henley Street, a lovely half-timbered house beautifully restored and retaining a great deal of Elizabethan timbering. Then there is Hall's Croft in Old Town, a Tudor house with a walled garden where Shakespeare's daughter Susanna and Dr John Hall lived. Apart from its associations, you will find a visit well worth while for the period furniture, which makes the house look very much as it must have done at the end of the sixteenth century.

Outside the town, but within easy reach, you can visit Anne Hathaway's cottage at Shottery, one mile, and Mary Arden's house at Wilmcote, three miles distant. The former, the early home of Shakespeare's wife and the scene of his courtship, is a spacious farmhouse which remained in the Hathaway family until near the end of the nineteenth century, when it was purchased by the Shakespeare Birthday Trust. Inside you will find some furnishings which formed part of the Hathaway home. Mary Arden's house, in which Shakespeare's mother lived, came into the possession of the Trust even more recently, in 1930. It is a really magnificent half-timbered farmhouse of the Tudor period, with a farming museum in the barns, a historic place in its own right.

Finally, there is New Place in Chapel Street. Only the foundations of Shakespeare's last home are preserved in a garden setting adjacent to the house of Thomas Nash, who

the afternoon the whole of Stratford goes gay and some streets are closed to traffic, so great is the throng of people who come in honour of the bard and witness the moving ceremony of the flags. At a signal the flags of the nations are unfurled from the tall standards planted down Bridge Street; a band heads a mighty procession of townspeople and visitors led by the mayor from Shakespeare's birthplace in Henley Street to place floral tributes on his grave in Holy Trinity. It is indeed a festive day; you will be amazed at the number of Stratford people who take part in honouring its most distinguished son.

Mary Arden's house, Wilmcote

Exhibition of country dancing at the Shakespeare Birthday Celebrations

married the poet's grand-daughter Elizabeth Hall. Nash's house is maintained as a museum of local history and Shakespearian relics. The knot garden is one of the finest of its kind in the country.

There is still doubt about the early history of New Place. It was most probably a residence of the Clopton family, whose name is remembered in Clopton Bridge, and dates from the fifteenth century. The one thing certain is that Shakespeare bought it in 1596 for less than £100 and retired to it, restoring on a more modest scale a house which had once been a magnificent mansion but had been sadly neglected and had fallen into decay. When the poet died in 1616 he was still resident there, and left the house and grounds to his daughter, who in turn left it to her daughter, Lady Barnard. But this grand-daughter of Shakespeare had been bequeathed the larger Nash's house by her first husband, and New Place once more became the property of the Clopton family. New Place as restored by Shakespeare was demolished and a new house built on its site, but this too was pulled down in the eighteenth century. That is why the site (which was purchased by the Birthday Trust in 1861) is only a garden surrounding the foundations of the old house. Shakespeare planted a mulberry tree in the garden of his home. There is still a mulberry tree in New Place garden, a lineal descendant of Shakespeare's planting. A well-founded tradition is that Shakespeare wrote *The Tempest* in the knot garden, which must certainly have been in existence in his time.

These five places have differing times of admission. All are open between April and October on weekdays from 9 a.m. to 6 p.m. and on Sundays from 2 p.m. to 6 p.m. Shakespeare's birthplace and Anne Hathaway's cottage are sometimes open until 7 p.m. and are open on Sundays

from 10 a.m. Between November and March the hours are shorter, generally between 9 a.m. and 12.45 p.m. and between 2 p.m. and 4 p.m. On Sundays only Shakespeare's birthplace is open, from 2 p.m. to 4 p.m.

As Levi Fox has said, 'Shakespeare belongs to the world now. And the world has responded marvellously to his four hundredth birthday. The Shakespeare Centre, the permanent memorial, can be called a birthday present from the world. Gifts come in daily. The spirit here is terribly exciting. All the art and decoration produced is modern – alive and very much a part of today.'

The Mop Fair

The life of Stratford revolves around the Shakespeare Festival, but quite apart from Shakespeare it is a festival town. At the beginning of May it stages elaborate May Day revels culminating in the crowning of the May Queen. The crowning of the Flower Queen at the annual summer flower show is another memorable occasion. But the Mop Fair takes pride of place in the list of annual events.

The 'Mop' is a survival from the Middle Ages, but has changed its character completely. It started in the reign of Edward III, when a law was passed in an effort to remedy the acute shortage of labour that all fit men should offer themselves at the nearest fair for service at a fixed wage. These were called Statute Fairs in some places and Mops in others.

In time the Stratford Mop, like all the other Mop Fairs, became an occasion for hiring house-servants by the year. It was only in the last century that the accent changed finally from the business of hiring servants to the equally absorbing business of making merry. Today the 12th October Mop Fair survives wholly as a festive occasion, though many of its old traditions are maintained, including exhibitions of country dancing. Ox-roasting too is traditional. Visitors – and there are thousands of them – are hungry people, but their mouths water in vain for the eight whole oxen and the eight pigs which used to be roasted on spits outside the principal inns. But there is plenty to eat from the stalls which line the main streets, from candy floss to jellied eels. You will also see the mayor in his robes and chain of office, preceded by the mace bearers and the town crier, leading the procession through the streets.

WARWICK – The Mop Fair

This is another medieval fair which is still held at or near its original venue – in this case by the market place. It served precisely the same purpose as Stratford's Mop Fair, first as a means of correcting the shortage of labour and enforcing fixed wages in the Middle Ages, then as a convenient place at which to hire servants by the year. It too became a pleasure fair in the nineteenth century, and recently it has been held on 12th October, its traditional date, and the two Saturdays following.

A special feature of interest is that Warwick still looks every inch a medieval town. However different the purpose of the fair today, its setting has not changed much in hundreds of years – and that in spite of a disastrous fire in 1694 which destroyed more than two hundred houses. The West Gate is wonderfully impressive, its lower stage dating from the twelfth century, its upper stage from the sixteenth. The East Gate with the fifteenth-century Chapel of St Peter above it (a medieval chapel also surmounts the West Gate) is picturesque as well as historic, the chapel of the 'brethren' of Lord Leycester's Hospital, than which there are few medieval buildings in the country less altered or more complete. Warwick town grew up quite independently of the castle and was incorporated by King Henry VIII, but the mighty castle on a cliff above the River Avon is an integral part of Warwick's beauty and deserves Sir Walter Scott's description of it as the 'fairest monument of ancient splendour uninjured by time'.

A Mop Fair also takes place in Chipping Norton, Oxfordshire. 'Runaway' Mop Fairs are held in Stratford and Warwick about a week after the Mop Fairs. According to tradition, these 'runaway' fairs owe their existence to the growing social conscience in the Middle Ages – to give servants and labourers who were unhappy in their new homes a 'second chance'.

COVENTRY – The Festival of Music

Several successful festivals have been held in this ancient city, which suffered so disastrously from incendiary bombs

Morris dancers near Shakespeare's statue in Bancroft Gardens

during the Second World War but has been rebuilt and is now one of the finest modern cities of England. The festivals are usually held in October, with orchestral concerts taking place at the Coventry Theatre and at least one concert in the Belgrade Theatre, one of the outstanding modern theatres of Europe. The scope of the festival is a wide one, aiming to bring orchestras and soloists of international fame to this historic city. The festival events are augmented by concerts given in the new cathedral, the controversial but highly successful and memorable building by Basil Spence, whose design was chosen in open competition and incorporates the ruins of the medieval parish church which later became Coventry Cathedral. These cathedral concerts are presented at intervals throughout the year, not only at the time of the festival. Details of programmes can be obtained from the Coventry Festival Society, Council House, Coventry.

In addition to the festival of music and the cathedral performances there is a carol service every Christmas Eve at which one of the songs sung is the 'Coventry Carol', adapted from one of the Coventry mystery plays. The latter are medieval miracle plays, one of the few collections of this kind in England. The performance of these plays, ten in number, was entrusted to a dozen of the city craft guilds in the later Middle Ages. Two of the plays, the only two which are intact, were revived in 1951, when they were performed in the ruins of the cathedral. Regular dates for performances have not been published since then, but details can be obtained, as of the music festival, from the Council House.

BIRMINGHAM – The Spring Festival

The Birmingham Spring Festival, which is held in Cannon Hill Park in the last fortnight of April, originated as a tulip festival in the spring of 1960 to celebrate the fourth centenary of the introduction of the tulip to Europe. Imaginatively, the tulip festival was also conceived as an opportunity for a festival of entertainment, primarily for the people of Birmingham and surrounding districts. The event was a success and has increased in scope and importance each year. It was supported from its outset by the Netherlands Government, who were invited to take part because of the special associations of Holland with the tulip. In more recent years contributions to the tulip festival have come from Italy and Sweden as well as from Holland, so that the Spring Festival is a truly international flower festival.

To coincide with the festival of flowers an exhibition of contemporary sculpture is usually staged in the park, and there are daily entertainments on the open-air stage and in the sports arena. In 1965 these included performances by the band of the Staffordshire Regiment and a Dutch band, folk dancing, exhibitions of professional wrestling, dance competitions, variety entertainments and concerts by such well-known pop stars as Marianne Faithfull. A beauty contest, a veteran car rally and firework displays are other regular attractions which bring many thousands of people to this lovely park, which was presented to the city in 1873 and covers an area of eighty acres, much of which is always given over to flower beds.

The Birmingham Tattoo

The first Birmingham Tattoo was held in 1962 in Handsworth Park. It is usually held in the second week of September for three days, with an evening performance on the Thursday and Friday and two performances on the Saturday. The tattoo is preceded by a half-hour concert by a military band. This is followed by a conventional tattoo programme, including gymnastic and motor-cycling displays, and special field displays by units of the Army, Navy and Air Force, together with music by massed bands. There is accommodation for seven thousand people under cover.

City of Birmingham Show

The first City of Birmingham Show was held in Handsworth Park in 1882. It was a flower show organized by the local horticultural society. Now the show is organized by a civic committee and sections are included for dogs, horses, rabbits, bees and caged birds. Covered stands have been built on four sides of the grand ring, in which there are floodlit show jumping competitions and military band displays. In recent years the number of entries in all classes exceeded fifteen thousand, including more than five hundred, the maximum that can be accepted, for the equestrian section. The show is normally held on the first Friday and Saturday in September. Further details of all the Birmingham events can be obtained from the General Manager, City of Birmingham Parks Department, Baskerville House, Civic Centre, Birmingham.

WELFORD-ON-AVON – May Day Revels

Dancing round the maypole originated as a Celtic festivity, but once Anglo-Saxon England was settled it became popular in every district, and was one of the few customs borrowed by the midlands from the far west. At one time maypoles stood on every village green, and May Day (heralding the approach of summer) was one of the great feast days in the rural calendar, celebrated by day-long dancing in which every young person—and many older ones too—took part, culminating in a feast at which everyone ate and drank as much as they could and often more than was good for them.

In the sixteenth century after the Reformation age-old restraints were forgotten and the May Day celebrations undoubtedly in some places could be described as 'riotous meetings' if not as 'orgies', which is how the Puritans of the Commonwealth referred to them. Perhaps the greatest impact which the Commonwealth had on English life was the throwing down of the maypoles. Not one was left. But after the Restoration, when old customs began to reassert themselves, they were raised again here and there, though the May Day celebrations never achieved quite the spontaneity nor the wildness which they had in the 'Merrie England' of Elizabethan and early Stuart times. Quite a number of maypoles survive in many parts of the country, and May Day is celebrated in the traditional way, often with exhibitions of morris dancing, the old folk dance which was introduced into England in the fourteenth century and is probably of Moorish origin. The true Celtic maypole was a live tree and the wooden posts which did service for the tree are a much later innovation.

Welford-on-Avon is one of the places at which the May Day dancing exhibitions take place, and the day is one of the best in the year on which to visit this attractive village, one of the most charming in the whole of the Avon valley, with its numerous half-timbered cottages and houses grouped about the ancient church. A gaily striped maypole on the green is the last in a long line of maypoles which have stood on this spot for at least the last two hundred years, and possibly since immediately after the Restoration.

Festival of the City of London.
'The Yeomen of the Guard'
at the Tower

London

2

In a sense there is a permanent Festival of the Arts in London – provided by the still numerous theatres, concerts in the South Bank's Festival Hall, the Albert Hall and numerous smaller concert halls, the newly fledged National Theatre with its headquarters at the Old Vic, performances by the Royal Shakespeare Company, and the Royal Ballet and Opera at Covent Garden. The many and varied art exhibitions complete the ingredients of the typical international Festival of Music and the Arts. The events which are described in the following pages are festivals in a very special sense of the term, events which highlight a particular facet of life in the capital or re-create the colour and pageantry of long ago.

City of London Festival

It was perhaps inevitable that sooner or later the City of London with its rich historic background should have its own festival. The festival of the City of London, of which Ian Hunter was the originator and the first artistic director, was founded in 1963. It was conceived, in Ian Hunter's own words, 'to show the beautiful and historic buildings of the "square mile" as a superb setting for the finest performances of music, opera and theatre, presented on a scale specially suited to the buildings'.

The Lord Mayor and Corporation of the City of London have been traditionally patrons of the arts (except when the Puritans drove the City's theatre into the Clink Liberty across the river in the sixteenth and seventeenth centuries). They have shown a positive and increasing interest in this festival, even though some of its events are centred on the Tower, which is, as it was when it was built in Norman times, outside the jurisdiction of the City. A spectacular outdoor production of *The Yeomen of the Guard* presented at the Tower was an important feature of the first festival and one repeated in the following years.

Concerts are given in many of the City's most famous buildings. The New Philharmonia Orchestra and Chorus presenting Verdi's *Requiem* in St Paul's Cathedral, the English Opera Group in Benjamin Britten's *Fiery Furnace* at Southwark Cathedral, the Schütz Chorale with Peter Pears rendering Schütz' *Resurrection Story* in St Stephen's, Walbrook, the City of London Choir and Orchestra in Stravinsky's *Mass* and Britten's *Serenade for Tenor, Horn and Strings* in St Sepulchre's, Holborn, and the London Bach Society rendering works by Britten, Bruckner and Stravinsky in St Andrew's, Holborn, are typical of the exciting musical programmes which are confidently expected of London's own festival.

Concerts are also staged at Guildhall, where Yehudi Menuhin and the Bath Festival Orchestra have made memorable appearances. Recitals in some of the halls of the City Companies, including the Fishmongers', the Goldsmiths', the Carpenters', the Clothworkers', the Apothecaries' and the Skinners', have given immense pleasure to thousands who continue to find these historic and architecturally significant halls ideal settings for recitals

Lime Street Fair, a feature of the first City of London Festival

by soloists or small ensembles. 'Restoration dances' at the Mansion House provide scenes of gaiety in the true spirit of festival. In the first years of the festival there was open-air dancing in the streets of the City, firework displays, a regatta, the roasting of an ox for a City feast and many other original features. The festival is presented for two weeks in mid July (11th – 23rd July in 1966).

St Pancras Arts Festival

The first festival designed to give Londoners the opportunity to hear music rarely performed even in London was

Military band playing on a float in the Thames during fireworks and, below, London Festival Regatta

held in 1955. Since then the St Pancras Festival has been an annual event. It still specializes in unfamiliar musical fare. Other features have been added – art exhibitions, poetry readings, opera and drama – but the accent remains on music. Performances are given in St Pancras Church, in St Pancras Town Hall, and the Friends' House in Euston Road, in the Camden School, and in other halls. There are concerts every evening throughout the four weeks of the festival and on some afternoons too (mostly about lunch time).

Highlights of recent festivals have been provided by the first performance in London of Paul Hindemith's *Chamber Music No. 4*, Opus 36, No. 3, by the English Chamber Orchestra; a guitar recital by John Williams, including works by Villa-Lobos and Giuliani; the first authentic revival of Debussy's *Pelléas et Mélisande*; some of the lesser-known works of Bach rendered by the London Bach Society; a Group Eight production of Phyllis Tate's *The Lodger*, with the New Opera Company Chorus and the English Chamber Orchestra; an organ recital by Barry Rose, the organist of Guildford Cathedral, with the Guildford Cathedral choristers; a concert by the new Philharmonia Orchestra, which included the first performance of Horovitz's Trumpet Concerto; and the Handel Opera Society Chorus's rendering of Rossini's *Il Turco in Italia*. Those items give some idea of the scope of the musical programmes, though far from doing justice to the great number of first performances in Britain and of works very rarely heard, which have given St Pancras such an important place in the festival calendar. There is usually also a concert of contemporary jazz and an exhibition of the work of amateur and professional artists living or working in St Pancras. Typical of the dramatic offerings was the performance in 1965 at the Hampstead Theatre Club of Euripides' *Hippolytus* in a new translation by Kenneth Cavander. Further details may be obtained from the Librarian, St Pancras Town Hall, Euston Road, London, N.W.1.

Commonwealth Arts Festival

The first Commonwealth Arts Festival was held in 1965 from 16th September to 2nd October in London, and simultaneously in Cardiff, Glasgow and Liverpool. There is every expectation that it will be staged as a triennial event, although probably different Commonwealth countries will be the hosts at subsequent festivals. In many ways it was the most important festival of the arts ever staged in Great Britain, certainly the most electrifying of all cultural links between the many countries of the Commonwealth. In all nearly fourteen thousand performers appeared from twenty-three Commonwealth countries and Colonial Dependencies.

The idea for the festival was conceived in 1956. It was

Commonwealth Arts Festival. Rehearsal for opening
concert and finale of Sierra Leone dance routine

the brain-child of Ian Hunter, now also known as the
organizer of the Bath and City of London festivals.
Between 1956 and 1962 he made various journeys to
Commonwealth countries to investigate the possibilities.
With financial backing from the London County Council
promised in 1962, he was ready to make definite plans for
this grandiose adventure. Later he received promises of
direct financial support from the Government, which was
later confirmed and increased by the Government in 1964.
There was a danger that a convention of performers from
so many countries speaking many tongues might become,
as Hunter said, merely a parade of national cultural events.
'I decided that the theme of the festival should centre on
contrast, contrast of artistic expression, of the various cultures contained in the Commonwealth, stressing the different ways in which different people express through the
arts the same basic emotions or ideas.'

The festival was presented by the Commonwealth Arts
Festival Society, with the Duke of Edinburgh as chairman

of the advisory council, Ian Hunter, director general and
Anthony Besch, artistic administrator. To make the project
possible Hunter undertook a 50,000-mile journey to every
part of the Commonwealth. In almost every case he had
assistance at Government level and fitted the innumerable pieces of the jigsaw together to make the inspiring
picture of contrast which he had conceived.

The Duke of Edinburgh spoke at the opening lunch
given in the Banqueting House and commented on the
enthusiasm for art which transcended the baser human
emotions, describing the festival as a great adventure and
wishing it every possible success. The word 'arts' was
interpreted as meaning every means of personal and communal self-expression, the spoken word and drama as well
as visual art and films, dancing and music in all their forms.
The Festival Hall on London's South Bank and the Royal
Albert Hall were the principal centres for performances,
but several theatres and halls were also pressed into service.

Concerts were given by the Sydney Symphony Orchestra
and the Toronto Symphony Orchestra, as well as by leading English orchestras, and groups of musicians from
several of the less developed Commonwealth countries
such as Ghana. Players from India and Pakistan illustrated
the vastly different musical traditions of Asia compared
with those of Europe. English opera was supplemented by
the extremely characteristic Nigerian folk opera. The most
successful and in many ways the most brilliantly conceived
part of the festival was, however, in the sphere of the
dance. The Australian Ballet and the Royal Winnipeg
Ballet were interesting foils for the wholly English tradition of the Royal Opera of Covent Garden. The Feux-
Follets of Canada and the Kathakali dancers from India
provided the necessary contrasts. An entirely different
phase of dancing (but not necessarily less sophisticated)
was provided by the Jamaican National Dance Theatre.

The most astounding performance, however, was that
of a company of three hundred dancers from eight countries who took part in the great dance gala, representing
the most varied and exciting tribal dances from Africa and
folk dances and music from the West Indies and Ceylon,
introduced rather curiously by members of the English
Folk Dance Society performing the Abbots Bromley Horn
Dance and other traditional English country dances.

In the world of the theatre, the Théâtre du Nouveau
Monde presented a comedy by Molière and a musical play
in French at the Old Vic, and the festival was made the
occasion for the world première of a new play at the
Theatre Royal by Wole Soyinka, one of the few African
dramatists who have been published in Great Britain. The
Indian National Theatre and the Eastern Nigerian Theatre
also contributed native drama.

The Queen at
the Trooping the
Colour ceremony

In the visual arts the Royal Academy Exhibition of Treasures from the Commonwealth was a spectacular introduction to the creative work of three continents, ranging from painting and sculpture to pottery and costumes.

The three other national centres which shared in the festival adapted their programmes to suit the artistic appreciation of Wales, Scotland and the north of England respectively. Many of the companies which appeared in London appeared also in all three. The great dance gala, for instance, was as big a success as it was in London's Albert Hall. In Cardiff the Welsh National Opera and the B.B.C. Welsh Orchestra appeared in place of the orchestras better known in London. In Liverpool three concerts were given by the Royal Philharmonic Orchestra; in Glasgow much of the musical fare was provided by Scottish orchestras. Liverpool staged the first Commonwealth military tattoo ever to take place. Glasgow arranged an eve-of-festival carnival and a Highland ball to close the festival. In all three centres the aim was to bring the people of the Commonwealth nearer to the people of Wales, Scotland and the north of England respectively.

Although, as Ian Hunter said on the last day of the festival, there were 'great shining moments and some depressing ones', the overall impression was of a great event well conceived, well carried out and brought to an uncommonly successful conclusion.

The Proms

A concert in which the audience is free to move about in the auditorium is a very old idea. It was adopted by nineteenth-century music halls which mostly had 'promenades'. The promenade concerts, as London knows them today, had their origin in the presentation in 1895 by Robert Newman of a series of concerts in the then recently completed Queen's Hall in Upper Regent Street, for which he engaged a young and promising musician, Henry J. Wood. Mr Wood became Sir Henry Wood in 1911. He conducted a season of concerts every year until his death in 1944. It was a happy inspiration to continue them after his death with the title Henry Wood Promenade Concerts. The Queen's Hall was the permanent home of the promenade concerts until the Second World War, when it was burnt out by incendiary bombs, and the concerts were transferred to the Albert Hall. This allowed many more people to hear the music, though the acoustics were less satisfactory than those of the Queen's Hall. The promenade idea was retained, and the floor of the Albert Hall was reserved for enthusiasts who elected to stand – and 'stand' was the operative word rather than 'promenade' because the audiences at the more popular concerts were so great that there was no room for 'promenading'.

The promenade concert season is now sponsored by the B.B.C. and has become a permanent part of the London musical scene. The last night of the Proms is a very special occasion. Sir Henry Wood set the tradition of performing his *Fantasia on British Sea Songs* at this last concert and inviting the audience to join in singing 'Jerusalem' and accompanying other items with clapping and stamping. It is a tradition which typifies the youthful enthusiasm which inspired the early Proms, and which more than thirty-five years ago the *Musical Times* described as 'customary and astonishing'. The great untrained choir, as Sir Henry called it, makes this event a national institution – 'we reach a climax which only Britons can reach'. The promenade concert season opens in mid July and continues until mid September. Further details can be obtained from the Royal Albert Hall, London.

Pageantry and Ceremonial Events

No city in the world can show the visitor such a wealth of colourful pageantry and ceremonial observances in keeping with a place which has a continuous history extending over two thousand years. The virtual rebuilding of central London in the twentieth century has only served to accent traditional aspects of London life, and to make Londoners from the Queen to the commoner even more determined to retain the age-old pageantry of events which link this modern world with the nation's storied past. Some of these occasions arise from the Sovereign performing ceremonies deep-rooted in the traditions of British life, others have survived in the conservative atmosphere of the City of London, which throughout the Middle Ages was a London quite separate from the Royal London of Westminster. Here

are a few of the most interesting and colourful ceremonies.

Trooping the Colour

The most exciting of all London's royal engagements, Trooping the Colour is held on Horse Guards Parade on the Queen's official birthday. This was celebrated on the second Thursday in June until 1958, when the day was changed to the second Saturday in June in order to avoid dislocation of traffic.

Trooping the Colour was once a daily regimental routine, the display of the regimental colours to the soldiers, but the modern ceremony, which dates from the time of George II, is a personal compliment and salute to the Sovereign. The first known parade was in 1755.

The Queen has a Sovereign's escort when she rides from Buckingham Palace to Horse Guards Parade. There she takes the salute at a march past of the Brigade of Guards and the Household Cavalry to the music of the massed bands of the Household Regiments, but only one colour is trooped, that of each regiment in turn. Finally the Queen returns at the head of the troops to Buckingham Palace.

Changing the Guard

Although in sober fact the security arrangements of London's royal palaces are in the hands of Scotland Yard, the ceremony of changing the military guard outside Buckingham Palace is maintained shortly before eleven o'clock in the morning to the music of a military band. The change-over involves intricate drill and is a colourful spectacle. The guard is also changed at St James's Palace, the official residence

Changing the guard at Horse Guards, Whitehall

'City of London Festival' by Barry Fantoni,
whose pop art view includes the Thames Regatta,
a performance of *The Yeomen of the Guard*, an
illuminated building, wine-tasting in Roman
costume, fireworks, a roast ox for a City
feast, the Thames course in tricolour, some
Beefeaters and the Tower on the City's
Cross of St George

The arrival of the royal procession for the State Opening of Parliament

of the court to which ambassadors are accredited, and at Horse Guards where the eighteenth-century building by William Kent is on the site of the seventeenth-century guard-house of the Palace of Whitehall. When the Sovereign is in residence in Windsor Castle a similar ceremony takes place there.

The State Opening of Parliament

There has been a State Opening of Parliament ever since the Sovereign first summoned a representative assembly to advise him. As the British Constitution developed the Sovereign's Speech to Parliament ceased to express the royal intention, and came to be the vehicle for the Government of the time to announce its legislative programme for the ensuing year. The panoply of the State Opening has, however, scarcely changed and takes place annually at the beginning of each new session early in November. The Queen drives from Buckingham Palace in the Irish State Coach escorted by the Household Cavalry, and the route is lined by the Brigade of Guards in dress uniform. The coach used for this splendid occasion, which rivals coronation processions in its magnificence, is called the Irish State Coach because it was purchased by Queen Victoria at the 1852 Dublin Exhibition.

The Royal Maundy

Observance of the Royal Maundy stems from an incident after the Last Supper, when Christ washed the feet of His disciples, bidding them to follow His example and 'do as I have done to you'. This act, interpreted as an act of humility, is commemorated in several ways in many Christian countries. In Jerusalem, for instance, the patriarch washes the feet of twelve senior clergy in the Church of the Holy Sepulchre on Maundy Thursday. In medieval England the custom was widely observed in the monastic houses and by members of the royal house. In the time of Queen Elizabeth I Maundy Thursday had become a day of elaborate royal ceremonial, including the washing of the feet of poor people, one of each sex for each year of the Queen's age, and the presentation of clothes, food and money. By the eighteenth century a money gift had been substituted for the clothes, and the Royal High Almoner, the Archbishop of York, performed the ceremony of washing the feet in place of the Sovereign.

From the time of Charles II maundy money was specially minted, and still is. When silver was no longer used in the manufacture of the ordinary silver coins, it was decided in 1946 to maintain the sterling standard in maundy money – in the silver penny, 2d, 3d and 4d pieces (all

The Yeomen of the Guard, the Sovereign's personal bodyguard, at the Royal Maundy observance

'silver' in general circulation is made of cupro-nickel). The maundy distribution is now quite substantial, the allowance in lieu of clothing being £2 5s for men and £1 15s for women, the gift in lieu of provisions, etc., £2 10s for men and women alike, in addition to the number of pennies in 1d, 2d, 3d and 4d pieces which make up the number of years in the age of the reigning Sovereign. The maundy money is presented in a white leather purse with red thongs.

The ceremony of washing is no longer carried out, although it has once more become customary for the distribution to be made by the Sovereign when possible, and nosegays are still carried by those taking part as a reminder of the washing ceremony.

King George V was the first Sovereign to distribute the maundy gifts for 247 years. After that it was distributed in 1936 by King Edward VIII, and seven times by King George VI. Queen Elizabeth II has carried out the ceremony in every year of her reign except in 1954 and 1960. The recipients are chosen by the Church authorities in the district in which the distribution is carried out. This was Westminster Abbey from time immemorial, but since 1952 has been the abbey only in alternate years. Churches selected for the distribution in the 'odd' years include St Paul's, Southwark, St Albans, Rochester and Chelmsford Cathedrals and St George's Chapel, Windsor. The Chapel Royal Choir in most distinctive costume and the Queen's Bodyguard of the Yeomen of the Guard play an important part in the ceremony. It is customary for the Sovereign

after the maundy service to walk the length of the choir and make the actual distribution in the nave, an act of humility consistent with the original purpose of the ceremony.

Installation of the Constable of the Tower
This ceremony, held every five years when a new Constable of the Tower is installed, takes place on Tower Green, usually in the first week of October (the next ceremony is due in 1970 unless the office falls vacant). Thousands of Londoners and visitors watched the ceremony on 6th October 1965 when Sir Gerald Templer succeeded Field-Marshal Lord Alexander of Tunis. The incoming Constable marches in procession from Queen's House to Tower Green, where are drawn up detachments of the Brigade of Guards, and the Yeomen Warders in full regalia headed by the Yeoman Gaoler armed with ceremonial axe. The Sovereign's Letters Patent are read, the new Governor is welcomed with full ceremonial, while military bands play traditional and martial airs.

Opening of the Law Courts
It is on the first day of the Michaelmas term following the long vacation (1st October unless this falls on a Saturday or a Sunday) that a special service in Westminster Abbey is attended by the judges of the High Court and other leading members of the Bar to mark the opening of the legal year. (Roman Catholics attend a similar service in Westminster Cathedral.) After the service a procession is formed from the abbey to St Stephen's Hall, where the Lord Chancellor holds a traditional breakfast (in modern times breakfast has become lunch). The procession, which

The Lord Mayor's coach standing at the Law Courts entrance

Remembrance Day at the Cenotaph

is headed by the Lord Chancellor, followed by the Lord Chief Justice and the Master of the Rolls, and the judges in their ceremonial robes of gold and scarlet and ermine, with full-bottomed wigs, makes a most impressive showing.

Lord Mayor's Show

The elaborate procession known as the Lord Mayor's Show, one of the favourite shows of the year for thousands of London children, takes place on the Saturday following 9th November, the day on which the Lord Mayor is installed in office and, until 1949, Mayoring Day all over England (now changed for the English boroughs to 23rd May). The processional way is from Guildhall to the Law Courts, where the new Lord Mayor takes the statutory declaration of office before the Lord Chief Justice and the judges of the Queen's Bench. The procession reaches the Law Courts at midday. The Lord Mayor rides in the official mayoral coach, a magnificent example of eighteenth-century craftsmanship, drawn by six Shire horses; his bodyguard is formed by the Company of Pikemen and Musketeers, and the rest of the procession is formed by detachments of the services and decorated floats which always illustrate a chosen theme – fruit in 1965, when all the major fruit-growing countries took part, including

Australia, Canada, France, New Zealand, South Africa, the United States and the West Indies. On this occasion girls carrying baskets and traders pushing barrows in the procession distributed several tons of fruit to the watching crowds. The return to the City from the Law Courts is by the Victoria Embankment and Queen Victoria Street to the Mansion House, the official residence of the Lord Mayor since 1753.

The Festival of Remembrance

Remembrance Day is the Sunday following 11th November (Armistice Day at the end of the First World War), a remembrance day for the dead of both world wars. The day before, Saturday, is Poppy Day, when the forty million artificial poppies and hundred thousand wreaths made by disabled Servicemen are sold throughout the Commonwealth. The Festival of Remembrance is held in the Royal Albert Hall on the evening of Poppy Day, when more than a million poppy petals, one for every man killed in the armed services since the beginning of the First World War, float down from the ceiling at the close of the festival. The programme, always watched by the Queen, includes a muster of past and present servicemen, a display of drilling and gymnastics, performances by military

'St Pancras Festival' by John Lawrence,
who studied at Hastings and Central Art
Schools, and is an illustrator,
print-maker and teacher

Navy League parade at Nelson's Column on Trafalgar Day. Nelson's famous signal flies from the plinth

bands and by choirs, and community singing. Founded in 1927 by the *Daily Express*, the festival has been organized by the British Legion since 1929.

On Sunday, Remembrance Day itself, a service is held at the Cenotaph in Whitehall, when the two minutes' silence is observed at eleven o'clock. The armed services, the British Legion, and other war-time organizations are represented. This ceremony also is by tradition attended by the Sovereign, who lays a wreath at the Cenotaph.

Honouring King Charles I
The statue of King Charles I by Hubert Le Sueur at the head of Whitehall is one of the finest of London's numerous statues. It has had a stormy history. Completed in 1633, it was removed by the Parliamentarians after the Civil War and sold to a brazier called John Rivit (or Rivett) for scrap. Rivit preserved the statue, which was re-erected after the Restoration on a day of great rejoicing on the site on which three of the regicides had been executed. The custom of decorating the base of the statue with wreaths and other floral tributes dates from 1892. With the exception of the year of Queen Victoria's death, 1901, the statue has been decorated in this way every year since then on 30th January, the date on which King Charles was executed

in 1649 on a scaffold outside the Banqueting House only a hundred yards from the statue. During the Second World War, when the statue was removed for safety, wreaths were still laid on the plinth.

Trafalgar Day Celebrations
The twenty-first day of October is the occasion for tributes to the memory of Lord Nelson, whose statue is on the summit of the Nelson Column in Trafalgar Square. His famous signal just before the battle of 1805 – 'England expects that every man will this day do his duty' – is flown above the plinth of the column when the commemoration of his death takes place, on the Sunday nearest to Trafalgar Day, and a naval parade from the Mall to Trafalgar Square is the prelude to a service and the laying of wreaths at the foot of the column.

At Portsmouth Nelson's flagship, the *Victory*, is dressed overall on Trafalgar Day and the signal is flown by ships in the dockyard.

Swan-upping
Many people must have seen, without recognizing the true nature of the occasion, the start of the annual swan-upping season. Skiffs flying flags and crewed by boatmen in distinctive and contrasting costumes start upriver from the

Swan-upping on
the Thames. The
Vintners' boats left,
the Dyers' right

Flower-decorated
floats at the
Easter Parade,
Battersea Park

Pearly King
and Queen at the
Easter Parade

City, usually on the last Monday in July. The background of this colourful flotilla is that the swan was classified as a royal bird in the Middle Ages, just as the sturgeon was a royal fish. A licence from the Crown was necessary to own one. Later the Vintners' and Dyers' Companies were given the right to keep swans on the Thames between London and Henley, but the licence has never been extended to others. Swan-upping means the placing of distinctive marks on the beaks of cygnets, one nick for the Dyers, two for the Vintners, and none for the other birds, which are still Crown property. Every year this practice is carried out by the Queen's Swan Master, and by the swan wardens of the two companies, who perform their duties in much the same way as in 1363, when swan-upping was first recorded.

Easter Parade

This is an annual festival held in the afternoon of Easter Sunday in Battersea Park. It is one of the most attractive and interesting of London's Eastertide celebrations. The highlight of the afternoon is the presentation of the Easter Princess and a parade in which decorated floats alternate with displays of traditional costume, including always those of the Pearly Kings and Queens. Further information may be obtained from the London Tourist Board, 29–30 St James's Street, London, S.W.1.

Veteran Car Commemorative Run

The veteran car run from London to Brighton commemorates the gallant band of pioneers who drove from Whitehall to Brighton on a singularly wet and inclement day in 1896 to celebrate 'emancipation', i.e. the passing of an Act making it no longer necessary for a car to be preceded by a man on foot. By no means all the horseless carriages which started from Whitehall reached their objective, but the event brought home to a vast public the fact that the motoring age had begun. The commemorative run is held on the first Sunday of November, and the start is from the Serpentine road in Hyde Park. Starting time has varied, but is currently 7.30 a.m. The 'finishing post' is Madeira Drive, Brighton. Both on account of the number of competitors and the number of spectators at the start, along the road and at the finish, the run is reasonably described as the most popular motoring event in the world. The 'old crocks', which are all of pre-1905 vintage, give a far better account of themselves than the horseless carriages of the original run.

The first commemorative run took place in 1927. After a brief period, when it was in the care of a motoring periodical, it has been organized by the Royal Automobile Club. The unceasing search for old motor vehicles which can be made serviceable on the road resulted in a steady

At the start of a Veteran Car Run, Hyde Park   Photo: R.A.C.

increase in the number of cars taking part, until in 1960 a record number of 265 was entered. The following year, in consultation with the police and local authorities, it was decided reluctantly that the number must be limited to 250 vehicles.

Cars assemble at the eastern end of the Serpentine road from 7 a.m. onwards. The start is staggered so that the last car gets away approximately one hour after the first. The route is by Westminster Bridge, Lambeth Town Hall (15 minutes), Streatham Station (22 minutes), Thornton Heath Pond (30 minutes), Croydon (45 minutes), Redhill (70 minutes), Gatwick Roundabout (85 minutes), Handcross (115 minutes), Brighton (170 minutes). These are the minimum times. In practice, near the approach to Brighton up to two hours separates the first car from the last.

There are three ways of seeing the run: by watching the cavalcade pass at a single vantage point, by following the cars down the A 23, or by seeing the start in Hyde Park and driving to Brighton in time to see the finish. The third of these is by far the best way, the second the worst. For those who want to see the start and the finish the R.A.C. signposts alternative routes to Brighton so that spectators can do the journey without being delayed by the crowds on the main road. One is by Leatherhead, Dorking and Horsham, the other by Godstone and East Grinstead.

The Pantomime

Boxing Day, the Feast of St Stephen, the day following Christmas Day, marks the beginning of the pantomime season, which has become a traditional part of Christmastide celebrations, though one far more firmly entrenched

'Leeds Pantomime Festival' by Sarah Quayle,
a child artist who went to the pantomime and
then painted this picture of Goldilocks

The Bank Holiday Fair at Hampstead Heath

in the provinces than in London, where the days when four or five pantomimes at leading theatres were offered are almost forgotten. So deeply rooted in people's affections has pantomime become that it is often overlooked that it is one of the more recent forms of English theatre. The character of Harlequin, around which all early pantomimes centred, was developed in 1717, when a famous actor-manager, John Rich, presented Harlequin and Cinderella, followed by adaptations of other fairy tales and legends with Harlequin as the chief character. The full regalia of pantomime with its principal boy (conventionally always a girl), principal girl, and its harlequinade relegated to a minor part, did not develop until the nineteenth century, during the last decades of which Dan Leno was one of the most honoured actors in pantomime.

More recently the story or fable has become no more than a thread binding together a song, dance and comedy show, increasingly sophisticated and hard to distinguish from the conventional revue or variety entertainment. One recent development of pantomime as a parade on ice has infused new life into an apparently dying tradition.

Fairs, Ancient and Modern

A century and a half ago every London suburb had its annual fair. Earlier still, London fairs such as St Bartholomew's and May Fair were world famous. These trade fairs degenerated into rather dubious entertainments; most of them were suppressed before the end of the nineteenth century. Today, however, the Battersea Festival Gardens keep alive the traditions of 'all the fun of the fair' for Londoners, while the Bank Holiday fairs on Hampstead Heath, the modern counterparts of the medieval fairs of Barnet and Pinner, and the famous though less ancient Mitcham Fair, bravely add their quota of innocuous if rather noisy amusement to London life. Pinner Fair obstinately maintains its traditional place in the main street leading up to the church, precisely where the medieval fair was held.

New Year's Eve

Scotsmen are not alone in celebrating the New Year with verve and high spirits. Vast crowds gather every 31st December round the steps of St Paul's, in Trafalgar Square and in Piccadilly Circus to welcome in the New Year. Scotsmen maintain that these are festivals of exiled Scots, but they are now embraced by tens of thousands of Londoners and visitors. As the clocks chime midnight a moment or two of silence falls on the crowds before they

Welcoming the New Year in Trafalgar Square

Photo: Keystone

join hands and herald in the New Year by the mass singing of Auld Lang Syne. This is one of the most moving ways of seeing the Old Year out and welcoming the New Year.

Royal Academy Summer Show

The summer show of the Royal Academy of Arts springs from the exhibitions of the Society of British Artists, which was founded in 1768 with the encouragement of King George III. It was not until 1886, however, that it was allowed to style itself royal. Until 1870 the exhibitions were held at Somerset House, but since then always in Burlington House, originally the town house of the Earls of Burlington built early in the eighteenth century. The summer exhibition, which is opened to the public in the first week of May and continues until mid August, is of the finest of British paintings submitted for the exhibition and selected by a hanging committee, which includes the President of the Royal Academy, always one of the most eminent of British artists, who is invested with his high office by the Queen, patron of the Royal Academy. Private viewing day, before the exhibition is thrown open to the public, used to be the first social gathering of the London Season. The opening of the summer show is still the first of the artistic events which bring thousands of visitors to London in late spring and early summer.

The Royal Tournament

This combined show of the armed services is an exciting exhibition of skill with musical accompaniment held at Earls Court for a fortnight in the latter part of July. It was founded in aid of service charities in 1880, when a military 'tournament and assault at arms' was held at the Agricultural Hall, Islington. This tournament was confined to the Army. The Navy first took part in 1896. Now it represents all the services, including the Royal Air Force and the Fleet Air Arm, with units from abroad (the pipes and drums of the Brigade of Ghurkas and the band and dancers of the Fiji military forces appeared in one year). The show continues to be in aid of service charities, and in the last twenty years has raised more than half a million pounds.

The bias of the show is on entertainment. Bands play throughout the performance; musical drives are highly popular and now traditional features. For the rest there are jumping competitions, gymnastic and drilling displays, feats of skill, such as manhandling field guns over difficult obstacles, and a recently introduced feature, a display by the police dogs (Alsatians) of the Royal Air Force. Full details may be obtained one month before the opening of the tournament from the Box Office, Earls Court Exhibition Building, London, S.W.5.

Horse of the Year Show

This event at the Empire Pool and Sports Arena, Wembley, takes place for a week in early October. It is the climax of the horse show season, though of comparatively recent foundation, and has become one of the most important international events in the equestrian year. It opens with a gala performance, generally including displays by units of the Household Cavalry, and features a number of jumping championships mostly sponsored by commercial firms, as well as competitions for hunters, Arabs, hacks and ponies. Special features are the grand parade of horses, a tribute to the champion horses of the year, and exhibitions of dressage. Further details and programmes may be obtained from the Box Office, Empire Pool, Wembley.

The Royal International Horse Show

This is one of the most lively and colourful pageants of the London year. It is held for a week in the second half of July at the White City. Show jumping is one of its most exciting features; the King George V Cup for men and the Queen Elizabeth II Cup for ladies are recognized as the most important individual awards in international show jumping. The King George V Cup was presented in 1911 and was first won by a Russian rider, Captain d'Exe. Since then it has been won by many of the most distinguished of the world's show jumpers but has only been won three times running by one man on the same horse – Colonel Llewellyn on Foxhunter, 1951–3. The coaching marathon and the amateur driving marathon are two other important events.

The International Horse Show was founded in 1907 and was held at Olympia until 1939. When it was revived in 1947 it was transferred to the White City so as to give a far larger number of spectators the opportunity to see it. In 1957, its Golden Jubilee year, it became the Royal International Horse Show. Full details may be obtained from the Box Office, White City Stadium, Wood Lane, London, W.2.

The Richmond Royal Horse Show

Recently called the 'Ascot of the show world' by a writer in *Horse and Hound*, the Richmond Royal Horse Show is always an occasion of beauty and social interest. It is a three-day show held in mid June in the lovely setting of the Old Deer Park. Leading riders from many countries compete in the jumping competitions and there are classes for all types, including hacks, hunters, mountain and moorland ponies and heavy draught horses. The coaching marathon and amateur driving competitions are highly popular, as are the parades of hounds and the sheep dog demonstrations. There is ample accommodation in covered grandstands, and car parking is far less of a problem here than at many comparable events. Further details may be obtained from the Secretary's Office, Richmond Royal Horse Show, 42 Shaftesbury Road, Richmond upon Thames.

Cruft's Dog Show

If the Richmond Royal Horse Show is the Ascot of the equestrian world, Cruft's Show is the Ascot of the world of dogs. It is the largest and most visited canine show in

The Royal Tournament at Earls Court, London

Great Britain and possibly in the world. Founded in 1886 by Charles Cruft, who had organized a similar show at the Paris Exhibition of 1878, it was held for some years at the Royal Aquarium, Westminster, and won the patronage of Queen Victoria. In recent years it has taken place at Olympia in early February. Well over ten thousand entries are received each year.

The Chelsea Show

Staged annually by the Royal Horticultural Society, this is the most famous flower show in the world. It is presented during the last week of May. Its central feature is a giant marquee covering about 3½ acres filled with displays of an immense variety of flowers, which include many new and rare varieties and examples of miniature but exquisite landscape gardening presented both by professionals and amateurs. The groups of flowering trees and shrubs, and the rock and formal gardens constructed by leading designers, make an unforgettable landscape. The first summer show of the Royal Horticultural Society was held in 1888 in the Temple Gardens. In 1913 it was transferred to the grounds of the Royal Hospital, Chelsea, the building designed by Sir Christopher Wren as a retirement home for old soldiers. Except for war-time breaks it has been held there ever since. Flower shows before and after the Chelsea Show are also given in the society's hall in Westminster.

Further details may be obtained from the Secretary, Royal Horticultural Society, Vincent Square, London, S.W.1.

International Motor Show

The very first motor show in Britain was organized by the Motor-Car Club at the Imperial Institute in 1896. That is a motor show which most historians have forgotten. It was a most important one, because for the first time it brought home to the many thousands of visitors the comparative safety of the horseless carriage. 'The cars', one report said, 'were brought to a standstill in a manner which secured the confidence of the spectators.' King Edward VII, then Prince of Wales, visited the show. His visit may well have overcome a great deal of the prejudice against motor vehicles, for on the following day nearly two thousand people attended the exhibition, and only a few weeks afterwards the hundreds of Members of Parliament who attended passed a Bill in Parliament allowing motor vehicles to use the roads without being preceded by a man on foot.

Six years later, in July 1902, the Society of Motor Manufacturers and Traders was founded in an effort to overthrow the last of the prejudices against motor-cars. This society is still responsible for the International Motor Show. The first under its auspices was at the Crystal Palace in 1903. The fiftieth show was at Earls Court in October 1965, when the total attendance was 660,257, breaking the previous all-time record of 612,952 in 1953. Further details may be obtained from the Exhibition Manager, Society of Motor Manufacturers and Traders, Forbes House, Halkin Street, London, S.W.1.

The motor show is one of the most popular of all London's shows and exhibitions, but there are scores of other interesting exhibitions during the year, mostly in the autumn and winter, firmly entrenched in the calendar of London events. These are included in the Festival Calendar at the end of this book.

Many of Britain's most important and thrilling sporting events are held in Greater London. Some, farther afield, such as the Henley Royal Regatta, Royal Ascot and the Derby Stakes on Epsom Downs, form part of London's sporting calendar. Though their venue is outside the boundaries of Greater London they are easily accessible and attract most of their visitors from the metropolis. They are described in their appropriate sections. The following is a short selection of some of the greatest annual events held in Greater London's own sporting arenas.

Oxford and Cambridge Rugby Football Match

Dark blue versus light blue is one of the show matches of the Rugby Union season. Originally Oxford played in white and Cambridge in pink. Some fifty thousand enthusiasts pack the famous ground at Twickenham, twenty minutes from Waterloo Station, to see the match which, excluding the war years, has been played annually since 1872.

All England Badminton Championships

Started 1899 with doubles only. Now men's and ladies' singles and doubles, mixed doubles. After various venues, now settled at Empire Pool, Wembley, over four days during the last week in March. Strong international entry.

Tideway Head of the River Race

Putney to Mortlake on the Saturday before the University Boat Race. Founded by the famous oarsman Steve Fairbairn in 1926, this race for amateur eights has had entries of more than 250 boats on several occasions. It is probably the most popular event of its kind in the world.

Oxford and Cambridge Boat Race

Putney to Mortlake on a Saturday at the end of March or beginning of April. First rowed in 1829 at Henley, the University Boat Race has been an annual event except in war-time since 1839 and was transferred to the present course in 1845. The river bank is a fine grandstand near the finish or tickets can be obtained for the launches, most of which start from Westminster Pier and follow the race.

The crowd at
the Motor Show,
Earls Court

Daily Mail
Ideal Home
Exhibition,
Earls Court

A corner of
the *Daily Express*
National
Boat Show at
Earls Court

The University
Boat Race on the
river Thames

Amateur F.A. Cup Final

Started 1893, played at Wembley Stadium since 1949 on a Saturday in the middle of April. Climax to country-wide competition, open to all wholly amateur clubs, belonging or affiliated to the F.A., arranged on knock out basis from preceding September onwards. Bishop Auckland ten times winners.

F.A. Cup Final

Also played at Wembley Stadium on a Saturday in late April or early May. Admission to ticket-holders only. Community singing by a capacity crowd of nearly 100,000 precedes the kick-off.

Oxford and Cambridge University Sports

First Oxford versus Cambridge meeting was in 1864. Now takes place at White City, London, early in May. Comprises about seventeen track and field events, track up to three miles. Results, up to and including 1965: Cambridge 43, Oxford 42.

Rugby League Cup Final

Played at Wembley on a Saturday in early May, usually the week after the F.A. Cup Final. Admission to ticket-holders only.

Stock Exchange Walk

London (Westminster Bridge) to Brighton on the third Saturday in May. First held in 1903, this competitive road walk still attracts a large entry. For several years it took place on May Day, which was a Stock Exchange holiday. It is still confined to competitors who are connected, however remotely, with stockbroking firms. The first man to reach the Aquarium in Brighton is presented with the Stock Exchange Cup, which is held for one year.

World Professional Ice Skating Championship

At Empire Pool, Wembley, one evening only in the third week of May. Speed skating and ice dancing by men and women champions are spectacular features.

Polytechnic Harriers Marathon

From Windsor to Chiswick during the second week in June (11th June in 1966). This is an international event, the leading race of its kind in the world. Held in conjunction with the A.A.A. Championships. The winner is therefore the A.A.A. champion.

All England Lawn Tennis Championships.

Wimbledon during the last fortnight in June. This is the premier amateur tournament in the world, and attracts entrants from every leading lawn tennis playing country. The winners of the men's and women's singles events are the unofficial amateur champions of the world. The tournament is presented by the All England Tennis Club, which is the lineal descendant of the England Croquet Club. Suggestions to make it an open event have been resisted strongly.

British Games

Organized by the A.A.A. at the White City, London, and take place on the afternoons of Whit Saturday and Whit Monday. Incorporating the Counties Athletics Union championships. Invitation international events attract world-class athletes.

W.A.A.A. Championships

Held annually, usually on the first Saturday of July at White City, London. Tickets available there or from the Hon. Secretary, 41 Hayward Court, London, S.W.4. Open to athletes of all countries. Entries are usually about 350.

A.A.A. Championships

Started officially in 1880. Held at Stamford Bridge till 1931. Now held annually, over two days usually in the second week of July, at White City, it is open to all nationalities. Some 500 entries annually and includes track and field events.

Doggett's Coat and Badge

From London Bridge to Chelsea Bridge, at the end of July or early August. This is said to be the oldest established competitive rowing event in Britain, and has become part of the pageant of London. It was founded in 1716 by Thomas Doggett in honour of the accession of King George I (1st August). Doggett presented an embroidered coat and arm badge to the winner of the race, which was (and still is) for watermen who have completed their apprenticeship during the previous year. He bequeathed funds for making the race for similar prizes an annual event; the funds are in the trusteeship of the Fishmongers' Company. Added colour is given to the occasion by the barge which follows the race carrying past winners in the full Doggett regalia.

Professional Indoor Tennis Championships

At Empire Pool, Wembley, from a Monday to Saturday in September. Prize money, £10,000. Under the auspices of the L.T.A., who arrive at seedings from competitors' previous six months' play and make the draw. Visitors to this event can be sure of seeing 'world-class' tennis.

Home Counties

3

Unlike many parts of England, the south-eastern corner occupied by the five Home Counties is almost entirely Anglo-Saxon in its cultural tradition. It has nothing comparable with the Celtic traditions of Cornwall or the equally strong Viking ones of Yorkshire. When south-eastern England was colonized after the dark age, which followed the break-up of the Roman Empire, the invading Anglo-Saxon tribes drove what remained of the Celtic population before them. Kent was settled largely by Jutes, the remaining counties by Anglo-Saxon tribes.

Essex became a petty kingdom in its own right, the kingdom of the East Saxons, its capital in London. At one time Middlesex, the kingdom of the Middle Saxons, now absorbed into Greater London, was also a semi-independent state.

Kent has the proudest record of them all, for the tribes which settled it were more advanced than most of the Anglo-Saxon tribes. For a time, before and after St Augustine was invited to the court of King Ethelbert at the instance of his wife Bertha, a Christian princess of the Franks, to preach the Christian faith, Kent was the leading state in the realm and received tribute from all the Saxon kingdoms. Later the whole area came under the sway of Wessex. When the country was partitioned by the treaty of Wedmore between the English and the Danes the Home Counties remained English. It is not surprising, therefore, that there is not a single festival in the Home Counties which derives from any but the Anglo-Saxon or Anglo-Norman traditions.

The Home Counties are in a very favourable position for the success of modern festivals of the arts, because they can draw on the eight million people who live in Greater London for their audiences. So the Haslemere Festival of Early Music, the Stour Festival of Music and Painting,

the Dickens Festival at Broadstairs, are among the serious cultural events which have gone from strength to strength since they were founded, and fill a real gap in the artistic and literary background of south-east England.

Equally a considerable number of old customs, even though they are not so old as in some parts of the country, draw enthusiastic audiences. The distribution of the Biddenden Dole in Kent, the Pancake Race of Olney, Buckinghamshire, the Admiral's Court at Rochester, the Oyster Festival at Colchester, and a number of others, are firmly established in the festival calendar. Above all, the summer race meeting on Epsom Downs at which the Derby and the Oaks are run attracts hundreds of thousands of visitors from Greater London. Like Royal Ascot, it was an integral part of the London Season in the leisured days of the

The Olney Pancake Race started by the Pancake Bell

nineteenth century, but has lost none of its popularity in the changed conditions of the mid twentieth century.

Buckinghamshire

LITTLE MISSENDEN – Festival of Music and the Arts

This village festival, which takes place for a week in early October, was founded in 1960 and has been successful in giving encouragement to young Buckinghamshire musicians and artists, as well as pleasure to residents and their friends and a number of visitors. Little Missenden's position in a valley of the beech-clad Chiltern Hills makes it an ideal objective for a day's outing, and the musical fare provided is always of a high standard. The major events take place on the last four days of the festival week, from Thursday to Sunday.

In one recent year there was a performance of works by Mendelssohn, Schönberg and Richard Drakeford (whose octet was specially commissioned for the festival) by the London Octet, a recently formed group from the B.B.C. Symphony Orchestra, and a recital of works by Handel and Bach, with psalms by Niel Saunders, also specially commissioned for the festival, by Geraint Jones on the organ supported by strings and oboe. Both these concerts were given in the church, a lovely medieval building, one of the most interesting in the county.

A concert by outstanding young Buckinghamshire musicians, and a children's concert, were other interesting events. A recital by candlelight in honour of the four hundredth anniversary of the birth of Christopher Marlowe was also given in the church, and there were a number of interesting meetings in the village hall, including a talk by Marie Rambert, D.B.E., the founder of the Ballet Rambert. This gives some idea of the scope of one of the most instructive of the smaller community festivals of music which are becoming an important part of the cultural life of the countryside. Further details may be obtained from the Organizer, Dering Cottage, Little Missenden, Buckinghamshire.

OLNEY – Pancake Race

Shrove Tuesday, the day before Ash Wednesday, which is the first day of Lent, is the day appointed for this and a number of other festivals still carried out with all their old spirit. The word 'shrove' is derived from shriven—everybody in pre-Reformation days went to the priest to be shriven, i.e. receive absolution, before Lent, and Shrove Tuesday was a universal holiday in preparation for the fast days ahead. Shrove Tuesday and pancakes are inseparably linked for a very practical reason. Housewives used their surplus of butter and eggs for pancakes so as to conserve perishable food in their larders before the fast. A bell was rung to show that the holiday had begun and again towards sunset as an indication that it was over, and this bell came to be known as the 'pancake bell'. It is still rung at Olney to mark the beginning of the pancake race, an extraordinary survival of Shrovetide sports. At Olney only ladies who have resided in the town for some months are eligible. They must be clad in skirt and apron and wear a scarf or hat. The race is over a course of about four hundred yards, ending at the church porch. The competitors must run from their homes with the pancake still sizzling hot, tossing it once at the official starting point, again at the beginning of the short run up to the church, and a third time at the church porch. The pancakes which survive the journey are given to the bell-ringer, who pays for them with a kiss. The first to deliver her pancake is the year's pancake champion. The race is run just before midday and an astonishing number of people come to watch it. It is indeed a very amusing race, though regarded seriously by the contestants, many of whom have taken part for twenty years or more. The race is probably five hundred years old.

International interest has been given to the Olney pancake race by the observance of a similar custom in the community of Liberal, Kansas, U.S.A. The race there is run over a similar course, and there is keen rivalry between the two towns to score the best time of the day. Bodiam in Sussex and North Somercotes in Lincolnshire are two other English villages which have inherited a pancake race tradition.

Essex

SAFFRON WALDEN – Saffron Walden Festival

A general rather than a music festival, which originated in 1958, the Saffron Walden Festival has a twofold purpose, first in common with that of all festivals to provide a period of rich artistic entertainment primarily intended for people who live in the locality and, secondly, to demonstrate the vigour of the amateur cultural life of the district. Even when professionals are engaged artists are chosen whenever possible who have local connections. The festival is held biennially in the even years for a fortnight, usually in May (29th April–13th May in 1966). Apart from the music there is a wide variety of festival activities – a ball at the opening of the event, a procession of vintage cars and traction engines, musical dinners, dramatic performances and a film evening. Further details may be obtained from the Saffron Book Shop, George Street, Saffron Walden, Essex.

COLCHESTER – The Oyster Festival

This interesting event takes place on 20th October and is

The Mayor and party at one of the ceremonies during the Colchester Oyster Festival

one of the oldest traditional observances in the Home Counties. Its exact origin is unknown but it may well date from the time of King Richard I, who granted the Colne oyster fisheries to the burghers of Colchester. By the Restoration period it had become a time-honoured event which took place on the eve of St Denys' Day, the day appointed for the proclamation of St Denys' Fair, which was chartered in 1319 and was by far the most important fair in Essex, lasting originally eight days, though this was reduced in the seventeenth century to four days.

St Denys' Day is 9th October. The fair changed its date in 1752, when a variation in the calendar resulted in many fairs being put forward; 20th October became the date for proclaiming the fair and the Oyster Festival was moved to the same day, so maintaining tradition.

In the eighteenth century many ancient corporation feasts in Colchester were paid for out of public funds. This is the only one which has survived the axe of the Municipal Reform Act of 1835, although the Oyster Feast itself is now the responsibility of the mayor. The usual number of guests attending the feast in recent times is three hundred and fifty, who have included many members of the royal family. Attendance at the feast itself is by invitation, but the proclamation of the fair and the colourful procession of

mayor, aldermen and council to the town hall attracts many visitors. Concerts and other attractions are arranged to coincide with the feast.

The Oyster Feast should not be confused with the official opening of the Colchester oyster fishery, which takes place each year off Brightlingsea in September. At this ceremony an ancient proclamation is read by the town clerk declaring the fishery open for the season, and the company partakes of gin and gingerbread.

DUNMOW – The Dunmow Flitch Trial

A Whit Monday occasion, normally held in Great Dunmow, although it has also been held at Saffron Walden and Ilford, the trial is of ancient origin, but in its present form is popularized out of recognition. It was in the reign of Henry III that Robert Fitzwalter, lord of the manor, offered a flitch of bacon to any man who had not repented, waking or sleeping, of his marriage for a year. The hearing of the claim was entrusted to the prior and officers of Little Dunmow Priory, who were of course all bachelors. The people of Dunmow were invited to attend the hearing, and because it was a special occasion the day on which the trial took place became something of a public holiday. There are records of three recipients of the flitch before the

Reformation. There was a lapse of many years after the dissolution of the priory in the reign of Henry VIII, but periodic revivals of the trial have taken place. At one time the carved chair of the prior, now in Little Dunmow church, was used to carry successful claimants through the streets.

Before the Reformation the claim could be made only by a man, never by a man and woman together – that is something of which the first is heard late in the eighteenth century. The present revival has not pleased everyone. Charles Cox, writing in 1909, spoke of it as a vulgar bank holiday frolic. 'It is satisfactory to know that the ecclesiastical chair is no longer used on these farcical occasions.' However, the trial, at which the claims are adjudicated by a jury of six bachelors and six spinsters, is the excuse for a great deal of merriment and is well worth a visit. Two flitches of bacon are distributed, one to the couple who first establish their claim (and there are many unsuccessful claimants), the other divided among the unsuccessful couples on the ground that they deserve a reward for showing the initiative to face a public inquisition!

SOUTHEND-ON-SEA – Spring Flower Festival
Southend-on-Sea has always made a feature of the displays of flowers and flowering shrubs in its parks and gardens, but it is only in recent years that it has instituted an annual Spring Flower Festival. This is held in the last week of April, when every corner of Southend which can sustain a flower bed is gay and colourful. It is one of the best displays in the country. Bulbs and plants in hundreds and thousands transform the cliffs into a mass of colour, and a really outstanding display is staged in the Cliff Pavilion.

Annual Whitebait Festival
This is organized by the Southend Chamber of Trade and is held at the end of September. Once whitebait were plentiful higher up the Thames, but pollution in the Greenwich area has driven them downriver, to the whitebait nurseries by Leigh-on-Sea and Southend. Towards the end of the eighteenth century the Thames Whitebait Festival was transferred to Greenwich, but before that it took place at Dagenham, so that in a sense Essex has regained what was once its own. (The last Government-sponsored Whitebait Festival at Greenwich was held in 1894.) The main event of the Southend festival is the banquet, but there is also a blessing of the fishes, attracting many visitors, which takes place on the morning of the festival when the catch of whitebait is ceremonially blessed at the head of the pier, the longest in the world, reaching a mile and a third out to sea. For those interested who do not wish to walk so far, modern electric trains run to the pier head every few minutes.

The festooned illuminations on the front at Southend-on-Sea
Photo: Southend-on-Sea Corporation

The Autumn Illuminations
These are switched on in mid August and switched off in mid October, the display lasting from dusk each evening until 11 or 11.30. It is the largest display of illuminations in the south of England. The cliffs, promenades, kursaal, children's playground and pier are all the scenes of spectacular lighting effects. The pier lights have a special theme, different each year; the triumphal arches, numerous set pieces and the festooned multicoloured lights along the sea front create a scene of real beauty. 'Never Never Land' is a children's favourite and the cliffs are floodlit in colour, bringing new but never displeasing effects to the natural pattern of gardens, trees and shrubberies. An important point for motorists is that cars are permitted to traverse the sea front illumination route from end to end.

Hertfordshire

HARPENDEN – The Highland Gathering
Organized by the Hertfordshire Highland Games Society, the gathering is an annual event, usually held on the second or third Saturday in June. It dates back to 1947 and, it is claimed, is the oldest Highland Gathering outside Scotland. The first meeting was organized by Tom Nicol, an Ayrshire man farming in Hertfordshire. It was on a very small scale. In the following year a committee with Calum Gillies, John Morton and Iain Cameron was formed, and a much more elaborate gathering staged at St Albans in 1949. It moved to Rothampsted Park, Harpenden, in the following year, where it has continued to attract large audiences each year. Of the original

committee, Dr Gillies and Mr Cameron are still active in promoting it. The event is on the traditional lines of Highland Games in Scotland, its purpose being to act as a meeting place for Scots in the south of England and to raise funds for the Royal Caledonian Schools and other charities. Further details may be obtained from the Convener, The Highland Games Society, Fassifern, Holloways Lane, North Mymms, Hatfield, Hertfordshire.

Kent

WYE – The Stour Festival of Music and Painting

'The artist is not a special kind of man but every man is a special kind of artist' (A. K. Coomaraswamy). This, said Alfred Deller, who, with John Ward, R.A., and the late Christopher Hassall, founded the Stour music festival, is what Stour music is about. It was founded in 1963 as a one-day festival to provide an opportunity to hear music rarely heard even at the great international festivals. The Stour festival has gone from strength to strength and is now a four-day event held towards the end of June (23rd–26th June in 1966).

The type of music commonly performed is well illustrated by the programmes for 1966, which include a Mozart recital on the unique Colt collection of early keyboard instruments at Bethesden by Paul Badura-Skoda, a Mozart concert by the Arriaga String Quartet, and the first performance of a string quartet by Robert Johnson introduced by the composer. The Concentus Musicus instrumental ensemble from Vienna with the internationally famous Deller Consort gave the Bach 'Brandenburg' Concerto and

Purcell's *Masque in Dioclesian* in the concert hall of Olantigh House. A performance of Handel's *Messiah* in its entirety was conducted by Alfred Deller in Wye church. A concert of instrumental music by the Concentus Musicus, and an organ recital by Christopher Dearnley, organist of Salisbury Cathedral, in Ashford parish church, complete the music programme, but there are also illustrated talks on musical subjects, dramatic performances and an exhibition of paintings. The concert of medieval poetry and music given in Boughton Aluph church in 1965 with the Deller Consort and the Renaissance Instrumental Ensemble from Germany was a special triumph.

This festival is an outstanding example of what can be achieved by local enthusiasm and the generosity of foreign artists, many of whom have waived their fee. Although it started as a festival of music given by friends for friends, it has already won an international reputation as a perfect medium in which artists can forge a real link with their audiences in the intimate atmosphere of Olantigh House and the parish churches of Ashford, Wye, Boughton Aluph and Chilham, all perfect settings for the kind of music performed in them. Further details may be obtained from the Hon. Secretary, Stour Music, Tanglewood, Lower Vicarage Road, Kennington, Ashford, Kent. Brochures are available each year in March.

CANTERBURY – The Canterbury Festival

Canterbury was chosen as one of the festival cities in the Festival of Britain year, when the municipally owned Marlowe Theatre was opened with a resident repertory

The Deller Consort

Photo: John Vickers

A scene from *The Boy from the Catacombs*, first presented at the Canterbury Festival

Photo : Kentish Gazette

company, which is still active. It was decided to hold a civic festival every ten years, although in actual fact the 1961 festival was postponed to 1962 in order to coincide with the Magna Carta celebrations. Apart from this there are three separate weeks in the year when special annual events are staged in Canterbury.

Festival of the Friends

This unique festival was founded in 1928 by Dean Bell, with the underlying idea of uniting the arts of music, poetry and painting as an offering in the cathedral. In subsequent years the Friends commissioned many plays which have since gained world-wide renown, including T. S. Eliot's *Murder in the Cathedral*. In 1965 a specially commissioned opera by Dean Ridout, *The Boy from the Catacombs*, was written for and played by the boys of the choir school. So the character of the festival varies from year to year, but it remains in essence an offering of talent and service to the cathedral. It is held for one week in June each year, normally from Tuesday to Saturday. Further

information may be obtained from the Secretary, The Friends of Canterbury Cathedral, 3 The Precinct, Canterbury, Kent.

The King's Week Festival

This takes place in the last ten days of the summer term, normally the third week in July, when the King's School presents a dramatic and musical programme. In 1965, for instance, the King's School Players performed William Shakespeare's *The Tempest* on four evenings in the garden of Chillenden Chambers, while the choral society and orchestra with visiting professional soloists gave Mendelssohn's *Hymn of Praise* and Handel's 'Chandos' Anthem in the nave of the cathedral. Dudley Moore with a trio presented an evening of light entertainment in the Shirley Hall, and the Allegri String Quartet gave a concert of chamber music, including quartets by Beethoven, Mozart and Debussy. The King's School Madrigal Society gave a serenade in the cathedral cloisters, and the King's School Orchestra a symphony concert of works by Brahms and

Haydn. On the final day the Auerbach Knabenkapelle gave a characteristic Bavarian programme.

A number of school exhibitions are also open to the public and the school's valuable collection of manuscripts may be inspected by appointment with the librarian. Further details of this distinguished festival may be obtained from the Manager, King's Week, The King's School, Canterbury, Kent.

Canterbury Cricket Week

This begins on the Saturday preceding the first Monday in August, when two three-day county matches are played at the St Lawrence Ground. Details from the Office, St Lawrence Ground, Canterbury, Kent.

BROADSTAIRS – The Dickens Festival

Charles Dickens lived for many years of his life in the rather stern-looking Bleak House, which overlooks the attractive fishing and pleasure-boating harbour of Broadstairs, midway between Ramsgate and Margate. In Broadstairs, too, high above the harbour, where survives one of the medieval defensive gateways complete with portcullis grooves, is Dickens House, the home of the original Betsey Trotwood in *David Copperfield*.

The festival lasts for a week in June and is organized by the Broadstairs branch of the Dickens Fellowship. It is largely the brain-child of Gladys Waterer, who for many years has been the honorary secretary of the Broadstairs Branch, and whose home appropriately is Dickens House. The centre-piece of the week's celebration is the performance of a play adapted from one of the novelist's works. In Miss Waterer's own words: 'The festival is unique in that it is the only Dickens Festival in Europe. It's a completely local effort. The whole town joins in. In 1936 we put on the first Dickens play. After the war I wrote *Christmas Carol* and that was really the start.' It was a very good start too.

For many years a different play was staged each year. In 1964 the wheel turned full circle and *Christmas Carol* was staged again. In 1965 it was *Our Mutual Friend*. The players are members of the Broadstairs Dickens Players' Society. The adaptation and rehearsals take on average nearly eight months. The result in the modest Festival Theatre is always satisfying, throwing a new and original light on the novelist, who is still one of the favourite writers of hundreds of thousands of people, young and old.

Gradually the scope of the festival has been extended, though the play remains its most important part. Bleak House and Dickens House are both open to the public throughout the week. There is a Dickensian garden party in the grounds of Bleak House, with prizes offered for the best costumes. There are concerts of Victorian music, talks

Canterbury Cathedral
Photo: Friends of Canterbury Cathedral
Broadstairs beach, with
Bleak House in the background

A scene from *The Pickwick Papers* at the Broadstairs Festival
Photo: Album of Gladys Waterer

Dickensian costume in the streets of Broadstairs
Photo: Roy Capel

on Dickens and his work and a Victorian exhibition. A festival dance is organized in the grand ballroom, and the proof of Miss Waterer's assertion that the whole town joins in is well illustrated by the number of Dickensian exhibits in the shops and the number of people, especially the shop-keepers, who wear Dickensian costume, in spite of the difficulty in modern times of moving about in crinolines! A stagecoach on the front is a sign that the festival is in progress. It is a replica of the kind of coach in which many of Dickens' characters travelled, and in which he must have made many of his journeys to Broadstairs. Further details of the play and other features of the festival can be obtained from the Hon. Secretary, Broadstairs Festival Committee, Dickens House, Broadstairs, Kent.

The Festival of Music
This festival, held in July (5th–12th July in 1966) at the Memorial Hall, is a relatively small and intimate one. Its purpose is quite simple, to promote and encourage good music and the arts in general. In addition to recitals (Colin Horsley, piano, Osian Ellis, harp, and the Willison Trio appear in 1966), there are evenings of ballet and various artistic and cultural exhibitions. Further details can be obtained from the Organizing Secretary, 29 Green Lane, Broadstairs, Kent.

The Carol Festival
The Broadstairs Carol Festival is of special interest because it was first organized by Edward Heath, better known in later years as a politician than as a musician, when he was an Organ Scholar at Balliol College, Oxford. Since then Edward Heath has not missed a year, and continues to conduct a choir, which now numbers sixty, and an orchestra of twenty, with orchestral arrangements by himself before an audience of six hundred or more. The festival is normally held on a Sunday before Christmas in a local hall (the Grand Ballroom in 1965).

BIGGIN HILL – Battle of Britain
R.A.F. stations throughout the country are thrown open to the public on 15th September in commemoration of the 'Few' – the fighter pilots who repulsed the onslaught of German bombers in 1940. At some airfields exhibitions are staged and an insight is given to visitors into the operation of modern high-speed aircraft. Biggin Hill is one of the most popular of the airfields within easy reach of London, because it was from here that so many of the 'Few' started on their missions. At the White Hart in the nearby village of Brasted the signatures of many of these war-time heroes can be seen.

ROCHESTER – Medway Ceremonies
Rochester is one of England's most ancient and historic towns. It was a Roman settlement, and an important Anglo-Saxon township, where a bishopric was founded soon after the conversion of Kent by St Augustine and the foundation of Canterbury Cathedral. It was a Norman castle town and later an important river port and commercial centre. The ruins of its Norman castle are magnificent in their size and strength. Nearby is the medieval cathedral which succeeded St Augustine's seventh-century church. It is a splendid Norman church with Gothic additions. The seventeenth-century red brick guildhall represents the city's latter-day prosperity, together with the many houses dating from the seventeenth and eighteenth centuries.

One of Rochester's proudest boasts is that it has commanded the River Medway from time immemorial – from the time, in fact, when the Romans first bridged it and built a fort to defend the bridge. (The Norman castle served the same purpose by defending the lowest point at which the river could be forded.) A charter granted to the city in 1446 by King Henry VI created the mayor of the city Admiral of the River Medway. That charter defined the boundaries of the admiral's jurisdiction from Hawk-wood to Sheerness. The former is six miles upstream from Rochester Bridge, Sheerness is fourteen miles downstream. A monumental stone by the river at Hawkwood marks the boundary and is inscribed with the words 'God preserve the City of Rochester'. Modern Sheerness is built away from the old town to the east; in practice the jurisdiction of the Admiral of the River Medway ends at Garrison Point, where the Medway enters the Thames. An interesting fact is that the jurisdiction of the mayor as admiral is recognized by the Lords Commissioners of

Formation flying at Biggin Hill during Battle of Britain week

Rochester Admiralty Court in session near the bridge
Photo: Chatham News

the Admiralty, though it must be many years since it was exercised. But the city retains absolute authority over the fishing rights within the area.

Two distinct ceremonies take place each year. One is the ceremony of beating the bounds of the admiral's jurisdiction, which is normally held on a Sunday in September. The mayor, in full regalia as admiral, travels in his barge (accompanied by the many craft which regularly use the river) from Rochester to Sheerness, back to Rochester, then to Hawkwood and back again (sometimes the directions are reversed according to the state of the tide). In one recent year eighty-four river craft participated, including units of the Royal Navy, the Medway Conservancy Board, the Kent Police Authority and the Kent Fire Authority, as well as a number of yacht clubs. It is a brave sight to see this great flotilla moving up- and downstream. The mayor, flying his flag as Admiral of the Medway, generally has a naval barge placed at his disposal by the Flag Officer Medway complete with Royal Navy crew. Cannons are fired at Hawkwood and Sheerness, and the occasion is made an opportunity for displays along the bank by Boy Scouts and similar bodies.

The second ceremony is the holding of the annual Admiralty Court, generally on the morning of the first Saturday of July. The court is held in a barge moored in the river above Rochester Bridge, just off Rochester pier. It consists of the mayor as admiral assisted by the city aldermen, and a jury of the free fishermen. It is in the form prescribed by the Oyster Fishery Act of 1728 and regulates both the oyster fishery and the floating fishery in the River Medway. These are free fisheries in the sense that only freemen of the river are entitled to fish. One can only become a free fisherman by serving seven years' apprenticeship with an existing free fisherman.

Invariably large number of visitors watch the colourful proceedings in the barge, in which of course the mayor and the aldermen are all in their robes of office. The sides of the barge are decorated with flags and the arms of the city. The precise date differs from year to year, but intending visitors may obtain full details from the Town Clerk's Office, the Guildhall, Rochester, Kent.

NEWINGTON – Blessing the Cherry Orchards

Nowhere in Britain is the beauty of cherry orchards in blossom better seen than in Kent, and especially in that part of the county which lies between Watling Street (the Roman road from Rochester to Canterbury) and the estuary of the Thames. At Newington a Rogationtide service is held on a Sunday when the cherry blossom is at its finest (there is no fixed date). Before evensong the vicar and congregation walk from the church to one of the orchards which surround it. There the vicar blesses the orchards and a short service is held before the procession returns to the church for evensong.

BIDDENDEN – The Biddenden Dole

Every Easter Sunday after morning service in the lovely late Gothic church a ceremony is held commemorating the Biddenden Maids. The legend is that Eliza and Mary Chalkhurst were born in this village in 1100, joined at the shoulders and hips, the first recorded instance of Siamese twins in Britain. They lived, the story goes on, until the age of thirty-four and bequeathed to the church a field about twenty acres in extent, the rent from which was to be devoted in making an annual gift at Eastertide of bread

The cherry blossom at blessing time near Newington Church

and cheese to the poor of the parish. The plot of ground is still known as Bread-and-Cheese land; the distribution, still carried out every Eastertide, has attached to itself a number of refinements. So now not only is a 'dole' given to the needy—for the land still produces a sizable rent – but small cakes or biscuits stamped with the imprint of the Chalkhurst twins are distributed to all the villagers and the many visitors who attend this interesting ceremony. The detail of the service and distribution, incidentally, has not changed since 1825 when William Hone, the artist and author, reproduced the design on the cakes in his *Everyday Book* and described the ceremony just as it is performed today.

The intriguing thing about the Biddenden Dole is that there is no real reason to doubt the truth of the legend except in one detail – the date of the institution of the dole. This cannot have been in Norman times. A suggestion is that 1100 is a misreading in an old record for 1400 or 1500, or a similar set of figures.

HYTHE – Venetian Festival

This spectacular water festival on the Royal Military Canal is held every second year on a Wednesday in mid August (17th August in 1966). It is presented by the Hythe Venetian Fête Society, a charitable organization under the presidency of the Mayor of Hythe, and is staged by voluntary workers. It has a history which began before the First World War, was revived in the nineteen-thirties, and since the end of the Second World War has extended its scope until it is now unique among British festivals. Hythe is a most historic town. It was, and indeed still is, a 'head port', i.e. one of the five original Cinque Ports. Its earliest charter is dated 1278 and the mayoralty was established by charter of Queen Elizabeth. The canal on which the

Historic set piece on one of the floats in the Hythe Venetian Festival
Photo: Jack Adams

Consort of viols and harpsichord, with Carl Dolmetsch, recorder
Photo: Colin Futcher

tableaux are paraded was cut during the Napoleonic Wars to enable British ships to sail from the Deal roads into the English Channel without being exposed to the risk of attack by French privateers off Dungeness.

The setting of the fête is a beautiful one, the tree-lined waterway of the canal, with ample space for spectators in enclosures on both banks. The mainspring of the event is a series of carnival floats, many presenting complex tableaux of historical, local or merely humorous interest. Prizes are awarded in each of a number of classes. In addition there are challenge trophies for the best exhibits on parade irrespective of the classes in which they are entered. The opening ceremony is at six o'clock and is followed by a daylight parade of the tableaux, then at dusk there is another parade of all classes with the tableaux illuminated and a display of aquatic fireworks. The festivities end about ten o'clock. A feature of the festival is a draw – 'The Grand Venetian Draw' – in which the first prize is a holiday in Venice for two. Further details may be obtained from the Publicity Secretary, Hythe Venetian Fête Society, 124 High Street, Hythe, Kent.

HASLEMERE – The Haslemere Festival

Arnold Dolmetsch founded the Haslemere Festival with a family group in 1925. Since then it has been held every year without a break and currently lasts for about ten days in mid July. It is thus one of the longest established music festivals in the United Kingdom, and is an international occasion renowned for the presentation of authentic performances of early music on the instruments for which it was written, including the harpsichord and clavichord, chamber organ, viola da gamba, the lute, the recorder and the family of viols. It was directed by Arnold Dolmetsch until his death in 1940, since then by his son Carl, who with his family and associate artists continues his father's life work, not only at Haslemere but in world tours which have included the United States, Australia, New Zealand and almost every European country. Thus an ever widening interest in early music and instruments is fostered.

The festival is sponsored by the Dolmetsch Foundation, an international society which was established in 1928 to assist Arnold Dolmetsch in his work. Membership has grown steadily, and there are few parts of the world where a representative cannot be found working to ensure that the tradition and practice begun by Arnold Dolmetsch can be carried forward confidently into the future.

Arnold Dolmetsch summed up the underlying purpose of the festival when in answer to the question, 'What are the conditions under which sixteenth-, seventeenth- and eighteenth-century music can produce its real effect on the listener?' he said, 'It must be presented in its original form, for obviously nobody can improve it. It must be played upon the instruments for which it was intended, in the conventional manner of its own period, free from the uncongenial ideas and modes of expression of our own time. Even then it will not be understood at a first hearing, nor even at a second. . . . The auditors must hear enough of it to become familiar with the tone of the instruments

Derby Day on Epsom Downs

and the style of the music.' That is an objective which can only be accomplished in practice at a festival in which the music is heard at concert after concert. Arnold Dolmetsch's ideal became a practical reality. After the first festival he said, 'Performers and auditors were transported to another sphere where pure joy and rapture replaced the cares of life. People from alien countries, who had looked upon one another with suspicion, became friends.'

That is equally true of modern Haslemere festivals, which are still very much family affairs with at least five members of the Dolmetsch clan performing, but with a leavening of professional musicians outside the family supporting them. Nor has the general shape of the festival altered much. In 1926 it consisted of eight concerts, two devoted to the works of Bach, one to various German composers, one to French, one to Italian and three to English music. In the 1965 festival there were nine concerts, of which one was devoted to Bach and his contemporaries, one to Italian music, one to French, one to Bach and Handel, and another to Bach, Mozart and Scarlatti and two to English music. One of the other two concerts commemorated the quarter-century since the death of Arnold Dolmetsch and concentrated on his compositions, the other presented a programme of dances from the court of Charles II in costume devised by Nathalie Dolmetsch, including scenes from John Blow's masque *Venus and Adonis*.

A Sunday concert is given in the parish church and includes choral and organ music from the sixteenth to the eighteenth century, while a recent and successful innovation is the staging of two concerts for children in which Carl Dolmetsch introduces music for recorders and viols, harpsichords and other old instruments, played mainly by members of his family.

During the festival the Dolmetsch collection of early instruments together with others loaned for the occasion are on view at the Haslemere Museum, while the Dolmetsch workshops are also thrown open to visitors. Here it is possible to see a vast number of the modern recorders, viols and other instruments which are made at the workshops for amateur as well as professional performers, and perpetuate the tradition of craftsmanship which was founded here more than eighty years ago. Further details and programmes can be obtained from the Secretary, Dolmetsch Foundation, Greenstead, Beacon Hill, Hindhead, Surrey.

TILFORD – Festival of Music

Founded in 1952, the Tilford festival has always had as its first aim the presentation of the music of Bach and his contemporaries in a style consistent with the composers' lifetime. The performances are of chamber music proportions, using the number and type of instrument for which Bach wrote, including the harpsichord, viola da gamba, etc. The Tilford Bach Festival Orchestra is a group of professional musicians who have specialized in this type of presentation. The festival choir is one of about fifty voices trained for the express purpose of singing at the festival. The setting of this completely unsophisticated festival is the small parish church of Tilford, but there were also performances for the first time in 1965 in the great hall of Farnham Castle and in Guildford Cathedral, where the *Mass in B Minor* was presented in a setting worthy of it. The festival is held on three or four consecutive days in the first half of May. Full details may be obtained from the Hon. Secretary, Tilford Bach Festival, Ling Lea, Shortfield Common, Frensham, Farnham, Surrey.

EPSOM – Derby Day

Epsom Downs have been well known for their race meetings at least since the reign of Charles I, who was a patron of racing. With the discovery of medicinal springs about the same time Epsom became fashionable as a place to visit and in which to live. The modern fame of Epsom as a racing centre really began in 1779, when the 12th Earl of Derby instituted the Oaks, and in the following year the Derby Stakes. Both these races form part of the summer meeting held at the beginning of June. The traditional day for the Derby is a Wednesday, for the Oaks Friday.

Derby Day is *the* day of the meeting, attracting an incredible number of people not normally interested in racing. Going to Epsom Downs for the Derby, on which it is said more money is laid in bets than on any other single race in the English racing calendar, has in effect become part of the Festival of London in its widest meaning. It is, of course, an immensely valuable race which attracts entries of Irish-bred, American-bred and French-bred horses. The extent of the foreign challenge is shown by the fact that French horses won the race six times between 1946 (when racing was resumed after the wartime break) and 1965.

The scene on the Downs attracts many visitors as strongly as the racing itself – the surging throngs in which fashionably dressed people rub shoulders with racing tipsters, the stalls and booths, traditionally the province of gipsies – though the gipsy population has decreased in recent years – the gay and colourful and noisy maelstrom of humanity. Whatever the reason, Derby Day has not lost a whit of popularity since Frith painted his famous picture of it. There is no other race meeting in the world quite like it; 1966 witnesses the running of the 186th Derby Stakes and 187th Oaks Stakes.

Eastern England   4

East Anglia, virtually an island within an island, bounded on two sides by the North Sea and the Wash, and on a third by what was once the impenetrable morass of the Fenland, has its traditions deeply rooted in the soil, the rich corn-growing soil of Norfolk and Suffolk and, since the draining of the Fens, the still more fertile black earth of the land drained by the Old and New Bedford Rivers and the intricate pattern of dikes and drains which supplement these great artificial cuts. It is a relatively thinly peopled countryside with few towns and no great industrial centre. In Norfolk, Norwich and King's Lynn, both ancient settlements, one the traditional capital of East Anglia, the other its chief port throughout the Middle Ages, are by far the most populous towns. Each has its important festival – the Norwich Triennial Festival of Music and the King's Lynn Festival of the Arts – which has made a permanent impression on the cultural life of the countryside and draws visitors from much farther afield.

The university city of Cambridge too, as one would expect, has a festival, or rather several festivals, ranging from the beautiful carol service in King's College Chapel on Christmas Eve to the rumbustious Poppy Day Rag with its spectacular carnival processions and air of spontaneous gaiety.

In Suffolk the Aldeburgh Festival of Music and the Arts is a host in itself, reflecting the genius of Benjamin Britten and his associates, a festival for friends given by friends, yet one the fame of which has spread to every corner of the western world, and which directly and indirectly has brought to thousands of people greater appreciation of contemporary and classical music. The Long Melford Festival, at first glance an offshoot of Aldeburgh, has developed in a few short years a tradition of its own.

In a lighter vein but in its own way just as beautiful an event, the festival of flowers at Spalding reflects the more recent traditions of Fenland, so like parts of Holland in appearance and so similar in the gorgeous display of its tulip show fields, as much as in the more formal displays of festival time.

Cambridgeshire

CAMBRIDGE – The Cambridge Festival

Founded in 1960 and held during July each year (14th–30th July 1966), the Cambridge Festival is designed to represent the arts in the city and university, to build a bridge between the two, and to provide a festival of music for the people of Cambridge and for a wider national audience. The period of the festival falls outside the university terms so that events can be arranged in the college halls and cloisters, in the college chapels of King's and St John's, and in the senate house of the university. Other events are staged in the guildhall, and also in Ely Cathedral. Apart from concerts given by major orchestras, recitals are given by the choirs of King's College and St John's College. Further details may be obtained from the Secretary, Cambridge Festival Association, The Guildhall, Cambridge.

Festival of Carols

The Festival of Nine Lessons and Carols was first presented in King's College Chapel on Christmas Eve, 1918. Since then it has been an annual event, its theme a tribute to God and all His acts, from the creation to the incarnation. It differs from other festivals in that it does not seek to attract visitors owing to the limited room in the college chapel. You can share in its beauty, however, through gramophone records and broadcasts, and visitors are welcome at the choral services held during the rest of the year

'Cambridge Festival of Carols' by Janet Archer,
a young artist who came to London after getting
her diploma from the Newcastle College of Art

Students collecting funds during the Cambridge Poppy Day Rag
Photo: Keystone

in term time, when there is also an opportunity to appreciate the character of what is commonly regarded as the most magnificent of all the churches built in the final style of medieval Gothic architecture. (It was founded by Henry VI in 1446 and took almost a century to complete.) Some of the events of the Cambridge Festival also take place in the chapel (*see above*).

Poppy Day Rag

It is customary for the University Rag Day to be the Saturday preceding Armistice Sunday, whence the name Poppy Day Rag. The proceeds of the rag and of the house to house collections organized by the university have been devoted to the Earl Haig Fund. The rag takes the form of set pieces, processions, firework displays and a great variety of informal entertainments. It is a day when the life of the city is subordinated to the high spirits of the university – most definitely a day to remember.

Many undergraduates can have no memory of either the First or the Second World War; of recent years there has been a growing movement to divorce the University Rag Day from Poppy Day so as to devote the proceeds to other charitable organizations as well as the Earl Haig Fund. A possibility is that in future years the university will have two rag days, the Poppy Day specifically for the Earl Haig Fund and a rag on quite a different day, for funds to be distributed among other charities.

NEWMARKET – The Town Plate

This, the only race in the English racing calendar under Jockey Club rules for women riders, is run at the mid October meeting, traditionally the second Thursday in October. This was the day appointed for the race by King Charles II, who founded and endowed it in a moment of humorous admiration for the equestrian prowess of his many lady friends, one of whom, Nell Gwynn, frequently stayed in Newmarket.

Lincolnshire

SPALDING – The Flower Parade

Sometimes known as the Tulip Festival, the Spalding Flower Parade came into being in 1959 and usually takes place on the first Saturday in May, the exact day being dependent on the weather during the spring which determines the growth of the tulips. The procession starts at about three o'clock, and consists of a mile-long parade of tulip-decorated floats on a four-mile course. Six million blooms are used annually for the display, many of the set pieces in which are animated, a gay and original pageant. The floats are left on view for three days after the parade. For those who cannot attend the Flower Parade, a twenty-acre show garden, known as Springfields, was opened to the public in 1966 providing a spectacle of all kinds of bulbs, from the beginning of April to the end of May. Full details may be obtained from the Hon. Secretary, Spalding Flower Parade, 1 Broad Street, Spalding, Lincolnshire.

STAMFORD – Burghley Horse Trials

In 1966 the first ever World Horse Trial Championship takes place on 7th–10th September. It will then be held annually in rotation of countries. This is an event similar to the horse trials held at Badminton in Gloucestershire.

HAXEY – Haxey Hood Game

This is one of the most elaborate English traditional games, also known as 'Throwing the Hood'. It is played on 6th January, or, when that day falls on a Sunday, on the Saturday before. It is a real festival day in the village and usually attracts hundreds of visitors. Work stops at midday; after lunch the people assemble at Haxey Church Green, where the Fool, who with the Lord and eleven Boggins are the principal actors in the proceedings, begins to make a speech. He is shouted down by the crowd and a fire of paper is lit beside him. This part of the ceremony is known as 'Smoking the Fool'. Later the hood, which is a roll of leather about twenty-two feet long, is thrown into the crowd. The aim is to manhandle it into one of the goals which are the inns of Haxey, the patrons of each inn struggling to get it into their own inn's door, when the game is won and the hood remains hanging in the inn for a year. The purpose of the eleven Boggins is to supervise the proceedings. It is remarkable that in the wild scramble with the hood no one is ever known to have been seriously hurt. Like so many traditional events, it ends with drinks

One of the floats in the
mile-long procession, at the
Spalding Flower Parade
*Photo: South Holland
Horticultural Association*

at the inn – free drinks on the winning goal according to custom, though clearly there are limits! The game is said to date from the thirteenth century; the tradition connected with it is that a certain Lady de Mowbray lost her red hood while out riding in a gale and had it chased and rescued for her by thirteen passing labourers. Certainly the thirteen principal actors – the Lord, the Fool and the Boggins – always have red in their carnival costumes.

Norfolk

KING'S LYNN – Festival of Music and the Arts

The first King's Lynn festival was held in 1951, when the town was chosen as one of the British festival towns for the Festival of Britain celebrations. It has continued since then as an annual event held towards the end of July

Norwich Cathedral

(23rd–30th July in 1966), and has become an important part of the town's cultural life, attracting large audiences from all parts of Britain. Its primary purpose is educational, to bring to the people of this ancient and historic market town better knowledge of music and the arts, classical and contemporary, and in the case of visitors to give them also an appreciation of the festival's outstandingly interesting setting. Its only rule is that it is an artistic event at which only the best is permitted. Music has played a leading part in each festival, and concerts have been given not only in the town itself but in churches and country houses within easy reach of the town. In 1959, 1960 and 1963 concerts were given at Holkham Hall, the home of the Earl and Countess of Leicester. In 1965 an open-air concert was held at Oxburgh Hall. But the majority of the events take place in the Guildhall of St George, in the town hall, which dates in part from the fifteenth century, though several times enlarged and restored, in the Corn Exchange and in the fifteenth-century St Nicholas Chapel.

Highlights of musical King's Lynn have included a memorable recital by the late Kathleen Ferrier, a recital of sacred music by the Westminster Abbey Choir, the appearance of Miss Imogen Holst and the Purcell Singers, with Peter Pears, and the visits of Yehudi Menuhin and the Bath Festival Orchestra giving works by Handel, Bach and Mozart. The Hallé Orchestra, with Sir John Barbirolli and the King's Lynn Festival Choir, have made frequent appearances. In addition to the varied and satisfying musical programme, festival art exhibitions are staged at the Fermoy Art Gallery and in the King's Lynn Museum. At some festivals private collections, such as that of Sir John and Lady Heathcoat Amory in 1965, are shown, often providing the only opportunity for the general public to see a famous collection in its entirety. There are also exhibitions of historic films, and illustrated talks by such well-known authorities as John Betjeman, Emlyn Williams and Gerald Moore.

One of the most popular events of the festival has been the chamber concert by the King's Lynn Festival Ensemble, which consists of members of the Hallé Orchestra augmented by Sir John and Lady Barbirolli (Sir John playing the cello), and Ruth, Lady Fermoy, the festival chairman.

The annual flower festival in the parish church of Wiggenhall St Mary Magdalen, is held to coincide with the first Sunday of the King's Lynn festival.

NORWICH – Norwich and Norfolk Triennial Festival

Originally a choral event linked with the cathedral of this ancient capital of East Anglia, the festival was founded in 1824, with the object of raising funds for the Norfolk and Norwich Hospital. The choral tradition has been kept

'Long Melford Festival' by Roger Law, a visual journalist, writer and part-time teacher of graphic design at Hornsey College of Art

alive, though the range of the festival has been enlarged and includes chamber music concerts, dramatic performances and art exhibitions. The main events are held in St Andrews Hall and in the eighteenth-century Assembly House for a week, beginning near the end of May (27th May–3rd June in 1967, and similar dates in 1970). Further details may be obtained from the Hon. Secretary, The Norwich and Norfolk Triennial Festival, The Close, Norwich, Norfolk.

Suffolk

ALDEBURGH – Festival of Music and Arts

This highly popular festival is held for a fortnight in the latter part of June. Its presiding genius is Benjamin Britten, though the original suggestion for the festival is said to have come from Peter Pears in 1947 when *Albert Herring* was on tour in Europe. The idea was for an intensely personal festival with 'performances given by friends'. The festival has widened its scope considerably in two decades, but it has an intimate atmosphere which is an integral part of its fascination for visitors, who become indeed personal friends of the festival by the time they have attended it three or four years running.

The ancient borough of Aldeburgh on the Suffolk coast is a remarkably suitable place for a festival of this kind, with its long civic tradition dating back to the time when it was one of the most important seaports along the east coast. From the time of Queen Elizabeth until 1832 it had the privilege of returning two members to Parliament, though by then much of the old town had been swept away by the sea and the port had lost its importance. It has lived on as a quiet but distinctive seaside town, its ancient flint, brick and timber moot hall left high and dry on the promenade. The late Gothic parish church, where the poet Crabbe was curate for a few months, has been restored but is little different in appearance from what it was when Aldeburgh was at the height of its prosperity.

The first aim of the Aldeburgh festival is excellence, both of music and of performance. It has never aimed at a mass audience, but has won unstinted praise from every leading critic since 1947. One of its traditions is that it gives first performances of a number of works specially composed for the festival. *The Little Sweep* was the first opera which Benjamin Britten wrote for it and introduced what has become a feature of the festival, the inclusion of songs in which the audience is expected to and does wholeheartedly take part. This close link between audience and performers is made easier by the restricted number of seats available in the Jubilee or Festival Hall in which the main performances are given – three hundred still constitute a

full house. Although major acoustic and other improvements have been made, the policy has always been to keep the old atmosphere and to present concerts mainly 'by friends'.

In one recent year there were eleven first performances, but there are also programmes of early music, in which Byrd and Monteverdi always have a part. Although it is natural that people should associate Aldeburgh pre-eminently with the operatic works of Benjamin Britten presented by the English Opera Group, the festival is genuinely one of music and the arts in a wider sense. Concerts of chamber and orchestral music, programmes of lectures and poetry readings, and art exhibitions all form important parts of it. One of its most attractive features in recent years has been the number of concerts in local churches. The first was given in the church of St Nicholas in 1948. Now the parish churches of Aldeburgh, Orford and Blythburgh all form the background to many of the festival's most memorable performances. Full details can be obtained from the Secretary, Festival of Music and Arts, Aldeburgh, Suffolk.

LONG MELFORD – Festival of Music

Long Melford, a village of many ancient houses and cottages beside its green and along both sides of its main street, which is as long as its name suggests, has two famous buildings. One is the splendid late Gothic church, one of the finest in East Anglia, 180 feet long exclusive of the Lady Chapel, with almost a hundred large windows, and containing a number of interesting monuments, especially of members of the Clopton family in the fifteenth and sixteenth centuries. The other is Melford Hall, an Elizabethan house built by Sir William Cordell, who was Speaker of the House of Commons in the reign of Queen Mary and Master of the Rolls under Queen Elizabeth. It is said of this Sir William that he entertained Queen Elizabeth at Melford in 1578 and, as the historian Churchyard puts it, 'He lighted such a candle to the rest of the shire that many were glad bountifully to follow the same example.'

Both these famous buildings form part of the background of the Long Melford Week End Festival held in mid September and dedicated to giving more people the opportunity of hearing Bach played and sung in perfect surroundings. Let Benjamin Britten, who inspired the festival, speak for it. 'Although the links with Aldeburgh are close, and many familiar names will be found among the performers, this Melford festival already has a life of its own. It is as different from Aldeburgh as West Suffolk is from East. And Long Melford, the town itself as well as the great Perpendicular church and the Tudor hall where

Long Melford Hall, Suffolk

we hold our performances, provides the ideal setting for some of Bach's greatest music.' Particulars of dates on which future festivals will be held and programmes can be obtained from the Long Melford Festival Office, Aldeburgh, Suffolk.

BURY ST EDMUNDS – Cake and Ale Ceremony

The great interest of this ceremony is that it is linked with what is claimed to be England's oldest established charity. On the Thursday after Plough Monday (i.e. the Thursday after the Monday following Twelfth Night, 6th January) a special service is held in St Mary's Church and a sermon preached in commemoration of Jankyn Smith, who by his will endowed a sermon to be preached on the anniversary of his death in perpetuity. He was a great benefactor of the town and was responsible for the building of St Mary's chancel. His bequests were administered by a trust in the care of the Guildhall Feoffees, who instituted the custom of distributing a shilling to the poor of the parish on the occasion of the anniversary service. That custom has been maintained, even though the shilling is now no more than a token and worth perhaps a hundredth of what it was worth at the time of the institution of the charity. Another citizen of Bury St Edmunds, Thomas Bright, left an endowment in 1625 to provide cakes and ale for those taking part in the service. This custom lapsed, although it has been revived several times, but in recent years the traditional cake-and-ale distribution has been confined to the trustees meeting at the guildhall, and sherry has taken the place of ale!

HINTLESHAM – The Summer Festival

Hintlesham Summer Festival is usually held during the last three weeks of July, its principal venue Hintlesham Hall five miles from Ipswich. This Tudor manor house, its interior remodelled in the seventeenth century, its new front added during the reign of Queen Anne, became the centre of a festival of the arts in 1951 (founded by A. S. Stokes), since when the event has been an annual one, ever increasing in scope and interest. Now it is an international attraction distinguished in many ways, and not least in that it gives the opportunity of seeing something of all the arts in one brief period in one place and of appreciating the work of younger and less known artists, who often appear here for their first important engagement, together with those who are well established in their profession.

Performances are given on the open-air stage, which is set in the floodlit gardens behind the hall, or in the Queen Anne Saloon of the hall. A special feature is the presentation of a classical opera accompanied by the Hintlesham Festival Orchestra on at least six nights during the festival, while art exhibitions with special emphasis on modern and local work are held throughout the period. In addition there are concerts at the hall and also in Ipswich in association with the festival, performances of ballet (the Bolshoi Ballet in 1965) and usually a folk festival and folk music competition. The festival is preceded by a midsummer ball held in Hintlesham Hall. Details of the festival may be obtained from the Hon. Organizer, Hintlesham Hall, near Ipswich, Suffolk.

Windsor Horse Show. Parade
of the Household Cavalry

South Country   5

Just as Greater London's horizon stretches out to the festival towns of the Home Counties, so it reaches on occasion as far as the festival events of Sussex and Hampshire. The most famous, and incidentally one of the most important of south country festivals, the Glyndebourne Festival Opera, draws a large part of its audience from London. It used to be a matter of slightly ribald merriment among less enlightened members of the public when hundreds of ladies and gentlemen in full evening dress converged on Victoria Station at half past two in the afternoon to travel to Glyndebourne. The same is true today, except that far more travel by car and the reason for the early wearing of evening attire is known to almost everyone, whereas in the years before the war only a few were in the secret. So too the Chichester Drama Festival, another which has earned an international reputation for the excellence of its festival fare, is not strictly a local one but looks to Greater London and to the nearby seaside resorts for most of its audience.

The Southern Cathedrals Festival, held in turn at Chichester, Winchester and Salisbury, makes its appeal more strongly to local people. Even so, its fame has spread far beyond the confines of these three ancient cathedral cities, and visitors from farther afield are at least as numerous as from the cities themselves and the surrounding country districts.

The sporting events of the south country have just as widespread an appeal. 'Glorious Goodwood' is an absolute 'must' in the London Season for the diminishing number of leisured people to whom the London Season is still a time of festival and enjoyment. Royal Ascot is in the same category: so, to a lesser extent, is the Royal Windsor Horse Show, which in a quarter of a century has leapt to the forefront of equestrian events in its popular appeal and in the high standard of its entries.

Inevitably many of the holiday towns along the holiday coast of Sussex, Hampshire and Dorset have weeks in which civic efforts to entertain the visitor are redoubled and additional entertainments of every description are provided.

Two events stand out because there is nothing quite like them, dissimilar though they are. One is Cowes Week, the premier festival of yachting and one of the finest and most renowned yachting festivals in the world. The other is the Jersey Battle of Flowers, outstanding partly because of the fantastic size and scope of the floral procession and the battle itself, partly because of the good taste with which it is carried out.

The south country too has its quota of old customs jealously preserved, from the Hocktide celebrations of Hungerford, a day of merrymaking, to the far more serious proceedings of the distribution of the Tichborne Dole and the midsummer ritual at Stonehenge.

Berkshire

READING – Summer Festival of the Arts
This interesting project of the University of Reading takes place for a week towards the end of June. Its aim is to present the widest possible variety of art, with the accent on youth, but the performances are of a high degree of excellence. In a single festival Ballets Minerva, one of Britain's leading touring companies, gave a classical programme, John Ogdon a Beethoven piano recital, Jacqueline du Pré and Stephen Bishop a cello and piano recital, the New Departures Quintet, featuring some of today's most adventurous modernists, a forward-looking jazz concert. The Oxford University Etceteras gave a performance of their revue, and Chekhov's *The Seagull* was presented by the University Drama Society.

In addition there were exhibitions of modern British

painting, and of stained glass by John Piper and Patrick Reyntiens, the designers of the stained glass in Coventry Cathedral.

Performances take place in the university great hall, the town hall, the Rainbow Hall and the Whiteknights Theatre. Full details of future festivals and programmes can be obtained from the Secretary, Summer Festival of Art, St Patrick's Hall, The University, Reading, Berkshire.

ASCOT – The Royal Ascot Race Meeting

This is not only a famous meeting which includes a number of valuable races, but is one of the most colourful and best known of the events on the outer fringe of London which still form part of the London Season. The meeting is royal for two separate reasons. The racecourse and all the buildings surrounding it are on royal land, while the royal meeting, which is now held in June, has had royal patronage for more than three hundred years. It is often said that the Duke of Cumberland founded the Ascot meeting. Certainly under his auspices it achieved far greater importance than before, but the actual founder was Queen Anne, who saw the possibilities of this part of the royal estate as a racecourse and gave positive instructions to her counsellors to establish a regular meeting there. The first took place in August 1711, and the first race run was Her Majesty's Plate, of 100 guineas. The first race of the meeting is still the Queen Anne Stakes, in honour of the founder.

The Ascot Gold Cup, now the most important race of the meeting, is a long-distance race of more than two and a half miles. The cup was first offered in 1807 by King George III. Since then it has become one of the most valuable races in the English racing calendar, worth well in excess of £10,000 to the winner. The Queen Alexandra

Stakes were founded just over a century ago. The Royal Hunt Cup is another race which attracts an international entry.

Early in the nineteenth century the future of the course was in jeopardy when an Enclosure Act was being considered, but by royal direction a clause was inserted in the act that Ascot Heath should continue for ever as a racecourse for the public use. When the Prince Regent, one of the greatest friends that English racing has ever had, became king he instituted the royal carriage procession up the course before each day's racing begins – now, as then, one of the highlights of the meeting. The procession too is still a carriage procession, the open carriages being drawn by the famous Windsor Greys. In practice the royal party leaves Windsor by car and changes into carriages in Windsor Forest. The grandstand was built in 1839 with the royal box an integral part of it, accenting the growing democracy of the nineteenth century and the greater freedom with which the sovereign has tended to mingle with the people since then.

The personal interest of the sovereign has prolonged the wearing of formal dress at Royal Ascot long after it has fallen out of use on many less formal occasions. Morning dress is insisted upon in the royal enclosure and ladies wear beautiful summer dresses made by the leading couturiers of England and France. It is so much a special occasion that hundreds of visitors who come to Royal Ascot seldom attend another race meeting.

Until the present century the Royal Ascot four-day meeting was the only one held on Ascot Heath. After the closing down of many racecourses during the Second World War, however, the number of racing days was increased. With the provision of a steeplechase course, Ascot now has meetings throughout the year, but the June meeting is still Royal Ascot, and no other meeting has attracted public attention in the same way as this traditional one.

WINDSOR – The Garter Ceremony

St George's Chapel is the chapel of the Most Noble Order of the Garter, the most distinguished order in British Chivalry. The occasion of the annual service in June is one of royal pageantry in its most dignified form. The Order of the Garter was founded by Edward III in 1348. It is no more than a legend, but a most diverting one, that the king instituted the order to commemorate an occasion when he picked up a garter which had been dropped by the Countess of Salisbury, and rebuked his tittering courtiers with the words, 'Honi soit qui mal y pense' (Evil be to him who evil thinks), which is the motto of the order. An investiture when required is held in the throne room

The royal drive up the course at Ascot before the racing begins

of Windsor Castle. Afterwards a procession from the castle to St George's Chapel is formed, including the Sovereign and Consort, the twenty-five Knights of the Garter and foreign holders of the order, and the Military Knights of Windsor. The route is lined by detachments of the Household Cavalry.

The Royal Windsor Horse Show

An exciting outdoor event that originated as a 'Wings for Victory' special attraction. Since 1943 it has been an annual event. In the short period since its inception it has become one of the leading horse shows in the country and certainly one of the most generally popular. H.M. Queen Elizabeth II is patron, as was King George VI. The show ground is in the Home Park within sight of the battlements of the castle and the fine timber of Windsor Great Park. Musical rides by the Household Cavalry, concerts by the massed bands of the Brigade of Guards and a coaching marathon, have become traditional features, in addition to the usual show jumping competitions and equestrian displays. The show is a three-day event in the second week of May.

HUNGERFORD – The Hocktide Celebrations

Hungerford lies astride the London–Bath road, a pleasant place, but not one where most people would expect to find a colourful and unusual survival from the Middle Ages still carried out with enthusiasm every year. Hocktide is the second Tuesday after Easter Day. Once it was a countryside festival widely observed, one feature of which was that people of opposite sexes were tied together and released only after they had paid a forfeit according to their means. Today Hungerford is the only place which preserves a semblance of the custom in a day-long festival which has attracted to itself more elaborate observances than the simple Hocktide fun of yesteryear.

Festivities begin in the morning about nine o'clock, when the 'town crier' clad in a grey and scarlet costume sounds a horn at the Corn Exchange. The horn itself is a seventeenth-century one, a copy of that presented to the people of Hungerford in the fourteenth century by John of Gaunt as a token of pasture rights granted to them. A Hocktide Court is then convened. The members of the court retain medieval names. There is the Portreeve, the Constable, the bailiffs and overseers of the common land, and inevitably ale tasters. Two Tutti-men are elected by the court. After all disputed matters relating to common rights have been settled the Tutti-men (tutti is a corruption of tithe and the Tutti-men are tything men or tithe collectors) are given their 'badge of office', a staff decorated with ribbons and flowers. Their official dress is morning coat and top hat. They set out on their round of the town

The procession from the Castle to St George's Chapel during the Garter Ceremony at Windsor
The coaching event at the Windsor Horse Show
The Tutti-men at the Hungerford Hocktide celebrations

accompanied by an orange scrambler wearing a cocked hat and with a sack of oranges over his shoulder. Their right is to collect a tithe of one penny from every man in the town and a kiss from every girl. In return for the kiss the girl receives an orange.

During the civic lunch at a local hotel pennies and oranges are thrown from the windows and the boys of the town scramble for them.

The whole day is treated as a holiday and is the equivalent of a village carnival, so that visitors can share in the fun and marvel once more at the extraordinary way in which such distinctive traditions have survived in an age of uniformity.

ABINGDON – The Election of the Mayor of Ock Street

Set in the broad plain of the Thames and retaining some interesting fragments of its abbey as well as a lovely classical market house, Abingdon was the scene of St Edmund's Fair, one of the great fairs of the south country. The Election of the Mayor of Ock Street, which is held on the Saturday nearest to 20th June, is a survival of the festivities attendant on the fair of St Edmund, whose feast is 20th June. An ox was roasted, as at so many ancient fairs, and the possession of the horns of the ox was regarded as an omen of specially good luck and was hotly disputed. In time competition for the horns was removed from the sphere of brute force and became part of an elaborate ceremonial. In the eighteenth century the contest was decided by a lively and intricate routine of country dancing, the ultimately successful dancer being called Mayor of the Morris, or Mayor of Ock Street. The latter is still the name of a street in Abingdon, and the whole ceremonial has become a festival of morris dancing, the dancers travelling the whole length of the street in dance formations, one of them holding aloft a pair of ox horns as a symbol of the real purpose of the dance.

Abingdon is one of the few English towns to retain the modern equivalent of three medieval fairs. Apart from St Edmund's Fair there is St Mark's Fair on 3rd May, and a Michaelmas fair. The latter is a far, far different event from what it was in 1805, when the *Oxford Journal* reported that there were ten thousand people present on one day and a great number of dairymaids, who were hired at very low wages owing to the reduced price of cheese. For that matter the June Fair has changed since the eighteen-thirties, when the same journal reported that prostitutes, pickpockets and highwaymen 'made a large display'.

Dorset

ABBOTSBURY – Garland Day

Most people think of Abbotsbury as a village of stone-built thatched cottages nestling under the Dorset Downs, and as a place of unusual interest notable for the tithe barn and gatehouse of its medieval abbey, and for the hundreds of swans which make a charming pattern on the water of Fleet which separates the fields of the Dorset mainland from the stony expanse of the Chesil Bank. But Abbotsbury in fact has been an important centre of inshore fishing for many hundreds of years. The Chesil Bank, which seems to separate it effectively from the sea, is in fact its strand, and West Bay which it faces has always been famous for its fisheries.

That is the background of the Garland Day celebration on or about 13th May (the exact date each year can be obtained most easily from the British Travel Association) when garlands of flowers made by the village school-children in traditional and rather lovely shapes and patterns are carried in procession through the village street on poles, then taken down to the sea and thrown into it. This once marked the beginning of the local fishing season and was accompanied by the blessing of the fishes and elaborate ritual to ensure a good fishing harvest. Today it is largely a local festival the exact meaning of which some who take part in it have never known, though it retains to the full its colourful character.

Hampshire

WINCHESTER – Southern Cathedrals Festival

This annual festival brings together the choirs of Chichester, Salisbury and Winchester Cathedrals, and gives visitors the opportunity to hear something of the great choral tradition which draws its inspiration from the church. The choral repertoire ranges from seventeenth- and eighteenth-century composers like Purcell down to contemporaries such as Benjamin Britten and Michael Tippett. The festival is held at each of the three cathedrals every three years for three days – 28th–30th July at Winchester in 1966, 27th–29th July at Salisbury in 1967, 26th–28th July at Chichester in 1968.

The first year in which the choirs united was 1901, when with the choir of the Chapel Royal they joined to sing in Winchester to commemorate the unveiling of the statue of King Alfred. Three years later the first Southern Cathedrals Festival was held in Chichester to commemorate the recommissioning of the organ. The results were so gratifying that with only one break the festival became an annual event until 1914. It was revived in 1920 for some years, then lapsed, but was revived once more in 1960. The increasing interest in sacred music has ensured its present established place in the English musical calendar. The programme usually includes a sung eucharist on the first day, evensong with special settings on the last day, and at least two concerts devoted to a theme such as 'The

Glories of the Psalter'. There are also recitals by famous organists, such as Dr Thalben Ball in 1966.

The festival also has a number of fringe events, including exhibitions, films and plays. The whole festival gives visitors the opportunity to discover the vast extent of the contribution which cathedrals have made to the cultural life of the nation. Further details may be obtained from the Secretary, Southern Cathedrals Festival, 57B The Close, Salisbury, Wiltshire.

FARNBOROUGH – The Flying Display and Exhibition

Established in 1932 at Hendon aerodrome immediately following the R.A.F. display, and since the close of the Second World War held at the Royal Aircraft Establishment at Farnborough, the flying display is now a biennial event in the even years (1966 and 1968) under the auspices of the Society of British Aerospace Companies. Its usual date is the first full week in September (5th–11th September in 1966). Its main purpose is to sell British Aerospace products, but it is a fascinating exhibition for anyone with the slightest interest in aircraft. The display given each afternoon starts at about three o'clock. The flying demonstrations by test pilots are supplemented by displays arranged by the R.A.F. and the Royal Navy. In the most recent events well over three hundred members of the society have exhibited. The guided weapons park and radar demonstration site are also of exceptional interest. In the 1964 exhibition the Bloodhound and Thunderbird were exhibited, as well as anti-tank guided weapons, the Blue Streak and Blue Steel missiles and a meteorological research rocket. A co-ordinated display of electronic communication and control systems was also staged. Further details may be obtained from the Secretary, Society of British Aerospace Companies, 29 King Street, St James's, London, S.W.1.

TICHBORNE – The Tichborne Dole

Tichborne is a tiny sequestered village in exceptionally well-wooded country two miles from Alresford, with a church which shows traces of Saxon workmanship. The north aisle is the chapel of the Tichbornes, who have been lords of the manor since Anglo-Norman times. Their ancestral home, retaining some of the original twelfth- or early thirteenth-century masonry, survived until 1803, when it was dismantled and replaced by the classical style mansion which is still the home of the Tichbornes.

The dole, an annual distribution of flour according to age-old custom, is distributed with great ceremonial to the villagers every Lady Day, 25th March, outside the house. The legend is that Lady Mabella, wife of Sir Roger Tichborne, one of the earliest members of the family, on her deathbed asked her husband to give more help to the poor

Formation flying at Farnborough Air Display

Below, crowds viewing the static exhibits at the same display
Photo: Flight

Preparing for the start
of the Fastnet Race. A typical
occasion at Cowes

of the parish. Sir Roger seized a burning faggot from the fire and told her that he would dedicate as much land as she could encircle before the faggot burnt out. Lady Mabella accepted the challenge and, though too weak to walk, crawled round an area of twenty-three acres, and with her dying breath invoked a curse on the House of Tichborne if the land were ever put to any other use than for the relief of the poor. 'If this sacred gift is tampered with, the name of Tichborne shall be changed and the family will die out.' Those twenty-three acres are still known as 'The Crawls'.

It is a matter of historic fact that in 1799 Sir Henry Tichborne decided to divert the revenue from 'The Crawls' to church charities in place of the flour dole, which he thought was being abused. Lady Mabella had prophesied that as soon as the dole was discontinued there would be a generation of seven Tichborne sons followed by one of seven daughters. Sure enough, Sir Henry had seven sons, and his eldest son seven daughters. Not unnaturally the dole was restored. A ton and a half of flour is distributed each year to about two hundred villagers, a service in Latin is held on the steps of Tichborne House and the flour is blessed before distribution.

How seriously the curse is taken is shown by the fact that, when flour was rationed and the Ministry of Food, unmindful of curses, refused Sir Anthony Tichborne's request for extra units in order to continue the distribution, Sir Anthony was deluged with thousands of coupons from people living in every part of Britain.

ANDOVER – Christmas Eve Mumming
Companies of Christmas mummers were numerous in rural England until comparatively recent times. Now only a few towns and villages preserve the old custom. At Andover performances take place on Christmas Eve, Christmas Day and Boxing Day in the town's inns, the mummers dressed in paper streamers and enacting in mime with various degrees of skill a version of the medieval routine depicting the story of death and resurrection.

Isle of Wight

COWES – Regatta Week
This famous regatta is held at the beginning of August and is organized by the Royal Yacht Club, the only yacht club which flies the White Ensign. Yachting at Cowes dates back to the eighteenth century, but the origin of the pre-eminent place which Cowes Week holds in the British yachting calendar dates from the founding of the Royal Yacht Squadron there in 1812. For the first eight years of its existence it was the Cowes Yacht Club, but was given royal patronage in 1820. Since then many members of the royal family have taken a personal interest in the regatta, either by presenting trophies or by taking part in the races. William IV was the first to present a cup in 1834. King George V was among the most enthusiastic yachtsmen of English sovereigns, and in recent years the Duke of Edinburgh, who has sailed in many races, has maintained the royal tradition.

Sussex

GLYNDEBOURNE – Festival Opera
The inception of the Glyndebourne Festival Season was in 1934, when Mr John Christie, C.H., the founder, with eager support from his wife Audrey Mildmay, built an intimate opera house in the gardens of his home, which dates in part from the sixteenth century and lies in a most

Walking in the grounds during the interval at Glyndebourne

picturesque setting between Mount Cabourn and the main ridge of the Downs. The Festival Opera is accepted as one of the leading musical festivals in the world. John Christie's policy was the best of everything – the best libretti, the best voices, the best musicians and the best production. Quite literally money was no object to him – only the highest possible interpretation of opera performed in the highly favourable atmosphere of a small theatre in near-perfect surroundings.

At first the festival was primarily a Mozart festival, but gradually the repertoire was extended, especially after the Second World War, until the works presented ranged over the whole world of opera and included a number new to the British theatre. One of the most successful new productions in recent years outside the usual repertoire has been Rossini's *La Pietra del Paragone*, a newly revised version of the opera written by Rossini for La Scala, Milan, and first produced there in 1812.

The international character of the festival is illustrated by the fact that in the 1965 revival of this opera the leading singers included Michel Roux of the Paris Opera, Ugo Trama, the distinguished Italian singer, Heinz Blankenburg of the Hamburg State Opera and Josephine Veasey of the Covent Garden Company.

In 1965 too what has so aptly been called the 'Glyndebourne experiment' included first productions there of D. Cimarosa's *Il Matrimonio Segreto* and G. Donizetti's *Anna Bolena*, as well as revivals of Richard Strauss' *Der Rosenkavalier*, Mozart's *Le Nozze di Figaro* and Verdi's *Macbeth*.

The ritual of festival-going at Glyndebourne has always included the wearing of evening dress, which compels visitors from London and farther afield to change soon after lunch (some operas begin at 5 p.m. or earlier). There is a long interval during which dinner is served. This was the policy laid down by John Christie quite deliberately in order, as he put it, 'to give the public trouble. We take a great deal of trouble. The public must do the same.' That trouble is a vital ingredient, John Christie thought, in stimulating the mood to appreciate the artistic entertainment his company offered. The long interval was also wholly deliberate to enhance enjoyment of the operas. He believed that without such an interval the musical appetite became sated.

The success of the great adventure is proof of his wisdom. Until recently the festival opened in mid May and continued until mid August, with performances every day. From 1966 onwards a new policy is being pursued. The festival will have a shorter season extending only over the months of June and July, and the six operas which were presented in earlier years will be reduced to four. Of these four productions, however, three will be new to the festival and only one a revival. Mr George Christie, who is carrying on his father's work, said that it might appear that these reductions represent to some extent a retreat. In fact it was nothing of the kind. What the festival was doing was to take the bold step of discarding commercial considerations for artistic ones. The 1967 programme will include a new production of *Don Giovanni* and the introduction of an opera by the seventeenth-century Italian composer Cavalli, reworked by Raymond Leppard especially for the festival. The 1966 programme consists of new productions of Handel's *Jephtha*, Massenet's *Werther*, Purcell's *Dido and Aeneas*, with Ravel's *L'Heure Espagnole* as part of a double bill, and a revival of Mozart's *Die Zauberflöte*.

It is hoped that this ambitious programme will be supported by a Glyndebourne touring group consisting mainly of talented young British singers from the Glyndebourne chorus and understudies, bringing the conception of Glyndebourne Opera to a far wider public than has been possible before except through the medium of radio and television (the Glyndebourne Company was featured on radio and television more than 150 times in the thirty years following their first broadcast in 1936). Full details of festival programmes can be obtained from the Press Officer, Glyndebourne Festival Opera, Glyndebourne, Lewes, Sussex.

CHICHESTER – The Chichester Drama Festival
The initial idea for the Chichester festival derived from Leslie Evershed-Martin, a city councillor and past mayor

The Chichester Festival Theatre, the open stage and auditorium
Photo: National Theatre

'Glyndebourne Festival'
by Gaynor Chapman,
who is an illustrator and
mural artist

Chichester Festival.
A scene from
The Royal Hunt from the Sun,
with Robert Stephens
as Atahuallpa
Photo: Angus McBean

Chichester Cathedral
from the south-west

of the city, but the genius which inspired its success was that of Sir Laurence Olivier. Today it is one of the premier drama festivals in Britain, distinguished from all others by being presented in the first permanent open stage theatre, which was awarded the British Travel Association Trophy for the most outstanding tourist attraction of 1962.

From the very beginning critical acclaim and public enthusiasm were lavished on the performances in this new conception of a theatre, especially that of *Uncle Vanya*, which, in Sir Laurence Olivier's own words, 'was the real test. I often think anything written before the eighteenth century must inevitably be more successfully produced in amphitheatres, but Ibsen and Chekhov – that is a very different matter. . . .'

The theatre has nearly 1,400 seats, none of which is more than sixty feet from the stage. The casts are composed of some of Britain's most famous actors and actresses. With Sir Laurence Olivier as director, the policy of the festival has been to produce three plays each season, the only criterion for inclusion of a particular play being its excellence as a play and the availability of the best actors and actresses to perform it. So there has been a mixture of old and new. *Uncle Vanya* was brilliantly successful, so was *Trelawney of the Wells*, but Peter Shaffer's *avant-garde Black Comedy*, which appeared in 1965 in a double bill with Strindberg's *Miss Julie*, was equally popular with experts and laymen alike.

The festival is a summer one. For some years it has run from April to September, but more recently from early July to early September. Sir Laurence was succeeded as director by John Clements in 1966. In the latter's first year the season was extended, commencing on 24th May and continuing for sixteen weeks with four plays in the repertoire. Full details of productions may be obtained from the Secretary, The Festival Theatre, Chichester, Sussex, or from the Press Representative, The National Theatre, 22 Duchy Street, London, S.E.1.

Plough Sunday Celebration

Chichester Cathedral has been in the forefront of the revival of the celebrations linked with the ancient festivals of agriculture, of which 'blessing the plough' is the earliest in the year. It takes place on the Sunday immediately after Twelfth Night. Services, with attendant processions and celebrations, were held in hundreds of village churches before the Reformation but there have been no continuous survivals (though the corresponding Harvest Festival at the end of the season has always been observed). The traditional order of service is observed at Chichester Cathedral Plough Sunday Service, and there is always a crowded congregation of farmers and visitors.

Sir John Barbirolli conducting the Hallé Orchestra at Bexhill-on-Sea Festival of Music. Festival visitors mingle at a wine tasting

The climax of the service is when young farmers drag a plough to the steps of the chancel and the bishop and dean touch the plough and invoke God's blessing on it and on all who plough the fields. This ceremony is sponsored by the dean and chapter of the cathedral and by the Young Farmers' Club. There is a similar Plough Sunday service in Exeter Cathedral. These and a few others in village churches, where although visitors are welcome there is little room for any except the farming community, all stem from the work of the Council for the Church and Countryside, which was founded in 1943 and which has done a great deal through the encouragement of interest in the services linked with the agricultural year to bring back awareness of religious feeling in rural life.

Southern Cathedrals Festival

Chichester is one of the three cathedrals which share this festival, which is held in each of them every three years. (*See* page 68.)

BEXHILL-ON-SEA – Festival of Music

The Bexhill festival is a fine example of civic enterprise, featuring internationally famous orchestras and soloists with a number of fringe events coinciding with the period of the festival, which is normally held for a week in the second half of July. It was founded in 1960, its purpose to provide a wide range of music performed in the best possible way. Apart from that it has no axe to grind. In recent years the Hallé Orchestra under Sir John Barbirolli, and the B.B.C. Concert Orchestra under Vilem Tausky, the Bournemouth Symphony Orchestra under Rudolf Schwarz have been featured.

Though orchestras vary from year to year, the festival takes a similar course, with a civil procession and opening service at the parish church of St Peter on the Monday afternoon, a symphony concert in the evening and on most other evenings until the Friday, with sometimes one evening devoted to a piano or violin recital. All these events take place in the concert hall.

Lectures are arranged every morning on musical topics by outstanding authorities such as Stanford Robinson, Anthony Besch and John Gardner. The festival club is open each day for the convenience of festival patrons and there are usually wine tastings for visitors at noon each day. Pre-concert dinners are served each evening in good time for the concert, and after the concert there is dancing with licensed bar until midnight. In this informal and relaxed atmosphere musical celebrities and the man in the street are encouraged to mingle in discussion and social activity so that many new friendships are made. An art exhibition is also staged, and festival coach tours are arranged to places of interest in the district. Further details may be obtained from the Festival Administrator, De La Warr Pavilion, Bexhill-on-Sea, Sussex.

GOODWOOD – The July Meeting

'Glorious Goodwood', as the Earl of Suffolk called it in 1886, and as it has been called ever since, is the last event in what used to be called the London Season, even though Goodwood racecourse is on the summit of the Sussex Downs almost seventy miles from London. The first races were run here in 1801, when the 3rd Duke of Richmond, Colonel of the Sussex Militia, made this part of his estate available to his militia officers and members of the Good-wood Hunt for 'race riding'. That first meeting was a great success. It became an annual event, though until the middle of the nineteenth century it was of wholly local importance. Gradually the beautiful setting of the race-course, one of the loveliest in England, began to attract people from farther afield, and by the turn of the century King Edward VII (while Prince of Wales) gave it the seal of his approval, describing it as 'a garden party with racing tacked on', and made it fashionable overnight.

Goodwood is often compared with Ascot, but the atmosphere is very different. King Edward before his accession was irked by the formality of the occasion and the need to wear morning dress. Directly he succeeded to the throne he abolished what he called the 'dress parade' and wore a soft hat and tweed suit for the meeting. He felt this was more appropriate to the rural surroundings. And so it has remained ever since, a gay, carefree event in the racing calendar as well as a fashionable one, with accommodation for thousands of the general public on the 'open-air grandstand' of the Trundle Hill, which overlooks the course and is capped by the entrenchments of a prehistoric fortified village. The meeting is a four-day one held at the end of July.

HASTINGS – Blessing the Sea

Hastings has always been pre-eminently a fishing town, as it still is. In spite of its growth as a seaside holiday resort, the Old Town remains much as it has been for centuries, and the still numerous fishermen, though they eke out their livelihood by taking visitors on summer boating trips, depend on the harvest of the sea for most of the year.

The ceremony of blessing the sea is a survival of the numerous observances in the rural calendar connected with Rogation-tide and coincided with the beginning of the local fishing season. The ceremony takes place in the evening on or about 26th May (the exact day can be obtained most easily from the British Travel Association). About 7 p.m. a procession leaves the two parish churches of the Old Town, All Saints' and St Clement's. It comes to a halt in the fish market, where the bishop of the diocese blesses the fishermen and their nets, and prayers are said for a good harvest from the sea. No records exist of the origin of the custom, but it almost certainly goes back to the Middle Ages.

RYE – Scrambling for Hot Pennies

Rye can claim to be a medieval town as reasonably as any town in the south country. Once an important port, it has been left high and dry by the sea. It is a place which is still largely contained within the former circuit of its medieval walls and retains part of its ancient fortifications, including gates and walls, and narrow cobbled streets as they were a century ago. It is also the scene of a ceremony watched by hundreds of visitors every year on Mayoring Day in the last week of May (officially 23rd May), when at about one o'clock streams of 'hot pennies' are thrown from a window of the town hall, or from the balcony of a neighbouring

hotel, to crowds of children waiting in the street. The custom originated when Rye, like many other important towns, minted its own coins and is a reminder of this ancient privilege. The coins were always thrown from the windows of the mayor's parlour on Mayoring Day. The chief difference between the past and the present is that in the past hundreds of adults as well as children were waiting to scramble for them. The story is told that one day the supply of coins ran out; a messenger was sent to collect a fresh supply and returned with a sack full of coins which were hot from the mint.

Sussex and Kent

LEWES, RYE, EDENBRIDGE – Guy Fawkes' Night

Guy Fawkes' Night is celebrated in every town and village. A few places, especially Lewes and Rye in Sussex, and Edenbridge in Kent, have made the day an occasion for more elaborate displays than the usual backyard fireworks or bonfire on the village green. The background of Guy Fawkes celebrations is that on 5th November 1605 a papist conspirator, Guy Fawkes, was discovered laying charges of gunpowder under the chamber in which King James I and his Parliament were due to assemble for the opening of Parliament. He was tried and executed for high treason. Parliament decreed that the day should be a public holiday as a thanksgiving to God for the foiling of the plot. The name Guy Fawkes gave to later generations the word 'guy'; even today a part of all bonfire celebrations is to throw a guy on to the flames. At Lewes, Rye and Edenbridge bonfire societies organize the celebrations and provide truly remarkable displays of fireworks. At Edenbridge a procession of revellers in fancy dress and decorated floats with brass bands in attendance is a feature of bonfire night.

Wiltshire

SALISBURY – Southern Cathedrals Festival

This festival is held triennially at Salisbury, in turn with Chichester and Winchester; at Salisbury in 1967 and 1970, at Chichester in 1968 and 1971 and at Winchester in 1966 and 1969. (*See page 68.*)

Musical events are arranged regularly in the cathedral irrespective of the festival, for example Bach's *St Matthew Passion* during Lent.

Son et Lumière in the grounds of the cathedral school, formerly the palace of the Bishops of Salisbury, is a feature of the 1966 programme, from late in July until mid September. A cathedral setting has always proved the ideal one for this modern entertainment, which uses the techniques of the twentieth century to bring the history and the beauty of the cathedral into the compass of a single moving experience. Full details of this and other cathedral

'Chichester Festival' by Graham Byfield,
an artist designer who has used a technique
of *gouache*, pen and ink on scraperboard
for this drawing

events may be obtained from the Secretary, Southern Cathedrals Festival, 57B the Close, Salisbury, Wiltshire.

EDINGTON – Festival of Music

The priory church of St Mary, St Katharine and All Saints, Edington, is one of the most interesting and beautiful parish churches in Wiltshire. Lying immediately under the northern slopes of Salisbury Plain and once the church of a medieval monastic foundation, it retains a wealth of interesting stained glass and carved timber. The festival was founded in 1956 and from the beginning has owed a large measure of its success to the support and encouragement of Ralph Dudley, the vicar. Its purpose is to provide a week of services set to the finest church music and sung as beautifully as possible at a time when cathedral and collegiate choirs are on holiday. Edington is a singularly appropriate place for a festival of this kind, since the monastic church was built with the primary intention that daily choral services should be sung in it. When the festival was founded a tradition that had been lost was partly revived.

Two choirs, consisting of members of some fifteen cathedral and collegiate choirs, take part in the festival. The daily eucharist and evensong are sung by the choirs, while the music of matins and compline is sung by all those present. The festival ends on the last Sunday in August and begins on the previous Sunday.

The music ranges from the old English of Byrd and Purcell to the modern work of Tippett, Stravinsky and Hindemith. Visitors are welcome and no tickets are required. Further details may be obtained from the Hon. Secretary, Edington Music Festival, Edington Vicarage near Westbury, Wiltshire.

STONEHENGE – Midsummer Druid Festival

The midsummer ceremony of the modern English Druids is both historically intriguing and colourful to watch. The Druids gather on the eve of Midsummer's Day and keep vigil by the giant trilithons and blue stones of Stonehenge on Salisbury Plain until the sun rises, when they hold a service by the altar stone and another service at midday. The colour of the ceremony comes from the Druids' robes and the traditional banners. Watching for the sun to rise at Stonehenge on Midsummer's Day (in spite of the fact that in three years out of four there is too much cloud or mist to allow the sun to be seen as it rises) for many years attracted great crowds. Accusations of hooliganism and damage to the stones through incision of initials were made to the Ministry of Public Building and Works, which is responsible for the care of the monument, with the result that the public were barred from the neighbourhood of Stonehenge until just before dawn. Then in 1964 and 1965 the police were called in and barbed wire fences put up to keep the public out both before and after sunrise. More recently restrictions have been eased, and large numbers of people travel by car on the night of 23rd June in good time for the rising of the sun in the early hours of 24th June.

What does all this mean? The Druids have often been accused of making nonsense of history on the ground that Stonehenge is far, far older than the Druid religion, which was introduced into Britain just before the Roman occupation, whereas the trilithons of Stonehenge date from the

Midsummer morning at Stonehenge

beginning of the Bronze Age, about four thousand years ago. Recent research has shown that the original circle, doubtless a temple to the sun god, was subsequently enlarged several times and was certainly still used in the period before the Roman occupation, when Druid rites were practised widely in England. It is historically quite possible, therefore, that what originated as a bronze age temple was adopted by the Druids two thousand years later, as once more it has been adopted by them after nearly another two thousand years.

Midsummer's Day, however, is not scientifically the correct day on which to hold the celebration. Years ago it was celebrated at the summer solstice, 21st June. That is strictly speaking the correct day, for although the altar stone and the 'hele' stone outside the main circle are not strictly in alignment with the rising sun at the summer solstice it has been demonstrated by astronomers that four thousand years ago this was the case.

WISHFORD – Grovely Procession

This is one of the more rewarding of old customs for the visitor. It takes place on 29th May, Oak Apple Day, a day more usually associated with celebrations in honour of King Charles II's escape after Worcester, though the Wishford ceremony has no known connection with Charles II.

Wishford is about five miles north-west of Salisbury in the valley of the Wylye, near the point where this lovely stream flowing down from Salisbury Plain joins the Nadder before merging with the Avon at Salisbury. Immediately to the south of it and separating it from the Nadder valley, Grovely Wood (formerly Grovely Forest) is still a mass of undergrowth and thickets, a vivid reminder of the medieval oak forest into which the people from Saxon times until the later Middle Ages were allowed to drive their swine to feed on acorns in the autumn, and in which by a royal charter of 1603 the people of Wishford were given the right to gather firewood in perpetuity.

The Grovely Procession originated as a thanksgiving for that royal charter, one clause of which was that the rights granted would be renewed each year by representatives of the village going into the forest and formally cutting wood. This is still done in the early morning of 29th May and branches are carried back into the village. The procession starts at noon, with a local band leading groups of men carrying the branches and women bundles of wood, followed by schoolchildren in fancy costume. Some of the village homes are decorated with sprays of oak and flowers, and the traditional banner inscribed with the words 'Grovely, Grovely, Grovely and all Grovely' leads the procession, as it has done for hundreds of years.

Part of the floral procession before the Jersey Battle of Flowers

Jersey, Channel Islands

ST HELIER – The Battle of Flowers

One of the most colourful of all festive occasions, this is an annual event which originated as part of the celebrations to mark the coronation of King Edward VII and Queen Alexandra in 1902. It is commonly held on the last Thursday in July and in recent years has been watched by more than 100,000 visitors. The vast interest is not surprising, for this is an entirely different kind of pageant from anything offered on the mainland of Great Britain. Several million blossoms, it is said, are used, all of them grown without charge for the battle. The centre-piece of the festival is a procession of floral floats and coaches with a great number of set pieces all made from flowers – working models of windmills, peacocks spreading their tails and so on. One float carries Miss Jersey, who literally rises from a sea of blossom. Episodes in the island's history, especially the 1871 battle of Jersey, are featured on other floats. After the procession there is a real, almost unbelievable, battle of flowers with blossoms used as ammunition. The air is filled with colour and scent. A similar but less elaborate flower festival is held in Guernsey towards the end of August.

West Country 6

The west country has an enviable tradition of quiet prosperity from the earliest times to the present day; west country people have a vigorous tradition of independence. That is as true today as it was in Elizabethan times, when Bristol merchants were laying the foundations of the commerce which made their city famous. The nineteenth and twentieth centuries have seen industrial expansion, not on the unbridled lines of the Black Country or of north-east England, but solid and substantial enough to project the image of the later Middle Ages into the twentieth century. The west country prosperity has its roots in the rich soils of the Marcher counties, and the favourable climate modified by the shelter of the Welsh mountains, quite as much as in the growth of its medieval and modern trade and industry. The two are linked in Gloucestershire and adjoining counties, for the fleeces of the sheep which found admirable pasture on the slopes of the Cotswold and Somerset hills were the raw material of a woollen cloth industry, which has not died out and is centred today on the hill town of Stroud and reflected in the magnificent fifteenth-century churches with their proud and lovely towers beckoning to the traveller over the wide acres of Gloucestershire and Somerset.

The individual approach and intense local patriotism of west country people are mirrored in the exceptionally large number of festivals of the arts, which have shown in the last twenty years that culture in its widest sense affecting the largest possible number of people is certainly not the prerogative of eastern England. The Cheltenham Festival is one of the oldest established and one of the most successful. With its fellow the Cheltenham Literary Festival it embraces the whole world of self-expression. The Bath Festival arranged with Yehudi Menuhin has made an equal mark on west country life; its fame has spread equally to every part of the country. The Three Choirs Festival, held in successive years in the cathedrals of Gloucester, Hereford and Worcester, is one of the most illustrious of its kind. The Ludlow Festival re-creates in the ruins of its famous border castle the spirit of the seventeenth century, when Milton's *Comus* was first performed there. The Festivals of the Arts at Stroud and Bromsgrove are models of what local festivals should be yet still make an appeal to a wider audience.

It is a tribute to the progressive spirit of the western counties that the Bath and West Show was the first of the great agricultural shows to be founded after the Dukes of Bedford had shown the way with the Woburn sheep shearings. It is significant too that a west countryman, the Duke of Beaufort, should have founded the Badminton Horse Trials, which in a remarkably short space of time became the premier event of its kind in the country.

WORCESTER, HEREFORD, GLOUCESTER

The Three Choirs Festival, the earliest of its kind in Europe, was founded before 1719, and is held triennially at each of the three cathedral cities, Worcester (4th–9th September 1966), Hereford (1967) and Gloucester (1968). It opens with a service of praise and thanksgiving in the cathedral, with singing by a festival choir of three hundred voices accompanied by a symphony orchestra. During the ensuing week there are at least nine concerts in the cathedral and chamber concerts in a local theatre and neighbouring historic homes, as well as exhibitions and social events in agreeable variety. The works chosen for the music programmes, which have included many first performances, range from choral works of the Tudor period to recent British works such as those of Tippett, Benjamin Britten and Elgar. The earliest records in the first part of

'Three Choirs Festival' by Leonard Rosoman,
a tutor at the Royal College of Art, who has
had one-man shows in London and New York.
The Cathedrals are Gloucester (left)
Hereford and Worcester

the eighteenth century show that then, as now, it was held in succession in the cathedrals of Gloucester, Hereford and Worcester, and indicate that the choirs sang sacred music in the cathedral while secular concerts were given elsewhere. The pattern has changed very little in 250 years. In the eighteenth century the festivals were patronized by the 'nobility and gentry' and involved a system by which two or more of their number offered themselves as stewards and became guarantors. The pleasant fiction by which subscribers who take tickets for the week are called stewards is a survival of this two-hundred-year-old custom. The eighteenth-century stewards established the principle that money given at the doors of the cathedral after performances should accrue to the Charity for the Relief of Widows and Orphans of Clergy in the three dioceses. This deserving charity, first associated with the festival in 1724, still profits from it. Full details may be obtained from the Secretary, The Three Choirs Festival, at the festival city of the year.

Gloucestershire

CHELTENHAM – The Cheltenham Festival

The Cheltenham Festival celebrated its twenty-first birthday in 1965 and is now established as one of the most important music festivals in Great Britain. Its theme is contemporary British music. It has provided the platform on which many now eminent composers have first won recognition, and at which many famous musical works have been performed for the first time. It has made a major contribution to the development of English music, for it provides a heaven-sent opportunity for public performances of works which might otherwise remain unknown, a boon which the composers of no previous generation have enjoyed.

The magnitude of its scope is illustrated by the fact that in its first twenty-one years well over two hundred first performances took place. Many of these first performances have been of real importance as, for instance, that of Peter Fricker's First Symphony by the Hallé Orchestra conducted by Sir John Barbirolli in 1950. The performance established Fricker as a composer of real genius and the symphony as an inevitable part of the repertoire of contemporary music. It was a happy arrangement for that same symphony to be performed by the same orchestra under the same conductor at the twenty-first birthday festival.

Peter Maxwell Davies' *Sonata for Seventeen Wind Instruments* (*St Michael*) was first performed at the 1959 festival; Elisabeth Lutyens' *Quincunx for Orchestra*, Opus 44, saw the light of day at the 1962 festival; Stanley Bate's Symphony No. 3 was first performed at the 1954

Three Choirs Festival. Worcester Cathedral floodlit

Photo: Berrow's Newspapers

Three Choir Festival
at Worcester Cathedral
Photo: Berrow's Newspapers

'Cheltenham Festival' by Brian Norwood,
  who has a satirist's taste for old films and, like
  this specimen, old souvenir postcards

festival. Those are only three of the more significant works chosen almost at random from the two hundred first performances. Every year there is fresh excitement as new works appear in the programme. Benjamin Frankel, Gordon Crosse, Alan Rawsthorne and Roberto Gerhard have all made a number of specially valuable contributions.

When Sir Arthur Bliss became Festival President in 1965, he marked the occasion by conducting the B.B.C. Midland Light Orchestra in the first performance of his revised *Hymn to Apollo*. The twenty-first birthday festival was notable also for the presentation of a representative selection of Gustav Holst's work, for Holst was born in Cheltenham and was incidentally the doyen of its musical history. In one concert the great composer's daughter Imogen conducted the Purcell Singers in a performance of some of his choral groups. At another concert the B.B.C. Chorus gave a memorable rendering of Holst's *Hymn of Jesus*. That perhaps gives some idea of the musical range of the Cheltenham Festival which, because it comprehends the whole field of contemporary English music, finds room for a jazz concert. While the basic theme of the festival is the programme of new works by British composers, it concentrates almost equally on established works by British composers of this century.

The festival is held in the first half of July, opening on a Sunday with a festival service and ending with a final concert on the following Friday week. There are major concerts every evening, most of them at the town hall but some more specialized ones in Shaftesbury Hall or the Pittville Pump Room. There is also a series of lunch time recitals in the town hall by young artists lasting approximately an hour. This arrangement gives visitors adequate free time to explore the architectural landscapes of Regency Cheltenham, one of the finest and most spacious of English early nineteenth-century towns, and to take part in the variety of tours round the Cotswold villages which are arranged during the festival. On the Sunday in the middle of the festival the Cheltenham Society usually arranges a coach tour of Cheltenham, covering the principal places of historic and architectural interest.

There is a festival club at the town hall where receptions are held at the conclusion of the concerts, and bar and buffet refreshments are available until midnight. The club is open without further charge to those attending the concerts, its purpose to foster the friendly spirit which is essential to the success of a festival of this kind – that and the interchange of views between people of similar tastes. An art exhibition is staged in the club. One particularly exciting one was an exhibition known as 'Sound into Sight', in which over twenty European painters produced in line and colour the image of a musical composition of their own choice.

The Cheltenham Festival has a 'fringe', not in the sense of the more vociferous Edinburgh fringe, but in the sense of a number of ancillary entertainments given with the full authority of the festival organizers. There is a festival gala starting at 7.30 p.m. and ending at midnight, the first part devoted to an open-air variety show, followed by an ox-roasting, a fireworks display and dancing in the open air. A festival ball is given in the Pittville Pump Room. There

Cheltenham Festival fringe. The start of the road race

Photo: Cheltenham Newspaper Co.

Open-air dancing on the promenade at the Cheltenham Festival
Photo: Cheltenham Newspaper Co.

are exhibitions of painting, pottery and sculpture. Among the most successful of fringe activities in past years has been the veteran and vintage car rally on the middle Sunday, the festival road race which always attracts a large entry, and the Regency 'rout' promoted by the Cheltenham Society, in the Pittville Pump Room and Gardens, with a reception by the 'Prince Regent', orchestra, side shows and fireworks in the gardens, followed by dancing in the Pump Room, guests being asked, if possible, to attend in masks and Regency costumes. Open-air dancing on the promenade is a well-established and popular festival event.

Many notable concerts have been given in recent years by the Bach Choir in Cheltenham College Chapel. Folk song concerts in the Shaftesbury Hall have proved extremely popular. A score of other attractions are designed to enhance the enjoyment of visiting the festival.

Lovers of contemporary music are offered most attractive terms for the entire festival by becoming a festival guarantor. On payment of twelve guineas (subject to revision) priority booking is obtained for all concerts with two reserved seats at each without further payment, at a saving of more than a third. For the payment of six guineas a 'subscriber' is entitled to one seat with priority booking at each of the concerts. Full details of performances and booking arrangements can be obtained from the Entertainments Manager, Town Hall, Cheltenham, Gloucestershire.

The Festival of Literature

This unusual festival is held in early October and its most important features are talks and discussions by outstanding literary personalities. Literary luncheons are arranged, to which guest writers are invited, and there are book and art exhibitions. Full details of this also may be obtained from the Entertainments Manager, Town Hall, Cheltenham, Gloucestershire.

STROUD – The Stroud Festival

This is described as 'A Festival of Religious Drama and the Arts' and takes place for a week in the second half of October. The musical fare is contemporary and has been of an unusually high standard ever since the festival was founded in 1947. In one recent year the first performance was given of *Inscape*, a choral work by Edmund Rubbra specially commissioned for the festival; a hundred children from schools in Stroud joined with top-ranking professional singers in Holy Trinity Church to perform Benjamin Britten's *Noye's Fludde*, in which Owen Brannigan sang the part of Noah. *Noye's Fludde* epitomized one of the festival traditions, to mingle professional with amateur performances in the rendering of great works. The festival opens and closes with a church service, the opening one in the parish church, the closing one in a free church. A religious play is performed each weekday evening in the parish church by Gloucestershire amateur players. In 1965 this took the form of the first stage performance of Brian Miller's *Genevan Fall*. Exhibitions are staged in the Subscription Rooms, especially of the work of Gloucestershire artists, sculptors and craftsmen. One successful recent display was of the famous local product, Stroud cloth. Outstanding films, such as *Henry V* and *Becket*, are shown in the local cinemas for festival audiences and there are numerous illustrated art talks and poetry readings. Altogether the Stroud Festival is a most ambitious project. Further details may be obtained from the Hon. Publicity Chairman, Stroud Festival Committee, Stroud, Gloucestershire.

PAINSWICK – Clipping the Church

Painswick church is a singularly beautiful medieval building with over a hundred clipped yews in its churchyard. On the Sunday nearest to 19th September an age-old ceremony is carried out, when the parishioners form a circle round the church and dance round it singing hymns and traditional songs. The church is then said to be 'clipped' and a sermon is preached in the open air. Before the actual ceremony there is a procession round the churchyard boundary, in which hundreds of children carrying garlands of flowers take part, as well as the church choir and many of the parishioners with the town band in the lead. The ceremonial clipping of the yew trees is quite distinct from 'clipping the church', though the two are often confused. A similar custom is observed at Wirksworth, Derbyshire, on the Sunday following 8th September.

MARSHFIELD – Boxing Day Mummers

Performances of a medieval play in mime are given in Marshfield market place five times during Boxing Day. The mummers, like those of Andover, Hampshire, wear costumes decorated with paper streamers and the play is also similar. Here, however, there are singing and dancing as well as the formal mumming.

CHIPPING CAMPDEN – Scuttlebrook Wake

Chipping Campden, with its noble Gothic church, its classical 'market' and scores of stone-built inns and dwelling places, ranging in date from the sixteenth to the nineteenth century, is always worth a visit, but takes on new life and gaiety at the time of the Scuttlebrook Wake, which is on the Saturday after Whitsuntide. Until the Puritan revolution Scuttlebrook Wake, or Fair, was counted one of the most boisterous in England. Now it is only a shadow of its former self, but the old custom of crowning the Scuttlebrook Queen is maintained and there are various

entertainments, often including a fancy dress parade and competitions, serving as a reminder of the 'Cotswold games', which once included cock-fighting and bear-baiting. The name Scuttlebrook, incidentally, is that of a stream which once flowed along the High Street. At the point where it reached the High Street the queen was crowned. Another interesting point is that the word 'wake', which seems so archaic in this context, is retained in a modern but analogous meaning in the wakes of Lancashire and Scotland.

COOPER'S HILL – Cheese Rolling

The Cotswold Hills fall steeply to the valley of the Severn at Cooper's Hill a few miles from the city of Gloucester. Here every Whit Monday a custom is carried on which originated as a token of the immemorial rights of the people to graze their sheep on Cooper's Hill. At about 6 p.m. a starter, clad in a white smock and wearing the traditional beaver hat, starts the cheese, which is protected by a wooden case. Scores of young men and boys chase it down the hill, many of them falling headlong as they run down the steep grassy slope. The one who captures the cheese (it invariably beats its pursuers to the bottom of

The gathering for the cheese rolling on Cooper's Hill, near Brockworth

'Ludlow Festival' by Anthony Weller,
a sculptor who has carved this plaque
of the 'Prince' from the red sandstone
of Ludlow Castle itself

The Queen with the Duke of Beaufort watching a jumping event in the Badminton Horse Trials

the hill) retains it and there is also a small prize. The custom is said to be fully four hundred years old. Apart from emphasizing the right of the people of the parish to graze sheep, it is said to assert their right to dance round the maypole. In token of this a flagstaff was used to mark the starting point.

BOURTON-ON-THE-WATER – The Water Game
An annual game of 'football' is played in the stream of the River Windrush which flows alongside Bourton's village green. It takes place on the late summer bank holiday (29th August in 1966, 28th August in 1967) – the day on which the football club holds its fête. In spite of its recent fame, the Water Game has no long history. The parish records give no clue to any festivities earlier than the nineteenth century involving a game of this kind. F.A. rules govern the game, which is played by teams of six a side for fifteen minutes each way. Further information can be obtained from Mr D. Orchard, 72 Merville Street, Bourton-on-the-Water, Gloucestershire.

BADMINTON – The Badminton Horse Trials
The origin of the Badminton Horse Trials can be found in the poor showing of British riders in the 1948 Olympic Games. Its purpose was to encourage a progressive improvement in the skill of British riders. The Duke of Beaufort, the Master of the Queen's Horse, appropriately offered his park at Badminton as the venue of the proposed meeting; his estate is still the setting of one of the most important equestrian meetings in the world, which has consistently enjoyed the patronage and personal interest of the royal family. The three-day event is held in April, usually from Thursday to Saturday in the second week. On the first day there is a dressage competition; on the second an endurance trial, including a steeplechase and a cross-country gallop; the third day is show-jumping day. The event is a competitive one, the overall winner being the rider who has scored the largest number of marks in the three days.

Shropshire

LUDLOW – The Ludlow Summer Festival
This festival, which is usually held in the first two weeks of July, was inaugurated in 1960 with the production of Milton's *Comus* in the court of Ludlow Castle, appropriately since *Comus* had its first performance there in 1633. Shakespeare has held the stage in recent years (*Hamlet*,

Margaret Rawlings
as Gertrude
in *Hamlet* at the
Ludlow Festival
Photo: Guardian

1965, *Much Ado About Nothing,* 1966) and the scope of the festival has broadened. Thousands of visitors each year are drawn to Ludlow, partly to see the play in its lovely open-air setting surrounded by the historic walls of the castle, partly to see more of the town, which from the twelfth century onwards was the capital of the Welsh Marches, its castle the seat of the Lords President of the Marches, and which is famous today for its black-and-white timbered houses of the sixteenth and seventeenth centuries, and its many other handsome buildings which slope down to the River Teme where it runs through a narrow wooded gorge.

In addition to the Shakespeare play which is the centre-piece of the festival, several concerts are given by well-known orchestras and soloists, and an art exhibition is staged. Recitals are also usually arranged in neighbouring country houses. Ludlow enters into the spirit of the festival. Shops show special displays, the hotels remain open late and there is even a night club for the entertainment of visitors who join the festival club. Further details may be obtained from the Secretary, Ludlow Festival Society Ltd, 41 Mill Street, Ludlow, Shropshire.

Somerset

BATH – The Bath Festival

This is a festival as much of architecture as of music, for the setting of the concerts, the lovely buildings of eight-eenth-century Bath, the creation of the Woods, father and

son, is as interesting in its own way as the varied pro-gramme of music arranged for the festival with Yehudi Menuhin. The beautifully restored assembly rooms and the guildhall are perfect places in which to appreciate the same kind of music as that which beguiled the people of fashion who lived in or visited Bath to take the waters in the time of that most illustrious master of ceremonies, Beau Nash. For full measure there are concerts in the abbey and in Wells Cathedral. The potential audience of the festival music is extended by arranging at least one concert by a leading orchestra in nearby Bristol.

It seems incredible that the first Bath Festival was held as recently as 1959, so important has it become in the cultural life of the west of England. That it has achieved this enviable position is due in large measure to the art and energy of Yehudi Menuhin, who was the mainspring of the first festival, as he has been of every one since then, and has trained the Bath Festival Orchestra until it can take its place with the small orchestras of the world, and is applauded as vigorously in Paris and Vienna as it is in Bath. The music programmes inevitably reflect Menuhin's personal taste, with a strong accent on the work of Bach and his contemporaries and enthusiasm for Mozart. That does not imply a wholly classical discipline. Contemporary composers such as Michael Tippett and Benjamin Britten have been represented at several festivals. It is character-istic that in a single afternoon concert in the assembly rooms Menuhin and the Festival Orchestra featured the work of Beethoven, Purcell, Tippett and Mozart. No festival programme could be more adventurous than that. Concerts are given by many famous symphony and chamber orchestras in addition to the Festival Orchestra. The visit of the Moscow Chamber Orchestra in 1965 was of special interest.

Fringe activities are numerous. The festival ball is one of the most exciting, sometimes held at a historic home in the neighbourhood, such as Farleigh Hungerford Castle where in 1965 the ball took the form of a dance in celebration of the victory of King Henry V over the French at Agincourt in 1415. A historic pageant was staged in the forecourt of the castle and a fifteenth-century dinner was served to the guests. In the same year Sir Laurence Olivier's *Henry V* was shown at one of the Bath cinemas.

Youth concerts are arranged in conjunction with the local educational authorities, lectures and discussions are given at the guildhall, and there is a festival production at the Bath Theatre Royal.

The festival is held for ten days in mid June, usually from the second Wednesday in the month to the end of the third week. Further details can be obtained from the Spa Director, Pump Room, Bath, Somerset.

The Bach Festival

This, the most ambitious and certainly one of the most important Bach festivals in Europe, is staged only every five years. The first festival was held in 1950 and the last took place in 1965. The next one will be in 1970. It is generally held for eight days towards the end of October and has been organized by the City of Bath Bach Choir ever since the formation of the latter by Mr Cuthbert

Bath Abbey with part of the Roman bath in the foreground
Photo: Bath Spa Committee

Bates, a prominent Bath citizen and lover of Bach's music. So high is the esteem in which this festival is held that in 1965 many applications for seats came from American and European countries, as well as from all parts of the British Isles. More than half the seats available were booked a month before the festival was due to open. The Bach Choir, more than a hundred strong and augmented by members of the London Bach Choir, is supported by the Bath Festival Orchestra and up to forty international soloists. An aim of the performance is to explore every aspect of Bach's genius. Many items are included in the programmes which rarely, if ever, find a place in the usual repertoire, such as the Sonata in A minor for Solo Flute and the Suite in G minor for Lute. About eighty works are included in the seventeen concerts, including always the *St Matthew Passion*, for which Bath Abbey makes the

Yehudi Menuhin conducting the Bath Festival Orchestra in the Assembly Rooms

perfect setting. Details of the next festival can be obtained from the Spa Director, Pump Room, Bath, Somerset.

MINEHEAD – The Hobby-horse Festival

This is strictly a May Day festival but special entertainments and festivities continue throughout the following two days. Undisguisedly the celebration has become a way of attracting visitors to take an early holiday in this quiet seaside town, where the slopes of Exmoor reach almost to the sea. A beautifully decorated hobby-horse is carried through the streets. It is more than six feet long and is made of painted canvas picked out with coloured ribbons. Various dances are carried out around it to a number of traditional tunes played by the town band, or indeed by anyone with a musical instrument, professional or home-made. According to many authorities it is a survival of a fertility rite, as in a sense were all the Celtic May Day customs 'to welcome in the summer and the may-o' and to invoke divine favour for the coming harvest.

CARHAMPTON – Wassailing the Trees

Carhampton, an attractive village two miles from Dunster on the Dunster–Williton road where the outliers of the Brendon Hills fall towards Blue Anchor Bay, is the scene of an annual ceremony, held on 17th January, which probably originated in pagan times. The word 'wassail' is of Old English derivation and means to wish good health; 17th January is the old Twelfth Night, that is the feast of Epiphany, before the calendar was changed, but that does not imply a Christian origin. The early Christian Fathers were remarkably adept at placing pagan customs within the orbit of the Church by identifying a traditional event with a saint's day! The routine is for the villagers to walk into the cider apple orchards (cider has been the staple drink in this part of Somerset from time immemorial) and make a circle round one or more of the finest trees soon after darkness has fallen. Guns are fired through the branches of the tree, cider is thrown on its trunk, and cider-soaked toast and cake are placed on the forks of the tree and left there. The company then sings an incantation which begins:

> Old apple tree, old apple tree,
> We've come to wassail thee.

The leaders of the song then drink a toast. This may sound rather childish, but it is most impressive for those who are present, if only because of the obvious sincerity which underlies the observance. Probably the original purpose of shooting the guns was to drive away the evil spirits which might damage the apple crop, and the purpose of the cider-soaked bread to act as an offering either to the gods of the trees or to the good spirits as a thank-offering in advance.

Worcestershire

BROMSGROVE – The Bromsgrove Festival

The first Bromsgrove Festival was held in 1960 and has become established as a spring festival (it is held in May) which provides a varied and interesting programme lasting a fortnight. From the beginning it has featured the presentation of new musical works and the experimental direction of drama, new and old. Most events are staged in the hall of Bromsgrove College of Further Education. Special efforts have been made to encourage the interest of young people. Free admission, for instance, is offered to members of staff accompanying parties of schoolchildren, and a substantial reduction in ticket prices is given to bona fide full-time students. Under the presidency of Professor Lewis, and with Sir John Barbirolli as vice-president and Joseph Stones as festival director, uncommonly fine programmes have been provided.

It has been customary to include a foreign theme in each festival. In one year, for instance, it was Spain, when Antonia y Marino and the Spanish Dance Company were guests of honour and there was a fiesta masked ball with Spanish cabaret and Spanish food and wine. In the same programme the City of Birmingham Symphony Orchestra conducted by Joseph Stones rendered works by Mozart, Falla and Beethoven. There were folk music events and, as always, concerts by the Festival Choir and the Festival Symphony Orchestra, also conducted by Joseph Stones – all that in addition to a number of individual recitals, a play presented by the Festival Drama Group, a performance of the Royal Ballet Demonstration Group and, presumably to ensure that all tastes are catered for, a concert by the Temperance Seven.

It is a wonderful achievement for a town which has only about ten thousand inhabitants, though it is well worth visiting to see its magnificent late Gothic church standing high on a cliff overlooking the market place, its many gabled houses and the famous boys' school which was founded in 1527. Further details from the Festival Secretary, 28 Victoria Road, Bromsgrove, Worcestershire.

GREAT MALVERN – The Festival of Drama

Famous for the Shaw festival which achieved its greatest success in the years immediately before and after George Bernard Shaw's death, the Malvern Festival Theatre now presents a more varied programme of plays during the summer months. The 1966 summer season was due to open on 3rd June and continue until 8th October, with Shaw's *The Doctor's Dilemma* included in a repertoire embracing modern English, French and American drama. Further details from the Malvern Festival Theatre, Worcs.

Cornwall and Devonshire 7

Cornwall is the Celtic England of tradition; Devonshire shares in that tradition and inherits also in its eastern marches the Anglo-Saxon traditions of Wessex. In the days of the Anglo-Saxon kingdoms the south-western peninsula was an independent state known as West Wales, which gives some idea of the close link there has always been between Cornwall and the southern counties of Wales, especially Pembrokeshire.

The Normans advancing from their strongholds in the eastern counties never effectively overcame the resistance of the Celtic people of the south-west. Launceston was the farthest point west at which they dared to build a castle; even the Anglo-Norman lords of Launceston became absorbed largely in the cultural life of the countryside they had been sent to subdue, and Celtic ways and customs continued to prevail east of the Tamar as well as in Cornwall itself. So it was, right through the later Middle Ages until very recent times. Cornishmen and Devonians have migrated in the nineteenth and twentieth centuries to London and Birmingham and the other growing industrial towns, but they have brought with them something of their own countryside, tenacious as ever of the traditions of their ancestors.

Before the nineteenth century there was little reason, still less encouragement, for migration. The Cornish settlements were situated on or near the indented coastline and on the banks of rivers which penetrated into the heart of the moorlands. Road communication was never fully developed, the water the principal, and in many parts the only, medium for travelling from one place to another. Like the Viking settlements on the Yorkshire coast, the Cornish fishing villages, Polperro, Mevagissey, St Ives and scores of others, were virtually impregnable to attack from the land, their only possible enemies the pirates and freebooters who occasionally sacked their ports and carried away plunder during the centuries of war with France. In a few cases a ship from another country was driven ashore (for the rounding of the Land's End peninsula was a perilous

Close-up of the Padstow Hobby-horse and its traditional teaser

adventure in the days of sail) and thus foreign elements were integrated into the Cornish and Devonshire strains. Such was the crew of a Spanish vessel which was cast ashore in Beer Cove in the seventeenth century after the village had been decimated by the plague. The Spaniards settled there, marrying local girls and resettling this quaint Devon fishing village, so that writers in the early part of

Helston Furry Dance

the nineteenth century commented on the swarthy appearance of the descendants of these castaways.

With this singular and distinctive historic heritage it is not surprising to find that Devon and Cornwall are the last homes of many Celtic festivals, celebrated with all the old fervour, but with perhaps an eye to the hundreds of thousands of people who spend their holidays in the south-western peninsula. Even so, many of them are genuine survivals from a time before St Augustine first preached the Christian faith in England. Devonshire too retains more fairs of medieval origin than any other county. Because Devon and Cornwall were so remote until the building of the railways, local markets and annual fairs meant more to the people and kept their original purpose for a longer time than those of central and eastern England. Today most of the fairs have become pleasure fairs, like those of every part of the country, though the local markets are as vigorous as ever.

Cornwall

HELSTON – The Furry Dance

'That quaint old Cornish town', in the words of the popular song, is famous for one of the most characteristic festivals dating from pre-Christian times in the Celtic tradition. This is the Furry Dance, often misnamed the Floral Dance, held on 8th May, unless this falls on a Sunday or Monday. It is the great day in the town's civic calendar. The streets are decorated with flags and bunting; the town band, a very fine one, turns out bright and early; concerts and special exhibitions are arranged for the afternoon and the sound of music is never far away throughout the day.

The festivities start early when groups of Helston people go into the surrounding countryside picking flowers and gathering branches of trees. Later in the morning many couples, the men in morning dress, the women in garden party dresses and picture hats, assemble in front of the market house, and with a band playing the accompaniment the Furry Dance begins:

> And we will go to the merry green wood, O!
>   And see what they do there, O!
> For we were up as soon as any day
>   For to fetch the summer home,
> The summer and the may, O!
>   For summer is a-come, O!

They dance up and down the streets of the town, in and out of the houses. Every door is left open and the couples dance in at the front door, out at the back and so round again to the street.

After lunch the civic festivities begin, but the Furry Dance is the essence of this exciting day. The Furry Day song is probably as ancient as the dance, which originated as a Celtic May Day festival to welcome the beginning of the season of growth. The custom lapsed during the eighteenth and nineteenth centuries, but in its present forms is as firmly established as ever.

PADSTOW – Hobby-horse Festival

This festival is more elaborate than the corresponding display at Minehead (*see* page 92). It takes place on the morning of 1st May. In this case the hobby-horse is not a manufactured article but a man covered in a full-skirted costume with a black hoop and a grotesque mask, rather after the style of the hobby-horse in the Abbots Bromley Horn Dance and the gee-gee of children's pantomime. As in the case of Helston's Furry Dance, there is a traditional song which accompanies the progress of the horse, his teaser, a choir, dancers and musicians:

> Unite and unite, let us unite
> For summer is a-cuman today.

The words of the song give the clue to the festival as a genuine Celtic May Day festival welcoming the season of growing things. An interesting legend which may have some truth has been grafted on to the May Day revels. The story is that during the Hundred Years War, in 1346–7 (accounts differ), most of the men of Padstow were away from home in the king's service at the siege of Calais. A French privateer took the opportunity to raid a number of Cornish ports, but its crew were frightened away at Padstow by the sight of this grotesque 'Obby 'Oss dancing vigorously on Stepper Point at the mouth of the harbour. As one writer puts it, 'The Frenchmen fled in terror from what appeared to be the Evil One.'

ST COLUMB, ST IVES – Hurling the Silver Ball

Although known by the same name, these two exciting annual events have no known common background, although according to some authorities they are both survivals of pagan sun worship, the silver ball representing the sun. All that is certain is that the games have been played from as long as there are records. Some think that the St Columb game is a last survival of the ancient Cornish game of hurling, which was rather similar to Rugby football, except that the ball was never kicked but only thrown or 'hurled' through the air.

At St Ives the game takes place on Feast Monday, i.e. the Monday following the first Sunday of February, which is the festival of St Ia, the patron saint of the town, one of the Irish saints who came to Cornwall at the end of the fifth century. The Cornish name of St Ives is Porth Ia. The parish church of St Ives, which is dedicated to this holy lady, is said to be on the site of her oratory. On Feast Monday at about 10.30 a.m. the silver ball, roughly the size of a tennis ball and made of wood covered with silver leaf, is thrown by the mayor into the crowd, in recent years mainly of children, though within living memory hundreds of the adults scrambled for the ball. The ball has to be passed from hand to hand (in practice it is usually thrown) and the game continues until noon, when whoever holds the ball as the church clock starts to chime takes it to the guildhall and is rewarded with a small prize by the mayor.

The hurling at St Columb is a far more boisterous affair for adult players. It takes place on Shrove Tuesday and on the second Saturday afterwards, and usually begins about 4 p.m. The ball, which is of similar composition to that used at St Ives, is inscribed with the words 'Town and country do your best, for in this parish I must rest.' The teams may number as many as five hundred a side, one representing the town, the other the country. The goals are a mile apart and the play is vigorous, with Rugby type tackling allowed and the rule derived from Cornish hurling that the ball must not be kicked, only thrown. If no goal is scored – and not unnaturally that is often the case – the winning side is the one of which a member has been the first to capture the ball and eluding all opponents places it outside the parish boundary.

Devonshire

BARNSTAPLE – St Giles's Fair

Barnstaple has been one of the most important towns in Devonshire for more than eight hundred years, and one of its busiest ports until the building of the railways robbed many of the ports in the south-western peninsula of their abounding prosperity. It is a most attractive town with many seventeenth- and eighteenth-century houses, and a bridge of seventeen arches which was built in the thirteenth century and, though widened, still carries the main road across the river. Barnstaple Fair is perhaps the most colourful and interesting fair of the west country. It has been held continuously for seven hundred years, and though it is now largely a pleasure fair the town is unusually gay at fair time, and the stuffed glove, as at Exeter and Kingsbridge, is on show outside the guildhall adorned with its garlands of flowers and ribbons. The gaiety of Barnstaple Fair is legendary, arising, it is said, from a reaction against the strong moral tone of the town for the rest of the year in times past, when it was one of the first and loyalest strongholds of the Plymouth Brethren. The fair is a three-day event which starts on the Wednesday before 20th September (14th–16th in 1966). On the Saturday, the day after the end of the fair, the town stages an elaborate carnival.

DAWLISH – Dawlish Arts Festival

Founded in 1954, and usually presented in the last fortnight of June, the Dawlish Arts Festival originated as a friendly event for performer-audience participation, designed primarily for local people. Through the years it has increased its scope and now welcomes enthusiasts from many parts of the country. Before the festival was founded it was the custom for the choir of Dawlish parish church to engage each year a professional orchestra for the rendering of Tudor and Restoration period anthems. The spacious church is still the centre-piece of the festival, for which it is ideally suited owing to its admirable acoustics. Many famous players, such as Dr Thalben Ball, have performed on its magnificent organ. The festival always opens with a special commemorative evensong, and concerts are presented in the church and other halls by well-known soloists and ensembles. A production by the Dawlish repertory company is an added attraction of festival fortnight, and there are lectures, recitals, exhibitions and illustrated talks. Further details may be obtained from the Hon. Secretary, Dawlish Arts Festival Society, The Moorings, Dawlish, Devonshire.

EXETER – The Lammas Fair

The Lammas Fair was one of the most important trade fairs in the south-western counties, partly because of the many roads which lead from all parts of Devonshire and from central and eastern England to the county town. The traditional date of its opening, Lammas Day, was also a time of festival – the Loaf Mass in the Anglo-Saxon rural calendar, that is, the feast of the first-fruits, when harvest time began and the first grain was offered to the church in the form of a loaf. The fair itself may date from Saxon times. It is likely that the ceremony of 'displaying the glove', common to several west country fairs, may have originated at Exeter. John Hooker, writing in the sixteenth century, says the custom was of great antiquity. A large white stuffed glove, decorated with garlands and ribbons, is carried on a long blue-and-white pole through the streets of the town when the opening of the fair is proclaimed in the various wards and at the gates of the city, then displayed in a prominent position in front of the guildhall. The glove was a symbol of safety for medieval traders on their way to and from the fair, a guarantee given by a law passed in the reign of Edward I, when the very existence of the medieval fairs was threatened by the footpads and robber bands who were attracted to the vicinity of the fair towns. The royal guarantee was implemented by sending detachments of troops to keep the peace at the approaches to all the principal fairs. Exeter's Lammas Fair declined, like all other fairs, in the nineteenth century until there was no business left to be done. It ceased to be held in the middle of the century. But the old ceremony of proclaiming the fair, not on Lammas Day but on the Tuesday before the third Wednesday in July, was and still is maintained with all the traditional pageantry of parading the glove through the streets. A small band is in attendance, and the officials are dressed in their robes of office as they walk in procession for the proclamation to be read at various points in the city, including the Cattle Market, Exe Island, Fore Street and the site of the East Gate. Interest in the fair, incidentally, was revived in 1939, when the Exeter Chamber of Trade adopted it to initiate a local shopping week.

Plough Sunday Celebration

A traditional service at which a plough is drawn to the altar steps and blessed is held in Exeter Cathedral, as at Chichester (*see* page 74).

KINGSBRIDGE – The July Fair

This is another formerly important annual fair which has become solely a pleasure fair, but the ceremony of the glove is maintained on the day of proclamation, and it is displayed outside the guildhall during the period of the fair, which is held in a picturesque position by the banks of the Kingsbridge estuary. An interesting sidelight on this fair is that local people believe quite sincerely that the significance of the glove is that while it is exposed no visitor will be arrested on a charge of being drunk and disorderly. Although this is not strictly true, it is an intriguing modern translation of Edward I's guarantee of safe conduct!

WIDECOMBE – Widecombe Fair

> Tom Pearce, Tom Pearce, lend me your mare,
>   For I want to go to Widecombe Fair . . .
>   With Bill Brewer . . .
>   Old Uncle Tom Cobleigh an' all.

There really *was* a Tom Cobley, who died at the age of ninety-six in 1794 and was buried in Spreyton churchyard on 6th March. It is pleasant to think that this typical Devonian song is based on an old tradition, but, alas, there is not the slightest evidence of a fair at Widecombe in Thomas Cobley's time. Widecombe, lying in a deep wooded combe on the southern fringes of Dartmoor in as lovely a position as any Devonshire village, is known to have had its fair only since 1850, when it started as an important fair for the sale of Dartmoor ponies. It is held on the second Tuesday in September and is still advertised as the Horse, Pony and Sheep Show, though a large part of its business is providing amusement for holiday makers. Tom Pearce's old mare is the theme of the village sign.

SIDMOUTH – Folk Festival

This attractive seaside resort, hemmed in by the red cliffs of South Devon, is the scene of an ambitious festival of folk dance and song which was first held in 1956. Organized by the English Folk Dance and Song Society, it is held in the first week of August (29th July–6th August in 1966) and aims not only to present a comprehensive programme of folk events but to give visitors the opportunity to participate. There are song sessions three times a day, dance displays twice a day, a square dance every night, two formal concerts, and a night-club open only to festival members. It is worth registering as a member before the festival opens. The fee of £1 gives the subscriber a season ticket valid for all events at which a charge is made, as well as admission to the 'Night Spot', open from 11 p.m. to 1 a.m. each night.

Further details may be obtained from the Director, Sidmouth Festival, 3 Barnfield Crescent, Exeter, or from the English Folk Dance and Song Society, Cecil Sharp House, Regent's Park Road, London, N.W.1, where particulars may also be obtained of the All England Folk Festival at London's Royal Albert Hall, usually held during the third weekend in February, and of other folk dance and song events.

Padstow Hobby-horse ceremony in progress

Start of the mountain race
at the Grasmere Sports

Northern Counties 8

The traditions of the north country spring from a more varied heritage than any other part of England. Anglo-Saxon kingdoms were centred on the east coast districts and on the west - one, Northumbria, stretching from the Humber to the Firth of Forth, the other, Strathclyde, reaching from the Firth of Clyde to Cumberland and Westmorland. The great central area of the Pennine moors, merging into the Cheviot Hills, was uninhabited, as it continued to be until improved farming methods were introduced in the eighteenth century, although even then the high moors defeated the husbandman, as they still do, except to provide summer pasture for sheep.

The Viking tradition was superimposed on the Anglo-Saxon. Norse warriors sailed across the North Sea to lay waste the monasteries and growing settlements of Yorkshire and Northumberland, and rounded Cape Wrath to descend on the fishing communities of Cumberland and Lancashire, penetrating inland into the valleys of Westmorland.

The Viking raids were followed by more ambitious expeditions in search of permanent settlements, and although after the Treaty of Wedmore the invaders accepted Christianity, they contributed much of their native culture to the northern counties. One can see the influence most easily in the Scandinavian-style carving of high crosses. One can also see it in the physical characteristics of the people of east coast fishing villages such as Staithes, who had little contact except by sea with the rest of England until recent times, and are descended directly from the Norse settlers of the ninth and tenth centuries. In the later Middle Ages the north was consistently threatened by Scottish arms, the boundary between the two countries often not clearly defined. In more recent times the native

cultures of Scotland and of northern England have been fused to an imponderable extent.

That is the background of the large number of ancient customs and ceremonies which are maintained to the present day. The Tynwald ceremony of the Isle of Man is a shining example of a survival handed down directly from the Norsemen, who superimposed their culture on the Celtic people of Man more than a thousand years ago. The medieval tradition is preserved in the triennial festival of mystery plays given in the lovely setting of St Mary's Abbey, York, and in the all too rare presentation of the Chester Miracle Plays. The ecclesiastical traditions of the Middle Ages are perpetuated in the rush-bearing ceremonies at Ambleside and elsewhere in the Lake District, and in the well-dressing ceremonies of Tissington and other Derbyshire villages. The May Fair of Gawthorne, the daily horn-blowing ceremony at Ripon and the Feast of St Wilfrid in the same city, are equally medieval survivals. So perhaps is the Shrovetide football of Ashbourne.

Modern festivals of music and the arts offer a great variety of entertainment. The music festivals of the spa towns of Harrogate and Buxton are perhaps the best known, but the more recently established Durham festival promises to be a successful venture in the presentation of all that is good in contemporary music and art.

Cheshire

CHESTER – The Chester Miracle Plays
The Chester Miracle Plays are presented by the Chester City Council in collaboration with the Chester Community Council. The policy is to present the plays every five years – 1967, 1972 and 1977. Performances are given on the Cathedral Green every day during the fortnight of the festival at the end of June and beginning of July.

The Chester plays are one of only three cycles which have survived the Reformation and the neglect of the following centuries. An Elizabethan prologue to the plays ascribes them to Randall Higden, a monk of Chester Abbey, and suggests that they were first presented about 1270. Modern research indicates, however, that they are probably the work of Henry Francis, also a monk of Chester Abbey, and were first performed in 1375. They were written in English and performed in the open air. The various episodes were undertaken by the craft guilds of the city. The stage for the plays was provided by a wagon or pageant cart, which could be and was moved from one part of the city to another, bringing the plays to the people rather than demanding that the people come to the plays. The Reformation spelt the death of miracle plays. The last full performance was in 1540, though isolated performances of an abbreviated version of the twenty-six episodes contained in the full cycle were given in 1572, 1575 and 1600. After that there were no more performances until the current revival was initiated as at York in 1951. The present version, which has been adapted by John Lawlor and Rosemary Sisson, is readily understood by modern audiences, yet it is one which has not lost the medieval spirit of the original. Of the twenty-six original episodes, twenty-four have survived, and these are presented as two full-length plays, the first dealing with the Old Testament episodes and the nativity, the second with Christ's ministry, leading up to the triumph of the resurrection (which springs inevitably from the apparent disaster of the crucifixion) and the last judgment, in which the devil leads the wicked into hell while Christ leads the faithful into the kingdom of heaven. The miracle plays are an experience which will live long in the memory, and give a wonderful insight into the life of the Middle Ages, when the audiences consisted of people whose church services were conducted in Latin and who could not read a word of the Bible.

The historic beauty of Chester is a fitting background for the miracle plays. The lovely red sandstone cathedral, the covered arcades known as 'The Rows' which converge on the market cross, the medieval walls which follow the line of the Roman walls, and the wealth of black-and-white timbered house, all contribute to the picture of a city wholly distinctive and wholly satisfying. Full details of the miracle plays can be obtained from the Town Clerk's Office, Town Hall, Chester, Cheshire.

Cumberland

KESWICK – Theatre Festival
The Keswick Theatre Festival was founded in 1961 as a world theatre. The plays are presented by the Century Theatre Company in their unique mobile theatre, an aluminium building with a small but well-proportioned auditorium which has extremely good acoustic properties. When the festival was founded it was described as an audacious venture in taking plays to the people, the theatre as something that must be seen to be believed. The 'audacious venture' has filled a long-felt want in the Lake District, and under Heinz Bernard as director of productions has achieved a considerable reputation. The season normally extends from June to early October, and the plays presented are mainly comedies of deliberately international character. In one recent season England contributed *Maria Marten*; France, Molière's *The Miser*; Germany, Carl Zuckmayer's *The Captain of Köpenick*; Russia, Chekhov's *The Seagull*; Switzerland, Dürrenmatt's *The Physicists*.

Performances are so arranged that there is a choice of at least two plays in each week. Further details may be obtained from the Century Theatre, 16 Station Road, Hinkley, Leicestershire.

County Durham

DURHAM CITY – Twentieth-century Music Festival
The Durham Festival of Twentieth-century Music was founded in 1964. It was an immediate artistic success and has become a firm date in the northern music calendar, lasting for one week at the end of August and the beginning of September (the dates are subject to alteration). Its aim is to promote interest in the performance of twentieth-century music of all schools without favouring any particular musical tradition. Thus the festival concerts include Schönberg as well as Hindemith, Debussy as well as Berio, Tippett as well as Boulez. It breaks away from most other festivals in which the time devoted to contemporary music can only be small without upsetting the ideal of a balanced repertoire. It has been particularly successful in promoting appreciation of many composers, especially French ones, whose work was previously almost unknown to the general public. It has proved that many of the so-called difficulties of modern music are ephemeral. Moreover several performances, notably one of the Stravinsky Mass by amateur musicians, have shown that the deep-rooted belief that most modern music is beyond the capacity of ordinary music lovers is a fallacious one.

Another important facet of the ideas which inspire the Durham Festival is that modern music must be given in the concert hall to be appreciated, and that the gap between the contemporary composer and his audience is largely due to the fact that most performances are heard canned, whether broadcast or recorded.

The festival was the idea of John Wilks, a lecturer of Durham University. He laid down the policy that the entire festival should be devoted to twentieth-century music without any earlier works to distract the attention. A summer school is run concurrently with the music festival, in which contemporary works are studied in classes and study groups. The classes are designed primarily for performers, but non-performers may 'observe' them and may join in the study groups. There are also a number of lectures.

All concerts are held in the great hall of Durham Castle and include individual recitals, ensembles, choral performances and at least one concert by a famous orchestra such as the Northern Sinfonia Orchestra. The festival ends with a concert given by the summer school choir and orchestra of works studied and prepared in the classes and study groups. Tickets for the concerts are available to members of the general public who are not resident or taking part in the summer school, but many lovers of contemporary music find it a great adventure to share in the excitement of the whole festival, the summer school as well as the concerts, staying in Durham Castle at charges far below those of most hotels. It is possible, incidentally, to stay at the castle for six nights for about two guineas a day, including admission to all concerts, without taking

part in the summer school. There is a festival club open to residents and non-residents with a club room, cafeteria and bar. All inquiries for programmes and booking forms should be made to the Secretary, The Music School, Palace Green, Durham City.

SEDGEFIELD – Shrovetide Football

This is a traditional game played on Shrove Tuesday, rather similar to the more famous one at Ashbourne but commonly of much shorter duration and of less spectator interest. It is, like all the Shrovetide games, a survival from the time when Shrove Tuesday was a public holiday, and is of particular interest because the 'pancake bell' is rung here, as it is at Olney to start the pancake race. In practice the bell is rung soon after midday to summon the players who, as at Ashbourne, have been on occasions hundreds strong, for there is no limit to the number taking part. A difference between this game and the one 'played' at Ashbourne is that the ball here is a small one about the size of a cricket ball, and can easily be kicked, while the goals are less than half a mile apart, one goal being a stream, the other a pond. Play begins on the stroke of one o'clock.

Some form of rather primitive football is, or was until recently, played on the same day in the streets of Chester-le-Street, County Durham, and Alnwick, Northumberland.

Derbyshire

BUXTON – The Festival of Music

This festival was founded in 1959 as a service to the thousands of 'music starved' people living in or within easy distance of Buxton and is held for a week in mid July. Its object is to provide the widest possible musical coverage to suit the most varied tastes. The mainstay of the musical offering has been the Hallé Orchestra conducted by Sir John Barbirolli, giving varied programmes of classical and modern music.

The festival normally begins and ends on a Sunday, opening with a festival service in the parish church and an opening concert by the Hallé Orchestra in the Pavilion Gardens Concert Hall. There are recitals every morning in the Pump Room, ranging from piano and violin recitals to chamber music concerts, with at least one morning devoted to an illustrated lecture on some special facet of music; in 1965 'The Lay of the Minstrels'. An evening of ballet music, a folk-dancing festival, a brass band concert, and an evening of jazz and rhythm featuring the Temperance Seven and Tex Matthews' Caribbean Rhythm, completed the list of the major events, although there were also concerts for schools and a recital by the Uxacona Singers in the Pump Room – altogether a very ambitious

Buxton. Country dancing in the Crescent
Photo: Entertainments Dept, Buxton Corporation

programme. Details of future programmes may be obtained from the Entertainments and Publicity Department, Pavilion Gardens, Buxton, Derbyshire.

Dressing of the Wells Festival

This is one of the outstanding events of Buxton's summer season, and is one of the attractions in a week which has many of the features of a festival week. It is generally held in the first or second week of July. The actual dressing of the wells here, as at Tissington, is a religious ceremony, first held in the town about eighty years ago. The attendant festivities include the crowning of a Festival Queen, a colourful pageant and procession, concerts and public dances. A fair with the usual roundabouts and conventional amusements coincides with the festival.

The wells are dressed in the traditional way, with large biblical set pieces surrounded by decorative frames made entirely of millions of flower petals and ferns pressed into a base of clay, the technique handed on from the older established well dressings. Further details may be obtained from the Entertainments and Publicity Department, Pavilion Gardens, Buxton, Derbyshire.

TISSINGTON – Well Dressing Ceremony

This is the original of the many Derbyshire well dressing ceremonies and is of great antiquity, although its actual origin is unknown. There are five wells in Tissington – the Town Well, the Yew Tree Well, the Hall Well, Hand's Well and Coffin Well (so called because of the shape of the trough which catches the water). The wells are dressed with flowers and greenery, berries and mosses, placed in a foundation of wet clay. The designs usually depict a biblical scene (but not always), and are often of exceptional beauty, transforming the appearance of this little grey village lying just under the hills of the Peak District and continuing to give it colour for some time after the day of the ceremony, which is Ascension Day, i.e. the Thursday before Whitsuntide.

The well dressing is essentially a religious ceremony, but it is made the occasion for entertainment in the village and for friends and relations from the surrounding countryside to spend the day in Tissington. A celebration service is held in the church. Afterwards the wells are visited in procession and a brief service is held at each. Undoubtedly this is a thanksgiving for the gift of water; a local tradition is that there was once a great drought, when the wells of all the villages around ran dry but the Tissington wells continued to give a supply of good water. It may well have foundation in fact. The temperature of the springs in Tissington never varies from about 47° F. in winter and summer, suggesting that the springs are deep-set and therefore unaffected by surface conditions. Certainly the wells have never failed in recorded time.

Another tradition is that the celebration was instituted when the village escaped a visitation of the plague, and people attributed this deliverance to the excellence of its water. The nearby village of Eyam had a terrible visitation in 1665, when five-sixths of the population are said to have died within a year. (The tercentenary open-air memorial service was held at Eyam on 29th August 1965.)

Whatever the origin, this charming festival of the wells is worth seeing. Nothing has changed appreciably since 1758, when Nicholas Hardinge, the Clerk of the House of Commons, wrote: 'The face of the whole country is picturesque. At Tissington we saw the springs adorned with garlands. In one of these is a tablet inscribed with a poem composed by the schoolmaster in honour of these fountains which, as Fitzherbert [the lord of the manor] informs me, are annually consecrated upon Holy Thursday.'

The ceremony of well dressing at other places seems to have grown up much later. A similar celebration is noted under Buxton. At Wirksworth, Youlgreave, Ashford-in-the-Water, Hope and Tideswell the festival is normally in June, the last two generally on the last Saturday in the month; at Belper and Dore it is celebrated early in July; at Bonsall, Stony Middleton, Wormhill, Eyam and Barlow in August. Exact dates of these festivals can be obtained from the British Travel Association.

CASTLETON – Garland Day

On Oak Apple Day, 29th May, a most picturesque ceremony takes place in this beautifully situated small town of the Peak District, dominated by the mighty keep of William Peverel's Peak Castle. The ceremony is held early in the evening, usually about six-thirty, when a 'king' and 'queen' ride through the town at the head of a procession to the accompaniment of a local band. The proceedings are enlivened by morris dancers, who have been particularly active in this district since the revival of morris dancing. The king is dressed in Stuart-style clothes, with a huge beehive-shaped garland of flowers resting on his shoulders. The procession ends at the church, where after more dancing the garland is hoisted on to a pinnacle of the church tower and left there for a week. The generally accepted explanation of this most diverting ceremony is that it commemorates the escape of Charles II after the battle of Worcester, when he hid for a whole day in an oak tree at Boscobel. The fact that it takes place on Oak Apple Day, Charles II's birthday, universally recognized as the day on which his escape is commemorated, supports this theory, but there is some evidence that the custom is older than Stuart times. It is possible that it is an echo of the

Well Dressing at Youlgreave

Forest Court of John of Gaunt, Duke of Lancaster, who held large estates in Derbyshire, and that this ancient custom was grafted on to the Carolean celebrations of Oak Apple Day. In either case, it is one of the ancient rural ceremonies most worth seeing.

ASHBOURNE – Shrovetide Football
This is a survival from the time when Shrove Tuesday was a national holiday in preparation for Lent. It is a boisterous game, with great spectator value but of rather unpredictable length. There is no limit to the number of players, the goals are three miles apart and the ball is large and heavy. Sometimes it seems as though the whole town were joining in the game, which starts at 2 p.m. The players are divided into two teams, the Uppards and the Downards. As there are several streams flowing over the 'pitch', and the ball is too heavy to kick across some of them, the teams are often literally bogged down at one or more of the crossings. The Henmore Brook is, as one writer observed, 'a favourable place for scrimmages'. Often the game goes on until night-fall, but there are records in the not very distant past of its

lasting two days! The game has a distinguished place in Derbyshire folklore. In 1929 it was started by the Prince of Wales, at other times by the Duke of Devonshire and the Marquis of Hartington.

MATLOCK BATH – Illuminations and Venetian Nights
This very attractive town in one of the limestone valleys which radiate from Kinderscout and the High Peak of Derbyshire is seen at its best on autumn evenings when the illuminations transform it into a fairyland of colour. The illuminations continue from the last week-end of August until the first week-end in October. The Venetian Nights entertainment is presented each week-end in September and the first in October. Approximately thirty thousand electric bulbs are used for the illuminations, which require some ten miles of electric cable, the display extending over more than a mile on the promenade and in the 'lovers' walks'. The Venetian Nights carnival is the direct descendant of the Venetian Fête, a one-night event instituted in 1903, and perpetuates the practice unique to Matlock Bath of making decorative superstructures for

Blackpool
Illuminations
Photo:
H. A. Hallas

rowing boats and illuminating the designs. The parade of boats on Venetian Nights is usually accompanied by a concert and on Saturdays by a display of fireworks. Further details may be obtained from the Hon. Secretary, Matlock Bath Illuminations and Venetian Nights Committee, Fernie Bank, North Parade, Matlock Bath, Derbyshire.

Lancashire

BOLTON – The Music Festival

The Bolton festival, held for three weeks at the end of April and beginning of May, is devoted to individual composers like Mozart and Brahms. It was founded in 1964 and was an immediate success. Designed primarily to introduce the people of this large industrial town and its satellites to the appreciation of good music, performed by some of the finest orchestras and soloists available in Great Britain, it has attracted many thousands of visitors from farther afield. In 1965, a typical year, there were orchestral concerts in the Victoria Hall, one by the Royal Philharmonic Orchestra conducted by Charles Groves; another by the Hallé Orchestra conducted by Sir John Barbirolli; a song recital, also in the Victoria Hall, by Ilse Wolf and John Shirley-Quirk; a series of six chamber concerts by the Loewenguth String Quartet, supported by viola and clarinet soloists, in the Civic Centre; and two piano recitals by André Tchaikowsky and John Ogdon. There were also two lecture recitals by Antony Hopkins. Each Tuesday and Thursday midday recitals on piano and violin were presented in the Civic Centre, to which the public were admitted free of charge. In addition a most interesting Mozart-Brahms Exhibition arranged by the libraries

committee was held in the central library throughout the festival period. Details of further festivals can be obtained from the Entertainments Officer, 1 Newport Street, Bolton, Lancashire.

PRESTON – Pace Egging Ceremony

This is one of the few places where the old custom of rolling eggs, or pace egging, at Eastertide is maintained. It takes place in Avenham Park on Easter Monday. Actual eggs are used, boiled extra hard, then painted red or green and rolled downhill over the greensward by scores of children. It is a custom rather similar to that of orange rolling on Good Friday at Dunstable, Bedfordshire, and may well stem from a commemoration of the rolling away of the stone from the tomb of Christ on Easter morning. Another theory is that the eggs are a symbol of life and rebirth, and therefore of the resurrection. It is interesting to remember that the egg as an Easter emblem is perpetuated in the giving of decorated Easter eggs today. The same symbolization is seen in the famous Pace Egg Play of Midgley, Yorkshire, a survival of medieval mumming representing the struggle between good and evil with the ultimate vindication of the good.

BLACKPOOL – The Illuminations

Illuminations were an innovation in Blackpool before the First World War, introduced as an additional attraction during the music festivals held in 1912 and 1913. It was not until 1925, however, that Blackpool conceived the idea of using the most modern decorative lighting as a spectacle for the autumn season. There was a gap during the Second World War, but the display was revived in 1949. It has been staged every year since then, growing in size and

'Blackpool Festival' by John Seares Riley,
who has chosen the illuminations as the
subject for this pop art impression

scope until now three times as many lights are used as in the first post-war revival. The 1966 display, the thirty-fourth, extending from the beginning of September until near the end of October, demanded equipment costing almost £500,000.

The main part of the illuminations is along six miles of the promenade, and consists of a series of panoramic spectacles, each devoted to a separate theme, such as the Wild West, Tavern Tales (featuring interesting and historic inn signs) and the Enchanted Grotto, a child's world of fantasy. There are also tableaux and a number of three-dimensional features, some of them motivated, including scenes from pantomime, motivated windmills, triumphal arches, illuminated landscapes and submarine panoramas.

Each year a well-known personality is invited to perform the switch-on ceremony. Since 1949 these have included in 1955 the Russian Ambassador, Mr Jacob Malik, and in 1957 the American Ambassador, Mr John Hay Whitney, as well as personalities of the stage and screen, such as Gracie Fields, the late George Formby and, of course, 'Mr Blackpool' himself, Mr Reginald Dixon.

The Blackpool illuminations, not inaptly called the greatest free show on earth, are a great event in the north country. Thousands of motor-coaches and hundreds of special trains carry visitors to see them, some coming from as far away as Wiltshire and Oxfordshire. The estimate of special visitors to the illuminations is four million each year. The statistics of the event are staggering: 375,000 lamps are used; the festoon strip is more than fifty miles long; more than seventy-five miles of wiring are necessary; there are five hundred scenic designs and features, and seventy large tableaux. Further details may be obtained from the Publicity Department, Town Hall, Blackpool, Lancashire. Similar, if less ambitious, illuminations are staged during the autumn months at Morecambe.

Northumberland

HEXHAM – The Abbey Festival
Previously a festival of music exclusively, Hexham Abbey Festival, reconstituted in 1964, now embraces all the arts. Its inspiration is the medieval abbey, which is at the centre of events and in which some performances are given. Its purpose is 'to encourage and promote knowledge, understanding and appreciation of the arts'. It is held during the last two weeks in October. In 1965 the programme included a concert by the Northern Sinfonia Orchestra, a recital by the Newcastle Bach Choir in the abbey, poetry readings, photographic exhibitions and the presentation of Molière's Miser by the Century Theatre. A special feature of interest to visitors is the recital of unaccompanied motets from the top of the midnight stairs, when the abbey is lit by candlelight. Art exhibitions are held in the vault of the Moot Hall, a fourteenth-century tower house. Further details may be obtained from the Hon. Secretary, Hexham Abbey Festival, Redhurst, Elvastone Drive, Hexham, Northumberland.

TWEEDMOUTH –
The Feast and Crowning of the Salmon Queen
Tweedmouth, now for administrative purposes part of Berwick-on-Tweed, which it faces across the estuary of the river, has preserved its ancient character to a remarkable extent, as befits a place which has for centuries been one of the most important centres of the Northumberland salmon fisheries and a great trading centre. The Tweedmouth Feast, including an elaborate procession, was derived from a medieval trade fair held in conjunction with the Church. The fair continued to be important until the building of the east coast railway, and for hundreds of years was at least as important as that of Berwick, protected as it was by the broad waterway of the Tweed from surprise Scottish attacks. This was particularly true in the thirteenth and fourteenth centuries.

The fair lapsed, but was revived in 1945, since when the third or fourth week in July, the period within which the medieval fair was held, is a festival week (commencing 25th July in 1966). It comprises many and varied sporting and social activities, including singing and music competitions, concerts, open-air dancing, sheep dog trials and an athletic meeting which attracts athletes of international standing. The highlight of the festival is staged on the Saturday, when there is a torchlight procession followed by the ceremonial lighting of a bonfire and a fireworks display. The ceremony of crowning the Salmon Queen takes place on the Thursday before the opening of the feast week. Further details may be obtained from the Secretary, Tweedmouth Feast Committee, 16 Kiln Hill, Tweedmouth, Berwick-on-Tweed.

Westmorland

LAKE DISTRICT – The Lake District Festival
The idea for this interesting and widely diffused festival was conceived by Mr and Mrs Robin Bagot of Levens Hall, Westmorland, one of the more beautiful of historic homes in the Lake District, famous alike for its sixteenth-century panelling and plaster decoration and for the ancient clipped yews of its formal gardens, which were laid out at the end of the seventeenth century.

The purpose of the festival is to foster a renaissance of music and the other arts in the Lake District, where it is far from easy for people to attend live concerts of the quality presented at the festival, of which Mr Geraint Jones is artistic director.

The festival is held biennially in the even years (21st–29th May in 1966). Concerts by artists of international repute are arranged at a number of widely separately centres – in the parish churches of Ambleside, Windermere, at Cartmel Priory, in Kendal Town Hall and elsewhere. In the past opera has also been presented at Levens Hall. Art exhibitions and poetry readings are arranged at several places, including Grasmere church which is used for readings of Wordsworth's poems. Artists taking part in these programmes have included Moiseiwitch, Gerald Moore, John Betjeman and the Alberni String Quartet. Full details may be obtained from the Publicity Secretary, Lake District Festival Society, Ings, near Kendal, Westmorland.

AMBLESIDE – Rush-bearing Ceremony

In the Middle Ages rush-bearing was a practical necessity as well as a traditional ceremony, since the floors of churches as of people's homes were strewn with rushes in place of the modern carpet or mat. It was an annual event in every parish, when hundreds of parishioners gathered rushes and carried them in procession to the church, where a special service was held. That is in practice what happens now at Ambleside and Grasmere in the Lake District, except that rushes are no longer carried, their place being taken by garlands of flowers carried in procession by the children of the parish. A service is still held, and at Ambleside the occasion is one of special celebration marked by the singing of a rush-bearing hymn in the market place:

> Our fathers to the House of God
> As yet a building rude
> Bore offerings from the flowery sod
> And frequent rushes strewed.

The Ambleside festival usually takes place on the last Saturday in July, the Grasmere one on the first Saturday in August. A similar ceremony takes place at Macclesfield, Cheshire, and a special rush-bearing service has been revived in recent years at Haworth, Yorkshire, on a Sunday in mid July.

GRASMERE – Old English Games

Grasmere, one of the most attractive villages of Lakeland, set in a fold of the mountains, has added attraction for visitors in one of the poet Wordsworth's homes, Dove Cottage, and the Wordsworth Museum (the poet's grave is in the churchyard). It is the scene of a famous Lakeland sports meeting, which is held on the nearby sports field in

A scene from the York Mystery Plays

Photo: York Festival Society

mid August. The value of the prizes offered for the one-day meeting, more than £1,000, assures a large entry. The most popular spectator events are the wrestling bouts under the rules of the association governing the Cumberland and Westmorland style of wrestling, with contests at all recognized weights. Apart from substantial prizes in all four groups – heavyweight, light heavyweight, middleweight and lightweight – a challenge cup together with an additional prize is awarded to the most meritorious competitor of the day, irrespective of weight. There are also boys' wrestling events for boys under fourteen and between fourteen and sixteen years of age.

The hound trail, under the rules of the Hound Trailing Association, is another popular event. In addition there are leaping competitions (the pole leap, the long leap and the high leap), and foot races from 100 yards to two miles. A silver cup, held for one year, is presented to the outstanding athlete of the meeting. More than twenty events are included in a programme starting at noon and ending soon after six o'clock – and, of course, there is the inevitable pipe and drum band. Further particulars can be obtained from the Secretary, Grasmere Annual Sports, Midland Bank Chambers, Ambleside. There are similar events at Ambleside, Westmorland; Keswick, Cumberland; and Ulverston, Lancashire.

Yorkshire

YORK – Mystery Plays and Festival of the Arts

The York cycle of mystery (or miracle) plays, which originated about 1350, was staged by the medieval craft guilds on Corpus Christi Day until 1570, a fact from which the name mystery play is derived (from the French *mystère*, meaning a craft). It is one of the two most complete cycles of mystery plays to survive. The revival of the plays began as part of the Festival of Britain in 1951, since when the festival has been a triennial event, taking place from 10th June to 3rd July in 1966 and on similar dates in 1969.

York is still essentially a medieval city, dominated by the minster, which exemplifies almost every period of medieval building. The central area of the city encircled by the medieval walls, which are pierced by several of the original gates, retains several of its cobbled streets, including The Shambles, the street of the butchers, which has altered remarkably little in the last three hundred years. One of York's loveliest corners is the garden of the abbey of St Mary, the venue for the performance of the mystery plays. It is an ideal site for the re-enactment of dramas which tell the story of mankind from the creation of the world to the last judgment.

The plays, in spite of their naïve simplicity, have a poetic beauty and grandeur of conception which place them in the first rank of early English drama. The adaptation by Canon J. S. Purvis loses little of the original beauty. Performances are given each night during the festival except on Mondays. One of the plays not included in the acted version is performed, in the medieval manner, on a wagon in the streets every day except Sundays and Mondays. The festival by tradition opens on a Friday, with a ceremony in the minster, in which the minster choir presents a short programme of sacred songs.

The presentation of the mystery plays coincides with an ambitious festival of music and the arts. The policy of the music direction is to range over the entire field of classical and modern music, with perhaps a slight accent on the work of Mozart, Bach and Beethoven. Well-known orchestras give concerts in the minster, where there are also organ recitals. There are morning, afternoon and evening piano and violin recitals and chamber concerts in the guildhall. Concerts are given too in some of Yorkshire's historic homes, such as Hovingham Hall and Castle Howard. The art gallery arranges a special festival exhibition and there are occasional recitals of light music in the festival club house and in local cinemas. A revue is staged in the Rowntree Theatre. Club and restaurant facilities are available until midnight to members of the festival club in the Assembly Rooms, one of York's most elegant Georgian buildings. Full details may be obtained from the Secretary, York Festival Society, Museum Street, York.

The Minster Diocesan Musical Festival

This impressive and spectacular one-day festival is held in York Minster on the first Saturday in July, when festival evensong is sung at six o'clock by a choir of approximately one thousand voices drawn from church choirs in all parts of the diocese. The service begins and ends with two processions of robed choristers, one from the chapter house, one from the south door, converging at the west end to form a double procession down the central aisle. The service consists of special settings of the *Magnificat* and *Nunc Dimittis*, and two anthems in addition to the usual evensong music. The sound of a thousand choristers, from small boys in cassocks and surplices to elderly ladies in colourful robes, is thrilling, not only to visitors but also to the participants.

The festival was instituted in 1928 to provide town and country choirs with the opportunity of improving their interpretation of sacred music under the skilled direction of the minster organist, who rehearses them individually and as a choir. Further details may be obtained from the Secretary, York Minster Diocesan Music Festival, 81 Leeds Road, Tadcaster, Yorkshire.

SELBY – The Selby Festival

This is one of the new-style genuinely local festivals. It was held for the first time in June 1965, and will probably be held at triennial intervals. Selby is an ancient and historic town which grew up round its medieval abbey. By the sixteenth century it was a flourishing trading centre, as it has remained ever since. After the dissolution of the monasteries there was a short period of decline, but it never fell into decay, and with the magnificent abbey church, with its splendid Norman and later medieval work still surviving as the parish church and the centre-piece of the town, it is a place which looks as historic and thriving as it is.

Music has been fostered by the abbey, especially since 1827, when the small orchestra which accompanied the services was superseded by the abbey's first organ. Quite apart from church music, Selby people have shown a greater than ordinary interest in artistic expression. An amateur operatic and dramatic society produced and staged a series of memorable musical plays between 1920 and 1935. But until 1965 there had been no actual festival of the arts, though the Selby Council had accorded direct financial assistance to efforts of cultural value for many years – ever since in fact it was made legally possible for it to do so, and it was the Selby Council which made the institution of a festival a practical proposition.

The idea was that of Mr D. P. Gedge, the organist and choirmaster of Selby Abbey and a local music teacher. He persuaded the art master of the local grammar school, Mr A. J. Doyle, to look after the interests of the art groups, and the urban district council to support the idea financially. And so the festival was born, an opportunity, as the festival organizers said, 'to enjoy a feast of music, to see and admire the sculpture of an artist of note, and paintings and drawings of Selby folk'. Although this festival was conceived as a local one for Selby people, to make them aware of their artistic heritage, it attracted large numbers of visitors and will doubtless do so again. In the course of a crowded week it presented a remarkably varied bill of fare centred mainly on Selby Abbey.

The abbey was the scene, for instance, of the interesting exhibition of ancient documents, paintings, drawings, photographs, etc., recording the activities and episodes that have made up the history of Selby and that of the nearby countryside through nine centuries. The abbey was also the scene of an exhibition of contemporary sculpture by Austin Wright. The festival art exhibition in the museum hall was of contemporary painting and designs by Yorkshire artists who formed a group to exhibit in Selby. Apart from Austin Wright, they included John Ridgewell and Marcia Tyler. There were exhibitions of the arts and crafts at the institute of further education, and illustrated lectures on Selby's history. Four films on forms of art produced by distinguished film units were shown. These included the life story of Vincent Van Gogh through the medium of the painter's work and an appreciation of Henry Moore, one of the finest films on the art of sculpture ever produced (*A Sculptor's Landscape*).

The concerts in Selby Abbey included a recital by the Sylvan Trio, a concert by the Northern Sinfonia Orchestra, the only permanent chamber orchestra in Great Britain, and a concert by the Selby Choral Society with the abbey choirboys, including works by Mozart and Holst. A recital was also arranged at the Selby High School by Cyril Smith and Phyllis Sellick. Further details and programmes of future festivals can be obtained from the Festival Secretary, Council Office, Park Street, Selby, Yorkshire.

BEVERLEY – St John of Beverley Festival

This festival is centred on the minster, aptly described as one of the finest Gothic churches in Europe. Its triple purpose is to make the beauty of the minster known to the widest possible public, to bring to Beverley a festival of

The medieval walls and the Minster at York

fine music irrespective of the country of origin or of its period, and to encourage local music-making groups to prove their worth. It coincides with the festival of St John of Beverley, the first Sunday in May, and lasts for a week. It starts with a festival service attended by mayors, town clerks and sheriffs from a number of Yorkshire towns, and usually includes an oratorio performed by local choirs with a professional orchestra and soloists, a concert by a professional orchestra (the Geraint Jones Orchestra in 1965), and an organ recital by a performer of international standing (Marie-Claire Alain in 1965), other individual recitals and chamber concerts, and a dramatic production. Further details may be obtained from the Director, St John of Beverley Festival, 30 Highgate, Beverley, Yorkshire.

SHEFFIELD – The Sheffield Festival

This ambitious festival of music, drama and films originated as a university event. It was adopted as a civic festival in 1965, but reverted to its original conception in 1966. Its primary purpose was to improve relations between the city and the university and to give the latter an opportunity to make a substantial contribution towards the cultural life of the city. The scope of the festival has always been ambitious, including a large number of events taking place both in the university precincts and in city halls and theatres. In recent years its fame has spread far beyond the confines of the city, and the university stresses that visitors from any part of Great Britain or abroad are welcome.

The 1966 programme, in which the University Union co-operated with the Sheffield Playhouse and the Sheffield Art Gallery, was imaginatively conceived to provide the spice of variety as well as serious interest – from an eighteenth-century cricket match to chamber concerts and poetry readings. Exhibitions of sculpture have been staged in Weston Park and general art exhibitions in the Mappin Art Gallery. Programmes of special late night films are given in local cinemas and special festival performances in the Sheffield Playhouse. The presentation of a miracle play from the Chester or York cycles is another unusual feature. Performances are also given by the university opera and theatre groups. In recent years plays by Seneca or Plautus have been given in the Mappin Hall in Latin. Concerts have been given by the New Sheffield Orchestra, the Midland Sinfonia Orchestra, the Aeolian String Quartet and many other famous symphony and chamber orchestras and ensembles. Finally, jazz and folk song concerts are included and a contemporary revue by a group of university students. The Sheffield Festival takes place usually in the last week of June (25th June–2nd July in 1966). Further details may be obtained from the University Union, Western Bank, Sheffield 10, Yorkshire.

HARROGATE – The Festival of Music

Harrogate is an ideal festival town. It became a famous spa in the nineteenth century and has remained a most distinctive inland holiday resort, with its attractive roadside commons known as the Stray and its flower-filled gardens of which Harrogate people are justly proud.

The twenty-first anniversary festival of music presented by the Hallé Orchestra with Sir John Barbirolli conducting was scheduled to take place in the Royal Hall during the week commencing Monday, 27th June 1966. It is one of the most popular musical festivals in the north and has played to ever larger audiences since it was founded. The aim is to present the finest of classical music of all nationalities, with a leavening of more modern compositions. Mozart, Mendelssohn, Beethoven and Brahms always find places in the nightly concerts, but the musical pattern is varied with the compositions of modern composers such as Ravel, Chabrier, Vaughan Williams and Elgar. One concert, usually on Thursday evening, is a gala night, at which patrons in the grand hall and grand circle are invited to wear evening dress. Otherwise the atmosphere is informal and at least one concert is devoted to the popular music of a particular country. In 1965, for instance, the Viennese tradition was accented in the final concert with works by Strauss and Léhar. Further details may be obtained from the Entertainments and Publicity Manager, The Royal Hall, Ripon Road, Harrogate, Yorkshire.

Festival of Arts and Science

The forward-looking idea of bringing the arts and science together and, incidentally, people primarily interested in artistic expression and scientific progress, inspired the first Festival of Arts and Science arranged for 11th–20th August 1966. The festival embraces music, drama and poetry, as well as science, which is represented by numerous exhibitions and lectures by leading scientists. The music offerings include symphony and chamber music concerts and recitals by famous performers. Art exhibitions, a writers' conference and a meeting of poets are other features of an event in which the audience is as much a part of the festival as the artists themselves. Further details may be obtained from the Administrator, The Harrogate Festival of Arts and Science, Riseley, Wormald Green, Harrogate, Yorkshire.

RICHMOND – Richmondshire Festival

The rediscovery and refitting of the Georgian theatre in this famous old town, dominated by its Norman castle and built round a cobbled square, is a story of real determination, the institution of a festival centred on a dramatic production in the theatre and held at the beginning of September, an adventure which deserved and has already received good support. Richmond Theatre is the sole remaining example in England of the classical Georgian playhouse, far more authentic than Bristol's Theatre Royal. It lies at the end of a narrow alleyway, little altered in the last 150 years, called Friar's Wynd. The theatre was built by the famous actor-manager Samuel Butler in 1788. The first performance was on 2nd September 1788. Until 1830 it had a highly distinguished history.

Theatres had been limited by law early in the eighteenth century, when politicians feared that they would be lampooned on the stage. Only theatres with a royal patent were permitted and these were relatively few in London and even fewer in the country. When the restrictions were removed in 1788 people flocked to the numerous new theatres that were built to partake of the long-forbidden joys of the theatre-goer.

Richmond Theatre was not of course open all the year, any more than it is now, but was associated with theatres in other Yorkshire towns. 'Festivals' were held in turn at the various theatres, the same company appearing in each.

Samuel Butler died in 1812, but his widow, son and daughter carried on the business until 1830. Then, with the popularity of the theatre waning, they were unable to renew the lease and there were only occasional performances between then and 1848, when the theatre was degraded into an auction room. After that it had a chequered career, and was in turn a corn-chandler's store, a furniture repository, and in war-time a salvage depot, the auditorium floored over and the pit converted into wine vaults. However, there was one happy interlude, when in 1943 a historical play was given in the unrestored theatre in honour of the 850th anniversary of the enfranchisement of the borough by the 2nd Earl of Richmond.

In 1960, chiefly through the enthusiasm of The Lady Crathorne, chairman of the Georgian Theatre Trust, an appeal was launched and the theatre restored to very much its original *décor*. It preserves the sunken pit and the narrow fore-stage which are the hallmarks of a theatre of the period, but to meet present-day ideas of comfort its capacity has been reduced from 400 to 232. Although the theatre has been open as a museum since 1962, the first Richmondshire Festival was held in 1965, with a presentation of *The Man of Mode* by Sir George Etherege, a Restoration comedy written in 1676 and not performed professionally since 1793.

Organ and choral recitals in the parish church, concerts at local halls and in nearby country houses in association with the National Trust, a ball to mark the close of the festival, lectures, art exhibitions and a popular music competition are other features which made the institution of the Richmondshire Festival a memorable event. Further details may be obtained from the Secretary, The Richmondshire Festival, Town Hall, Richmond, Yorkshire.

RIPON – Ceremony of the Horn Blower

Ripon is a small cathedral city of most distinctive character, a place of ancient foundation, its history centred on the cathedral and the market place. The latter is the scene of an interesting daily ceremony at 9 p.m. when the Horn Blower, clad in a fawn-coloured coat and wearing a three-cornered hat, walks briskly into the market place and sounds a horn of traditional pattern at the market cross and in front of the mayor's house. This is a custom which may be a thousand years old and certainly dates back to the Middle Ages.

At one corner of the square there stands a half-timbered house of fourteenth-century origin with later additions, known as the Wakeman's House. The wakeman of Ripon was the forerunner of the mayor. (The house is now a museum to which visitors are welcome.) The Horn Blower ceremony once marked the 'setting of the watch', that is, the time at which the city was in the wakeman's care for the night. If a robbery was committed after the watch was set it was the wakeman's responsibility not only to apprehend the criminals but to pay compensation to the citizen who had been robbed. Householders paid an annual toll for this security. In 1604 Wakeman Hugh Ripley was created mayor, but the Wakeman's House continued to be the mayoral residence for many years after that.

The horn used today is a beautifully curved buffalo horn made less than a century ago. On show in the mayor's parlour, however, is a far older horn, the Charter Horn, which some believe to be of Saxon workmanship. It is encased in velvet and silver, and is mounted on a belt studded with the emblems of wakemen and mayors from 886 to 1886, and decorated with the badges of the medieval

The Georgian Theatre, Richmond
Photo: Stockton-on-Tees Photo-Colour Society

'Scarborough Festival' by Oliver Elmes,
an illustrator, designer, painter and
fan of good cricket

trade guilds. It is a unique treasure. The Millenary Horn, similarly mounted, carries Ripon's history into its second millenium.

The Feast of St Wilfrid

This is another interesting survival, though its origin is less certain than that of the Horn Blower. It is celebrated on the first Saturday in August, and at the same time a fair is held in the market place. Early in the afternoon a man in medieval habit mounted on a white horse, taking the part of St Wilfrid, tours the city streets preceded by the local band. This ceremony is believed to commemorate the return of St Wilfrid, the founder of the cathedral in 681, after a long absence in Rome. The Feast of St Wilfrid was founded by royal charter in 1108, and the cathedral is dedicated to him jointly with St Peter.

OSSETT – Gawthorne May Festival

Originally a May Day celebration, the Gawthorne maypole ceremony is now held on any convenient day in the first week of the month. The elaborate ceremonial is centred on the famous maypole in Gawthorne High Street, where there has been a maypole from time immemorial and at least four different poles in the last hundred years. The predecessors of the present one, which dates from Coronation Year (1953), suffered variously from storms and local prejudice.

The main attraction of the festival is a procession in which the newly elected May Queen and the May Queen of the previous year ride on horseback with their retinue in the van of gaily decorated floats and lorries carrying set pieces and tableaux. The festival has been held continuously, apart from breaks during the war years, since long before motor-cars became general, and was once famous throughout the north country as an equestrian exhibition. The custom still followed by the May Queen of riding on horseback is a reminder of those early days.

SCARBOROUGH – Festival Cricket

The Scarborough festival, for long the premier English cricket festival, was founded in 1876, although there are records of cricket matches being played on the Castle Hill some years earlier. It is thus by far the oldest festival of its kind in the country. The underlying idea has always been to gather the best players from various parts of the country, plus touring teams when they are in England. As T. N. Pearce, the organizer of the festival for some years, has said, 'I think the Scarborough festival has become something of an institution, even a national institution. At the end of a season of serious competitive cricket it is a pleasant, very pleasant, way of reaching close of play.'

The festival generally consists of nine days' cricket in early September. The atmosphere is rather more carefree than in competitive cricket, the rate of scoring faster and the bowling always attacking rather than defensive. Certain courtesies or conventions have grown up, such as giving the batsman a chance to break his duck with an easy first ball, 'one to get off the mark'. These conventions have been criticized widely by sports writers, who have appealed again and again for games to be played 'flat out'. But cricket, after all, is a game, and a cricket festival is a

Ceremony on the Tynwald Hill, Isle of Man

series of games for the pleasure of the spectator, who always gets full value for money in the carefree but not frivolous festival atmosphere.

Some remarkable innings have been recorded at Scarborough. Cecil Pepper in 1945, in an innings of 168 completed in two and a quarter hours and including six sixes and eighteen fours, hit one ball over a four-storey house into Trafalgar Square. The same feat had been achieved by C. I. Thornton in 1886. In 1965 there was a fascinating innovation. One of the matches was between an England eleven and a Rest of the World team chosen by the public through the medium of radio and television. Players were brought from the four corners of the earth, and only two of those selected by B.B.C. audiences were unable to be present. Unfortunately the match was marred by rain, but it was a brilliant idea which will probably be repeated with greater success.

Altogether the festival is an exciting reason for a cricket lover to take a late holiday in Scarborough, always an attractive seaside resort, with its vast sandy beaches, attractive cliff walks and its medieval castle set high on the steep ridge which separates the South Bay from the North. Full details can be obtained from the Secretary, Scarborough Cricket Club, Scarborough, Yorks.

Isle of Man

For many motorists the Isle of Man is associated with the International Tourist Trophy Race round the famous island circuit, usually held in mid June, or with the Manx Grand Prix Race, held early in September. This historic holiday island, however, celebrates each year two important festivals, one a survival of its most ancient form of government, the other a modern celebration in honour of the Viking warriors who colonized it.

The Tynwald Ceremony

Tynwald Hill is a flat-topped eminence above the old capital town of Peel. It is the ancient meeting place of the Island Parliament, an open-air assembly as in all Viking communities, dating probably from the tenth century. The date of the legendary foundation of the Althing, the assembly meeting on the Thing-Bör, the Parliament Field, is 930, the same as that of the Icelandic Parliament, but there are no records earlier than the thirteenth century. The open-air Parliament of Iceland was abandoned more than a century ago and the Manx Tynwald is the only one surviving from the Norse tradition. It was held on Midsummer's Day, 24th June, but when the calendar was altered in 1752 Manxmen rejected the alteration and the meeting is still held on old Midsummer's Day, now 5th July.

Manxmen feared when the Duke of Atholl sold the lordship of Man to the British Crown in 1765 that the Tynwald would be held no more. There was indeed a gap of five years, and it was the governor who suggested its revival, since when it has been carried on without a break. In those days the governor rode to the assembly with a retinue of a hundred horse. Today the representative of the Crown is called the lieutenant-governor and travels by car. Otherwise the proceedings follow closely the order laid down by tradition. There is a religious service in St John's Chapel, a procession to the open-air (or rather canvas-covered) meeting place, where the Queen's representative sits on the highest point of the hill with the council, consisting of Bishop, Deemsters, representing the judiciary, two members nominated by the lieutenant-governor, and four elected by the Keys, or House of the People's Representatives. The remainder of the Keys, with their Speaker, sit below this *élite* gathering. Below them again are the High Bailiff, the local authorities and clergy, and finally the captains of the parishes, formerly the commanders of the militia. The titles of the Acts which have received Royal Assent during the year are then read out and a summary of their content in English and in Manx. Until 1914 no Act passed at Westminster came into force in Man until it had been promulgated in this way. In 1945 King George VI presided over the Tynwald in his dual capacity of English King and Lord of Man. The Queen Mother (representing the Queen) and Princess Margaret have also presided.

The Viking Festival

Instituted at Peel on 4th July 1961 to celebrate the fusion of the Celtic and Norse people into the Manx nation. In this first pageant four hundred Manxmen, women and children re-enacted the scene of the Viking landings and settlement, dressed in the costumes of the period and armed with replicas of the battle weapons of the ninth and tenth centuries. It attracted audiences estimated at nearly twenty thousand. It has been repeated each year since then, and has become a popular festival held in the first week of July within a day or two of the Tynwald ceremony. The festival opens with music by the Douglas town band and is followed by the pageant at 7.30 p.m. Sepcial entertainments are arranged before and after the pageant including a torchlight parade along the promenade late in the evening. Further details may be obtained from the Secretary of the Viking Festival, 23 Marathon Road, Douglas, Isle of Man.

Viking Festival at Peel

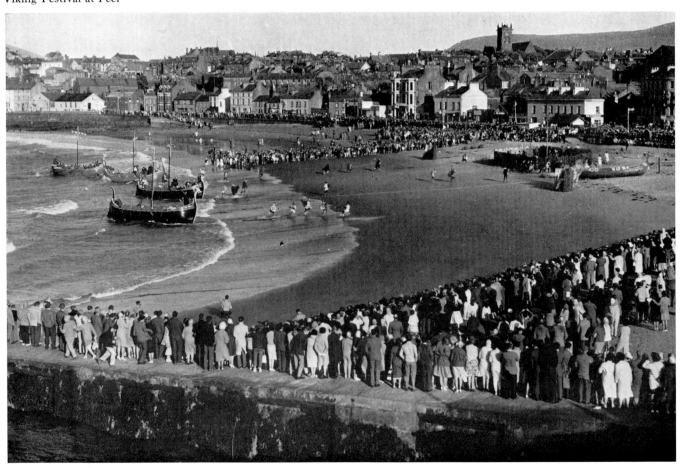

'National Eisteddfod of Wales' by John Wright,
head of Graphic Design, Newport College of Art,
whose four dominant themes depict the Crowning
of the Bard, an ancient Celtic sign, the
Gorsedd Circle (reputably of Druidic
origin) and the Welsh Harp

Wales

Wales is a small country compared with England or Scotland, its total population only a fraction of that of England, and concentrated in the mining and industrial valleys of the south and in the conurbations centred on Cardiff and Swansea. But Welsh traditions are those of the hill farming communities which emerged from the centuries of medieval warfare which preceded the Act of Union. It is not surprising, therefore, that few ancient observances have survived. On the other hand Wales is in the forefront of modern cultural development, its festivals of music and the arts comparable with the great festivals of England and Scotland, yet entirely individual. Welsh, after all, is a living language to a far greater extent than Gaelic or Erse. It is the language which you will hear in the streets and in the shops, still the language in which hundreds of thousands of Welsh people talk to each other.

The Welsh language tradition is perpetuated and embodied in the Eisteddfodau and in the dramatic festivals which have become part and parcel of the Welsh way of life in the present century. So on the one hand we have the Llandaff Festival and the Swansea Festival of Music and the Arts; on the other we have the National Eisteddfod and the Garthewin Festival of Drama dedicated to the Welsh language.

Wales looks to the future as much as to the past; though people whose only language is Welsh are relatively few, there is not the least risk of the language dying out. The youth movement 'Urdd Gobaith Cymru', which was founded in 1922, soon boasted of six hundred branches and a membership of more than 100,000. That movement was responsible for the organizing of junior local Eisteddfodau, culminating in the Urdd National Eisteddfod, still one of the most vital annual events in the principality, as well as fostering physical fitness in the Mabolgampau, the sports modelled on the Olympic Games.

Non-Welsh visitors to the National Eisteddfod might not perhaps realize that it is the culmination of a network of Eisteddfodau on a smaller scale, the very lifeblood of the villages and small towns of Wales. An Eisteddfod may take place in a chapel or schoolroom, or in a local hall. It is none the less a great event which gives the people of the district the things they most desire – contact with their fellows, gaiety and entertainment. Here, as in the National Eisteddfod, music and literature hold pride of place, two inseparable parts of a single whole. A visitor fortunate enough to attend one of these fascinating local gatherings, which have the same spontaneity as Irish feis, will enjoy a rich experience and in the atmosphere of audience/performer participation will learn something of the highly individual Welsh character. That is true to an even greater extent of the semi-national Eisteddfodau held annually in some of the bigger centres such as Carmarthen and Cardigan.

The Royal National Eisteddfod

In one sense the climax of the Welsh year, the Royal National Eisteddfod is held during the first full week of August alternately in North and South Wales at a different centre each year. Almost every form of music making, from brass bands and choirs to vocalists and instrumentalists, can be heard. Many famous artists have graduated

The Royal National Eisteddfod in session

A picturesque ceremony at the Royal National Eisteddfod
Photo: Studio Jon

from the National to the concert platforms of the world. Pennillion singing – folk songs with a harp accompaniment – and folk dancing are important parts of every Eisteddfod. The main events of the week are the Crowning of the Bard ceremony, usually held on the Tuesday, the Chairing of the Bard, usually on Thursday, a formal welcome to Welsh exiles on Friday and a day devoted to choral music, usually Saturday.

The Druids hold the stage at modern Eisteddfodau and it is the Arch Druid, resplendent in a flowing gown, supported by elders of the order, who takes the leading part in the ceremonies. A fascinating feature of the Eisteddfod is the welcome home which is given to hundreds of ex-patriate Welshmen who come 'home' from all parts of the world to attend. Some of their number occupy places of honour on the platform on the Friday and receive a vocal welcome as the name of each country represented is called.

The venue for the Eisteddfod is chosen two years in advance by the Royal Eisteddfod Committee, which considers invitations received from scores of towns and cities. The place selected for 1966 was Port Talbot, Glamorgan; for 1967 Bala, Merionethshire, on the shores of the five-mile-long Llyn Tegid (Lake Bala).

The bardic rites of the Gorsedd, which became part of the Eisteddfod early in the nineteenth century, presuppose a druidical origin at some time before the Christian era, or at least before the Roman legionaries carried out repeated offensives against the Druid religion in the first century A.D. The evidence for such antiquity is tenuous. The first Eisteddfod in the modern sense of the term of which there is positive evidence took place in 1451 at

Carmarthen. Queen Elizabeth I published royal proclamations to regulate the 'conventions' of bards, musicians and singers. By the end of the eighteenth century the Eisteddfod was well established in a manner akin to its present form. Then, and for the first decades of the nineteenth century, part of the proceedings was in English for the benefit of the English-speaking patrons of the meetings, but since about 1850 no effort has been made to pander to non-Welsh-speaking people. It is wholly a Welsh festival, evoking tremendous verve and enthusiasm and bringing out the latent gaiety of the Welsh people.

Throughout the week recitations and discussions take place in the Literature Pavilion and an arts and crafts exhibition is staged, with a notable display of Welsh paintings, sculpture and craft work. Further details may be obtained from the Permanent Secretary at the Eisteddfod office in the town in which the event is being held.

Urdd National Eisteddfod

Like the Royal National Eisteddfod, the Urdd Eisteddfod is held in alternate years in North and South Wales at a different centre each year in the first week of June (1st-4th June in 1966). The capital city of Cardiff welcomed the event for the first time in 1965; Holyhead was chosen for the 1966 Eisteddfod, and Carmarthen for 1967. The children and young people who contribute to the Eisteddfod are selected through the medium of the local aelwyd, or club, which is also a centre for the outdoor activities organized by the Welsh League of Youth. Every county in Wales is represented at the National Eisteddfod. Individual victories are not rewarded, but win points towards the

The crowning of the Bard at the Urdd National Eisteddfod
Photo: Western Mail and Echo

View of Royal Welsh Agricultural Show, Builth Wells
Photos: Studio Jon

total of each aelwyd and each county, the supreme award being made to the county which obtains the highest number of marks during the four-day festival. Further details may be obtained from the Urdd Director, Swyddfa'r Urdd, Llanbadarn Road, Aberystwyth, Cardiganshire.

Anglesey

LLANGEFNI – The Welsh National Drama Festival
This festival has similar aims to those of the Garthewin Festival. Founded in 1954, it takes place in the first week in October and is promoted by the Welsh Committee of the Arts Council in conjunction with the Anglesey Rural Community Council. The real purpose of Gwyl Ddrama Genedlaethol Cymru is to present Welsh plays in the Welsh language and original Welsh plays by Welsh authors. Further details may be obtained from the Secretary, Gwyl Ddrama Genedlaethol Cymru, Council Office, Llangefni, Anglesey.

Breconshire

BUILTH WELLS – The Royal Welsh Agricultural Show
The Royal Welsh bears the same relationship to Wales as the Royal Highland Show does to Scotland. It is one of Britain's most important agricultural events, attracting visitors and dealers from all over Britain and many foreign countries. On each day show jumping, parades and competitions alternate with adjudication in the main ring, and there is much to interest the casual visitor as well as the farmer. Until 1963 the Royal Welsh had no settled home. Since then it has had permanent headquarters at Llanelwedd near Builth Wells, in one of the loveliest parts of the Wye Valley, an area of unspoilt natural beauty within easy reach of the Plynlimon range and the Mynydd Eppynt. The show is held for three days in the second half of July (19th–21st July in 1966). Further particulars may be

obtained from the Secretary, The Royal Welsh Agricultural Society, Llanelwedd, Builth Wells, Breconshire.

Cardiganshire

CILGERRAN – The Coracle Week
Cilgerran Coracle Week is one of the gayest and most interesting annual open-air events in West Wales. Coracles, which are smaller than the Irish curragh but otherwise similar, are traditional craft used by fishermen and have had no change of design for at least two thousand years. They are still used for fishing on the rivers Towy and Teifi, where one can often see fishermen working in pairs with a net suspended between the two coracles. The Coracle Week which is held in mid August (14th–20th August in 1966) includes exhibitions of the craft of manœuvring the boats, and invitation and impromptu races. Cilgerran itself, though a wonderfully hospitable village, has little accommodation, but there are hotels and guest houses in nearby Cardigan. Further information may be obtained from the Wales Tourist and Holidays Association Ltd, 7 Park Place, Cardiff.

Denbighshire

LLANGOLLEN – International Music Eisteddfod
Founded twenty years ago, the International Music Eisteddfod is held annually during the second week of July near the small and ancient town of Llangollen in the lovely valley of the Dee, where it cuts a narrow gorge for itself through the Berwyn Mountains. Ten thousand competitors take part in the Eisteddfod. Audiences in recent years have numbered more than 180,000.

The original purpose of the festival was to bring the people of the world together through music and dancing, a fact symbolized by the festival's motto, 'Happy is a

International Musical Eisteddfod, Llangollen. Competitors in national costume rehearsing on the lawns of Plas Newydd

'Swansea Festival' by Geraldine Knight,
an art teacher who studied at the Royal
Academy Schools and won the *Prix de Rome*

world that sings, gentle are its songs.' The organizers bring the competitors from their point of arrival in Britain and accommodate them free of charge; but sacrifice and effort are needed on the part of many of the competitors to attend the Eisteddfod and to prepare the national costumes which bring brilliant flashes of colour to the proceedings.

The opening performance is generally given by a well-known company of dancers or a professional opera group. On the second day all sessions are devoted to folk singers and dancers from between twenty and thirty countries, nearly all in their national costumes. On the last three weekdays the day sessions are occupied with choral and instrumental competitions; in the evenings concerts by representative choirs of the different nations and dance routines offer varied programmes. The concluding concert on Sunday evening is a choral and orchestral performance epitomizing the whole festival.

Season tickets are available, entitling the holder to the same seat for all performances. Reserved seats for individual concerts can be obtained in advance. The official programme is published in June each year. Further details, and help in obtaining accommodation locally, may be obtained from the Secretary, Llangollen International Eisteddfod, Llangollen, North Wales.

GARTHEWIN – The Garthewin Drama Festival

The park lands of Garthewin rise steeply above the valley of the Elwy at Llanfair Talhaiarn. The mansion was built about 1710 and enlarged fifty years later for the Wynne family, who have held this part of Denbighshire for more than a thousand years. The mansion as it stands today is very much as it was built after restoration in 1930 by Clough Williams-Ellis, the architect of Welwyn Garden City in England, of Cushendun in Ireland and of Portmeirion in Wales. A Georgian barn adjacent to the mansion was restored along with the house and has become the permanent home of the Garthewin festival. The interior is still unmistakably Georgian, its 'nave' spanned by two great brick arches, one of which forms the proscenium. The Garthewin Players have inherited the traditions of the Welsh National Theatre Company, which was formed before the Second World War by Lord Howard de Walden. They stage a biennial festival in the even years, usually in early June, of Welsh and translated plays spoken, of course, in Welsh. Lectures are arranged to coincide with the drama festival. In recent years lecturers have included Robert Speaight, Huw Wheldon and Hilton Edwards of the Gate Theatre, Dublin. Further details may be obtained from the Secretary, The Garthewin Players, Wernol, Coed Coch Road, Old Colwyn, Denbighshire.

Glamorgan

NEATH – Craig-y-Nos Opera Festival

This festival, presented each year since 1963 by the Neath Opera Group, is staged in the Adelina Patti Theatre in Craig-y-Nos Castle, which the great singer made her home and described as the loveliest spot in the world. It is generally held during the first two weeks in July and features one opera (*La Traviata* in 1966). The standard of performance is high, the local opera group being assisted by a leavening of professionals. As at Glyndebourne, formal dress is preferred and there is a long interval during which visitors are able to walk over the terraced lawns and through the shrubberies which border the

Garthewin and its Georgian Barn Theatre

Photo: Country Life

winding River Tawe. In 1965 the production was Donizetti's *L'Elisir d'Amore*, in which Adelina Patti played a principal role at Covent Garden in 1866.

The festival is presented by the Friends of the Adelina Patti Hospital Society, formed in 1953 to provide additional amenities for the patients and staff of the hospital at Craig-y-Nos. The opera group were founded in 1960 for the express purpose of singing at the opera festival which was designed specially for the performance of works which music lovers have had little opportunity of hearing elsewhere in Wales. Further details may be obtained from the Secretary, Neath Opera Group, 6 Wenham Place, Neath, Glamorgan.

LLANDAFF – The Llandaff Festival

Founded in 1958, the Llandaff Festival is predominantly a cathedral festival centred on the Gothic cathedral church, which is on the site of a sixth-century chapel. The cathedral is in fact one of the most interesting sacred buildings in Wales. Although mainly in the thirteenth-century Gothic style, it retains considerable fragments of the Norman church which was begun about 1120. Yet in the eighteenth century it was a ruin, with an Italian temple-like structure erected inside its walls by John Wood, the builder of Georgian Bath. Restoration followed, but the great church was again reduced to ruins by enemy bombardment in the Second World War. Rebuilt once more, it shows little sign of the disaster it has suffered, but the famous sculpture, 'Christ in Majesty', by the late Sir Jacob Epstein dominating the interior, is an insistent reminder of the modern work of restoration.

The festival arose from a desire on the part of the Friends of Llandaff Cathedral to celebrate their silver jubilee in 1957. The result was the 1958 festival, fully two years before the thanksgiving service was held to mark the end of restoration. The success of this first festival, in which the Hallé Orchestra played an important part, was the determining factor in making the festival an annual event with a permanent festival council, the president of which is the Lord Bishop of Llandaff. Unlike most cathedral festivals, the emphasis at Llandaff has never been on choral works but on spreading the interest over a wide variety of music making. Oratorio plays its part; so equally do chamber music and orchestral works, while an international coverage has been attempted successfully with the visit of many foreign orchestras, such as the Czech Chamber Orchestra in 1966.

A festival service is held on the Sunday afternoon, and there are concerts in the cathedral on most evenings for the duration of the festival. Celebrity concerts have also been arranged on occasion in the City Hall, Cardiff, and

A concert in
the cathedral during the
Llandaff Festival
Photo: South Wales Argus

Charles Groves and the Royal Liverpool Philharmonic Orchestra in Llandaff Cathedral *Photo: Elsam, Mann & Cooper*

Concert at the Brangwyn Hall, Swansea
Photo: South Wales Evening Post

recitals there and in other halls. The festival club is open after concerts in the Llandaff Institute and art exhibitions are also staged. The exhibition of the religious paintings of Stanley Spencer in the Prebendal House in 1965 was one of outstanding interest.

The Llandaff Festival is held during the second half of June (15th–23rd June in 1966). Further details may be obtained from the Festival Secretary, Llandaff Festival, Well House, Penylan Newton, Cowbridge, Glamorganshire.

SWANSEA – The Festival of Music and the Arts

The first Swansea festival took place in 1948, when the opening concert was given by the London Philharmonic Orchestra under Sir Adrian Boult. That set the trend of subsequent festivals, which have established their reputation mainly on the strength of the first-class orchestral concerts which are presented in the Brangwyn Hall. Performances of choral music have also been a speciality, the visit of the Three Choirs Festival Chorus a particularly memorable occasion. There are also recitals by artists of international reputation, art exhibitions and illustrated lectures. Held in the second week of October, the festival makes a good opportunity to visit this once crowded commercial town, which was devastated by aerial bombardment in the Second World War and has risen, phoenix-like, from the rubble as one of the finest post-war urban reconstructions, with handsome and spacious shopping precincts along the roads which converge on the new town centre, the Kingsway Circle. The festival, with its insistence on the value of contemporary as well as classical art, expresses admirably the spirit of the new Swansea. Further details may be obtained from the Organizer, Swansea Festival of Music and the Arts, Guildhall, Swansea, Glamorgan.

CAERPHILLY – The Arts Festival

Caerphilly is an ancient settlement which grew up round its thirteenth-century castle, one of the most impressive medieval ruins in Britain, a perfect example of an Edwardian concentric castle. Modern Caerphilly, a market and commercial town, has spread out from its ancient centre, but the castle is still its dominant feature. A small band of enthusiastic pioneers founded a music festival in 1960, which since then has been presented every year and is sponsored directly by the urban district council. It was designed originally to provide the residents of the urban area with an opportunity to hear the best in music and see the best in art. It is still primarily a people's festival, catering for catholic tastes and at prices within the reach of everyone. Nevertheless professional artists of the highest standard are engaged to supplement the work of young Welsh artists and local amateurs. The festival is usually held in Whit week (28th May–4th June in 1966). A pattern has emerged in the few active years of the festival. There are always a festival service, a recital, a production involving soloists and local schoolchildren, a choral work in which local amateurs and professional artists share, a programme by an operatic star and a dramatic production. A firework display in the grounds of Caerphilly Castle ends the festival. Further details may be obtained from the Public Relations Officer, Council Offices, Caerphilly, Glamorgan.

CARDIFF – The Military Tattoo

The annual military tattoo held in the second half of August (15th–20th August in 1966) takes place in the court of Cardiff Castle. This impressive castle has been presented to the Cardiff Corporation by the Marquess of Bute. Inside its nineteenth-century outer wall, rebuilt in the spirit of the thirteenth century, there is the mound of the Norman fortress, a stronghold of the Marcher Earl Fitzhamon, Earl of Gloucester. Between the keep and the outer wall there are fragments of a thirteenth-century tower and the fifteenth-century octagon tower. There is no more apt setting for the military pageant of a tattoo than Cardiff Castle.

Edinburgh Tattoo,
with the castle floodlit in
the background

Scotland 10

Little more than a century ago a journey to Scotland was a great adventure for a southerner; a century before that few made the journey. The Highlands were a closed book to most Englishmen before they were opened out by the railways to Inverness and Fort William, even though a few intrepid travellers like Dr Johnson contrived to journey on horseback to their most remote parts. As recently as the beginning of the twentieth century there was comparatively little traffic except on business between London or Cardiff and Edinburgh or Glasgow. During the nineteenth century, however, Scottish culture was recognized by English people as something distinctive and admirable. Scotsmen who settled in England and Wales brought greater appreciation of their literary background. Scottish universities made their mark, 'Rabbie' Burns became a household name, Sir Walter Scott was read in every household in the land. The artistic communion between the Scots and the other peoples of the British Isles became a reality.

Now in the second half of the twentieth century, when many people think little of travelling a thousand or two thousand miles for a fortnight's holiday, Edinburgh and Pitlochry and Inverness are within easy reach of every British town. That has meant an amazingly increased two-way flow of ideas, more particularly since the Second World War. Though there has been integration there has not been the slightest trace of growing uniformity. British culture as a whole is one thing, Scottish culture another. Scotland is as tenacious of its traditions as ever and cherishes them as part of the national way of life, not as a self-conscious revival of things which have passed their useful life. The skirl of the pipes may not be the average Englishman's idea of a beautiful sound. To the Scotsman it is a reminder of his homeland, a sound than which there is nothing more wonderful.

Gradually Englishmen and Welshmen and Irishmen have come to appreciate the vast potential of the Scottish character, of Scottish art and literature, of musical and dramatic interpretation. That explains the enormous success of Scotland's premier festivals, such as Edinburgh and Pitlochry. It also explains why the traditional Highland gatherings now attract thousands to see their spectacle, where fifty years ago the audience was numbered in hundreds. It explains too why the few old customs and observances, such as the Common Ridings, which do not have much practical importance in the modern world, interest strangers as much as they do Scotsmen.

Scotland has been described as a land of romance. In a sense it is, although it is also a country of hard common sense. But there is something in its atmosphere, whether the atmosphere of Edinburgh or of a Highland moor, which stirs the imagination of almost every visitor.

New Year's Eve Celebrations

These have always meant far more to Scotsmen than to Sassenachs. New Year's Eve celebrations are correspondingly more vigorous and vociferous. That is true of New Year festivities in every Scottish town, from Glasgow to Inverness, from Edinburgh to Wick. A few special New Year's Eve customs (there must have been scores of others in the Middle Ages) survive. One of the most exciting is at Comrie in Perthshire, where a procession of people in fancy dress, led by pipers and torch bearers carrying lighted torches, marches to the central square, where a band plays and the audience sings until the torches burn themselves out.

At Stonehaven, in Kincardineshire, the ceremony of swinging fireballs is still observed. This is a fishermen's custom. Balls made of wire netting are filled with ropes and rags soaked in paraffin. These are set alight and are carried by young men who swing them from side to side and in a circular motion round their heads as they march through the town.

Hogmanay

New Year (Hogmanay) celebrations are far more universal in Scotland than in England, Wales or Ireland. Christmas

Hogmanay at Glasgow Cross

man and must carry a gift. Until recently the first foot was required to bring food, drink and fuel for the fire, but although some maintain the tradition of carrying bread and peat, the usual gift is a bottle of whisky or wine, or a canister of tea with a piece of New Year cake.

Aberdeenshire

BRAEMAR – Royal Highland Gathering

This, the most famous of all Highland gatherings, is held early in September (8th September in 1966). The royal patronage extended to it (the Queen and the Duke of Edinburgh are regular visitors from their Highland home at Balmoral) and its lovely situation where the broad valley of the Dee narrows into a Highland glen make it an important Scottish social event.

Queen Victoria was the first sovereign to give her patronage to the gathering, a fact which has led to the entirely erroneous impression that the games are of Victorian origin. In fact they are of great antiquity and, like the numerous other Highland gatherings, important links with the Celtic Scotland of tradition. The chief events of the gathering are Highland dancing and piping competitions and distinctively Highland athletic events. The latter include tossing the caber, a pine log up to 20 feet high and 120 pounds in weight, putting the stone, throwing the hammer and wrestling in the Cumberland and catch-as-catch-can styles. The 'march of the clansmen' in full Highland dress, which used to be a feature of the games, is still maintained at the Cowal Games at Dunoon and the Lonach Gathering at Strathdon. The athletic events were introduced in 1832.

Other Highland gatherings of early foundation or of special interest include the Edinburgh Highland Games in the third week of August (20th August in 1966), the Crieff Highland Games, also in the third week of August, the Cowal Highland Gathering at Dunoon in the last week of August (26th and 27th August in 1966), the Lonach Highland Gathering at Strathdon, also in the last week of August, the Aberdeen and Aboyne Highland Games in the first week of September, the Argyllshire Gathering at Oban in mid September (14th and 15th September in 1966). Further details may be obtained from the Scottish Tourist Board, 2 Rutland Place, West End, Edinburgh 1.

The Braemar Highland Festival

This is a festival of drama, films, music and dancing held at Invercauld, which adjoins Braemar. It was founded in 1953 by Mrs Farquhar of Invercauld and is under the patronage of the Queen. The numerous festival events are centred on the Invercauld studios and festival theatre and feature the Invercauld Players. In most years there is a

celebrations, which were banned by the Calvinists, have returned to Scotland in large measure, but many Scots work on Christmas Day and Boxing Day and have their winter holiday at the New Year. (New Year's Day is a public holiday.)

'Hogmanay' is a word of Norse origin, and the celebrations are derived from the Scandinavian festival of Yule, which also became identified with the celebration of the nativity. Until recent years there were vast gatherings on New Year's Eve in all the big towns to 'see the New Year in', but since the advent of television the numbers at these gatherings have decreased and Hogmanay is becoming increasingly a time for family gatherings.

However, there are still many hundreds to sing 'Auld Lang Syne' at Glasgow Cross. In Dundee, the most traditional-minded of large Scottish towns, some thousands assemble in the city square. One custom which has shown no decline is 'first-footing' from midnight onwards, sometimes until 4 or 5 a.m. The first person to cross the threshold of a house after midnight is known as the 'first foot', the good fairy, the Hogman of Norse Hogmanay. For good luck in the coming year the first foot must be a dark-haired

The Royal Braemar Highland Gathering

fortnight of drama in August, when modern plays and revues are presented. In 1965, for instance, one production was a comedy by Robert Kemp, taking the audience backstage at the Edinburgh Festival, the second a specially written play depicting episodes in the life of Mary Queen of Scots, a third was an up-to-the-minute revue.

The all-Scottish film festival continues from June to September on one evening a week except during the drama fortnight. Gaelic singing, piping and dancing and fashion shows also form part of the varied programme. Further details may be obtained from the Secretary, Invercauld Festival Theatre, Invercauld, Braemar, Aberdeenshire.

Angus

MONTROSE – The Montrose Festival
The festival in this attractive east coast resort spans eight days during the early part of June and includes concerts, art exhibitions and drama performances. It is one of the youngest of Scottish festivals, founded only in 1963, but has taken a firm place in the festival calendar. It features Scottish orchestras and soloists. The B.B.C. Scottish Orchestra, the Aberdeen Orpheus Choir and the Edinburgh University Singers have given some of its most successful concerts. The Montrose town band appears at frequent intervals throughout the festival. A military pipe and drum band is also engaged. The art exhibitions feature the work of Scottish artists past and present. Further details and programmes may be obtained from the Secretary, Festival Office, Town Buildings, Montrose, Angus.

Ayrshire

AYR – Burns Nicht Celebrations
Robert Burns was born in a cottage now open to the public at Alloway near Ayr on 25th January 1759. The Burns

Monument, a colossal temple-like structure in the Corinthian style, built in 1820, is by the Auld Brig o' Doon. In his own lifetime Burns became a national figure through his genius in expressing the feelings of his fellow Scots in verse and song. His birthday is a nationwide day of festivity comparable with Hogmanay. Every year in Ayr, and elsewhere, hundreds of Burns Nicht suppers are held. The pattern is invariably the same, including piping in the haggis, when a piper precedes the chef carrying the steaming dish to the top table, where the pudding is ceremonially cut open. Then follows Burns' own 'Address to a Haggis' and the toast 'The Immortal Memory' by the leading speaker. The latter is not a simple toast, but an

Burns Monument at Alloway

Dunvegan Castle, Skye
Piping at the
MacCrimmon Memorial
during Skye Week

occasion for prolonged and often poetic oratory which may last for half an hour or more.

Visitors to Scotland at this period should not miss an opportunity to participate in a Burns Nicht supper. The Scottish Tourist Board will furnish a list of the more elaborate suppers at which visitors are welcome.

Invernesshire

ISLE OF SKYE – Skye Week

The beautiful island of Skye, with its moors, a thousand lochs and its precipitous Cuillin Hills, is the easiest of all the western isles to reach, linked with the mainland at Kyle of Lochalsh by a remarkably efficient car ferry service, operating seven days a week. It is the island of the Macleods; Dunvegan Castle at its western extremity is the ancestral home of the Macleod of Macleods, who is now Dame Flora. In history it is remembered as the place to which Prince Charles Edward (Bonnie Prince Charlie) fled after Culloden in 1747 and had his last meeting with Flora Macdonald in a house which became the Royal Hotel at Portree.

Skye Week, which spans eight days at the end of May, was founded in 1950. Its underlying purpose is to show visitors in a friendly and only partly organized form the way of life of the islanders. One feature of the festival is the vast number of Macleods from all over the world who contrive to take part. The programmes follow a regular pattern. There is always a ceilidh of welcome at Portree where the week is declared 'open' by some distinguished visitor, with pipers in attendance, and a full musical programme and a dance to follow. There is a Highland gathering and piping competitions, concerts and craft demonstrations. In some years artistes are imported from abroad. In 1963, for instance, a troupe of Norwegian dancers gave a number of performances, underlining the link between Skye and Scandinavia (Skye was for centuries part of the Norse kingdom). Two special days have become traditional in the short time since the 'week' was founded: Dunvegan Day, when visitors are welcomed to the castle, and Borreraig Day, an occasion for pilgrimage to the MacCrimmon Memorial Cairn, where the most famous of all Scottish pipers founded the first school of piping, which was carried on by his family for many generations. Further details may be obtained from the Secretary, Skye Week, Portree, Isle of Skye.

Midlothian

EDINBURGH – The Edinburgh Festival

The Edinburgh International Festival, which is staged each year for three weeks in late August and early September (21st August–10th September in 1966), is without

'Braemar Royal Gathering'
by Abis, Sida and Stribley,
a young, enthusiastic team of
artists who all studied at
the Royal College of Art

dispute the most important musical and dramatic festival in Scotland and one of the most important in the British Isles. The idea for a festival of the arts in Britain to promote international goodwill originated from the directors of the Glyndebourne Festival Opera. Initially the project was discussed by Mr Rudolf Bing, Glyndebourne's manager, and Mr Harvey Wood of the British Council. Their suggestion to Mr John Falconer, the then Lord Provost of Edinburgh, was received with enthusiasm. From the time of the first festival, held from 24th August to 13th September 1947, the stress was on the international aspect of the festival.

The festival was made possible in the first instance by contributions from many individuals and firms as well as from the Edinburgh Corporation. Its success has justified the faith shown. in it and in the inspiration which lay behind it. As the Lord Provost of Edinburgh said in his message of welcome to visitors to the nineteenth festival, 'The citizens of Edinburgh join with visitors to the festival in the common pleasure of listening to and seeing great works performed by great artists.'

The great works and the great artists are truly international. The programme includes opera, drama, orchestral concerts, chamber concerts, recitals by individual artists and art exhibitions. Performances are given in Edinburgh's numerous theatres and halls – opera usually in the King's Theatre, drama in the Lyceum Theatre, concerts generally in the Usher Hall or the Freemasons Hall, or farther afield in the Leith Town Hall. The Gateway Theatre and the Assembly Hall are also used.

The international nature of the programme is illustrated in no department better than in opera. In one year the Bavarian State Opera of Munich presented Mozart's *Cosi Fan Tutte* and Richard Strauss' *Intermezzo*, the first performance of this opera in Great Britain, the English Opera Group the uncommonly English work by Britten, *Albert Herring*, and the Festival Opera in association with the Holland Festival, Mozart's *Don Giovanni* and Haydn's *Le Pescatrici*.

The reputation of Edinburgh for drama has not always been as high as for music and opera. Modern innovations, however, have been tremendously successful – none more so than the rather daring one of presenting an Italian comedy performed by a Genoa company in Italian in 1965. The first play presented in this way was *I Due Gemelli Veneziani* by Carlo Goldoni. One critic described this as the first play he had seen 'which is funnier if you do not comprehend the language in which it is basically spoken'. That surely represents the ideal of international co-operation and understanding.

The year 1965 too was the first year in which the Scottish National Orchestra opened the festival, a fully justified compliment to one of the most accomplished of British symphony orchestras. In that opening concert the Scottish Festival Chorus made its debut, no less than 380 voices chosen from amateur singers all over Scotland and trained in Edinburgh, Glasgow and Aberdeen. It is a safe prediction that the chorus, which was formed under the auspices of the Edinburgh Festival Society, will become an integral part of the festival's attractions.

Several orchestras are always engaged for the festival. In a single year, in addition to the Scottish National Orchestra, concerts were given by the New Philharmonia Orchestra, the B.B.C. Scottish Orchestra, the B.B.C. Concert Orchestra and, representing Europe, the Hamburg Radio Symphony Orchestra and the Netherlands Chamber Orchestra. The London Mozart Players gave performances not only of Mozart but of Haydn and other composers.

An innovation in the festival programme introduced only in recent years has proved extremely popular – the poetry readings given in the Freemasons Hall with the provocative title 'Poets in Public'. The policy so far has been to invite four poets to give readings at each session. Surprisingly large audiences attended when the readings first became part of the festival, the most successful of all those appearing being John Betjeman, who paradoxically made the crowded audience at the Freemasons Hall roar with laughter!

It is very much an achievement to present in public on one day John Betjeman, Martin Bell, David Wevill and R. S. Thomas, whose elegies on country life in Wales, incidentally, were remarkably well received. In the same year as these four distinguished contemporary poets appeared W. H. Auden and Norman MacCaig were also included in the full programme. The basic idea of 'Poets in Public' is to forge a link between modern poets and their readers, and to enlarge the rather restricted circle of people who enjoy modern poetry. The experiment has been brilliantly successful.

The magnitude of the festival organization is well illustrated by the fact that it is commonplace for 150 performances to be given under the official auspices of the Festival Society. Inevitably there is the occasional hitch, but the spirit of festival is not too serious, though certainly not over-frivolous. As Sir Thomas Beecham once said in Edinburgh, 'Every festival must be fun.' Edinburgh certainly lives up to that concept of a festival, even though the performances reach the highest level of artistic excellence.

Lord Harewood was artistic director for five years until 1965 (festival director in his last year), when he was succeeded by Peter Diamand, formerly director of the Holland Festival. Lord Harewood was responsible for many of the ideas which have enhanced while not radically changing the character of the festival in the nineteen-sixties. He, like his predecessors, saw it as a vehicle for devising memorable experiences for the layman and professional alike. 'We set out to produce a balanced series of programmes which would be enjoyable at more than one level.' That is the true spirit of festival, the provision of something for all tastes, an extraordinarily difficult object to achieve but one which Edinburgh attained with more than average success.

One of the interesting features of the Edinburgh festivals of the early nineteen-sixties, contributed wholly by Lord Harewood's genius, was the staging of what can only be described as a festival within a festival by concentrating on one or two composers or types of music. That is something which in a smaller festival would not be possible without destroying the spirit of the festival as a whole. At Edinburgh it proved to be successful, never more so than in 1965 when Pierre Boulez and Michael Tippett were the guests of honour. The idea underlying the festival within a festival was that it would assist in bringing the understanding of music to a wider audience if composers were invited to interpret their own work as well as that of other composers.

It is difficult to express in words the spirit of the Edinburgh Festival. Perhaps its main theme is, after all, something for everyone, whatever his tastes. Equally its success has depended on its balance – the balance between classical and contemporary music, between contemporary and established drama, between the art of today and that of yesterday.

The Fringe

A phenomenon peculiar to the Edinburgh Festival is the popularity of dramatic performances 'on the fringe'. Halls large and small have been pressed into service for performances mainly by young dramatists and actors, often of a very high calibre. One of these fringe presentations gave London and the United States the Jonathan Miller, Alan Bennett, Dudley Moore, Peter Cook production *Beyond the Fringe*. Several other fringe productions have reached the London stage.

The reason for the development of 'the fringe', even though it is unique, is fairly obvious. The festival brings to Edinburgh a large number of people interested in the theatre. Here then is a golden opportunity for hitherto unrecognized drama to reap its due reward of recognition. The shows are unofficial in the sense that they are not included in the festival programme, but they have been given official encouragement. Full houses are quite common. That is not so surprising as it sounds when one bears in mind that one of the most notable of the fringe enterprises,

the Traverse Theatre, has only sixty seats. Yet the Traverse Theatre Club has been productive of several lively contributions. Among many successes originating in Edinburgh, *Green Julia* has been presented at London's Arts Theatre.

As Lord Harewood has said, 'There are limits to the amount of drama the official festival can present. The fringe productions extend the range. Some of them are very good indeed.' That, after all, is an accolade even if not official recognition. It is well worth visitors' while to discover what are the current fringe productions in festival time.

Although relatively so recent in origin, the Edinburgh Festival already has a number of traditions. The opening ceremony, for instance, takes the form of a service in St Giles Cathedral, the medieval church of Edinburgh which has been the centre of its ecclesiastical life for many centuries. Flags mounted on tall flagstaffs are unfurled along the length of Princes Street to show that the festival has truly begun. The flower beds in the Princes Street gardens are at their brightest, the castle is floodlit like a fairy castle outlined against the black of the sky. Edinburgh looks a festival city, and there is a welcome for visitors from the people of Edinburgh – from hotel receptionists, boarding-house keepers and traffic wardens! There is nothing in Europe quite like Edinburgh in festival time – no city where the traveller is made to feel more at home, more at one with the people of the city.

Pipers at the Edinburgh Tattoo

The Military Tattoo

This floodlit spectacle on the esplanade of Edinburgh Castle is one of the most thrilling as well as one of the most popular events of the Edinburgh Festival. It epitomizes the traditions of Scotland and yet provides magnificent entertainment for every spectator, whether Scot, Sassenach or a member of some other nation. Its Scottish atmosphere is something to be felt and remembered for years afterwards. In the tattoo, as in the festival as a whole, the aim of the organizers is to provide something for the tastes of everyone. For many years an item has been included from overseas. One of the highlights of the tattoo in 1965 was provided by soldiers from the island of Fiji, whose dancing, singing and regimental band music proved a tremendous attraction. The audiences on the castle esplanade take the visitors to their heart and by their enthusiasm stimulate them to skills which their own people might have thought was beyond their prowess.

The high spot of the tattoo, however, is always the surge of colour and sound when the massed bands of the Scottish regiments march across the arena, the skirl of the pipes a sound never to be forgotten. The pipes and drums of famous Scottish regiments, Highland dancing by men of the Highland Brigade, with the Lowland Brigade also well represented, the sensation of movement and colour and melody all combined in one great exercise, spontaneous yet obviously well rehearsed – that is the very spirit of the tattoo. Four million people have seen the military tattoo since it became a regular event in the festival calendar. Every one of those four million has a vivid impression of military team-work and of music performed as perfectly in its context as any music can be.

The International Film Festival

This is held contemporaneously with the Edinburgh Festival, but is entirely separate from it. The nineteenth festival was held in 1965. It has become one of the leading events of its kind, with entries each year from about forty countries and a repertoire of two hundred films or more. The films are shown on weekdays at the Cameo Cinema, with gala performances on Sunday evenings. It is the policy of the film festival to provide national presentation performances of major film-producing countries, such as the U.K., U.S.A., U.S.S.R., France, Germany, Italy, Czechoslovakia and the Netherlands. Details of performances can be obtained from the Director, Edinburgh International Film Festival, Film House, 3 Randolph Crescent, Edinburgh 3.

The Edinburgh Festival Guild and Club

Visitors to the festival are invited to join the Edinburgh Festival Guild, which has been established to strengthen the bonds of friendship between supporters of the festival whatever their nationality. The basic idea of the festival is to contribute to international understanding and goodwill through the medium of the arts. The Festival Guild is an organization designed to make this dream come true. Members are sent all festival publications as they are issued and are guests at a guild garden party during the festival. Further details can be obtained from the Edinburgh Festival Society Ltd, 11 Cambridge Street, Edinburgh 1.

The festival club is a social rendezvous for all visitors to the festival. Its club headquarters has been for some years a music hall in George Street. It is a venue at which people interested in the festival activities meet, make friends and share ideas and impressions with others interested in the spirit of the festival. There is a restaurant with bars and dancing on most evenings after dinner.

The Royal Scottish Academy Annual Exhibition

Founded in 1829, the Royal Scottish Academy, which has a permanent home in a handsome Greek temple style building on the Mound by W. H. Playfair, a Doric composition, contrasting with the Ionic style of the neighbouring National Gallery, which was built thirty years later, is the Scottish equivalent of the English Royal Academy. Its annual exhibition takes place from April until the beginning of the Edinburgh Festival, when it stages the festival exhibition, usually a one-artist or one-school show (Corot in 1965).

Royal Highland Show

The Royal Highland Show is the Scottish national agricultural show and is presented under the auspices of the Royal Highland Agricultural Society, which was founded in 1784. The first show was held before the end of the eighteenth century. Until 1960 it took place on a different site each year, but, owing to the growing number of entrants, suitable sites became increasingly difficult to find and the show now has a permanent home at Ingliston (adjacent to the Edinburgh Airport) where it is presented in the second half of June (21st–24th June in 1966). It has been attended in recent years by nearly 100,000 visitors. Further details may be obtained from the Secretary, The Royal Highland Agricultural Society, Edinburgh.

Morayshire

BURGHEAD – Burning the Clavie

This is a traditional celebration of disputed origin which takes place on 11th January. One half of a tar barrel is filled with faggots then rolled downhill. As it breaks into fragments bits of the faggots and of the barrel itself are scrambled for by onlookers who regard them as tokens of good luck.

'Pitlochry Festival' by William McLaren,
well-known Scottish artist and illustrator,
who in 1951 designed the very first
Pitlochry Festival brochure

Peebleshire

PEEBLES – Beltane Festival

Beltane was one of the great feasts of the Celtic calendar, celebrated on 1st May, similar in origin to the May Day festivals of south-west England. It is said to derive its name from the pagan god Baal and the Celtic word meaning fire. The custom of washing the face in dew on the top of a hill at sunrise on May Day is still observed at several places, notably at the wishing well at Culloden Moor and at Arthur's Seat in Edinburgh, where a service is held for young people. A number of fairs were established to coincide with Beltane Day. Peebles Beltane Fair was one of the most popular. A royal charter of James VI gave the town the right to hold the fair from 3rd May. The celebrations, which include the crowning of the Beltane Queen on the steps of the parish church and processions with local bands through the streets, have been translated from the original date to a convenient day in June. Further details may be obtained from the Scottish Tourist Board.

Perthshire

PITLOCHRY – The Festival Theatre

Pitlochry's Festival Theatre was sixteen years old in 1966. It is the answer to all those doubting people who thought that good acting does not appeal to holiday makers in the mass. Today anyone who has been to Pitlochry for a holiday is likely to be asked 'What plays have you seen?' rather than 'Did you go to the theatre?' The idea of a dramatic festival at Pitlochry was one which John Stewart evolved during the Second World War. Stewart believed that the many thousands of people who come to the Scottish Highlands for their holidays would welcome a cultural centre in which drama took first place. He was right, as events proved.

Pitlochry was chosen as the geographical centre of Scotland and, more importantly perhaps, because it had a great number of hotels which could accommodate enough people to make a festival theatre an economic proposition. Pitlochry in fact has more than a score of hotels and a large number of boarding-houses and lies in a valley on either side of which the heather moors rise to the Scottish mountains. Today it is famous quite apart from the Festival Theatre as the nearest place to the River Tummel hydro-electric scheme, the man-made Loch Faskally and the famous salmon ladder where in season the young salmon can be observed through under-water windows leaping up the artificial ladder into the higher reaches of the river.

Even so it is probably true that the majority of people who come to Pitlochry do so for the sake of the Festival Theatre. John Stewart's idea became a reality in 1951 at a time when no new building was permitted. Undaunted, he decided to start his venture in a tent, and such was the response that two years later, when a building permit was issued, the idea of the tent theatre was preserved, but the tent was encased in an outer shell of durable material which stands today. The result is that the Pitlochry Festival Theatre is not only unconventional but uncommonly comfortable, far more so than most up-to-date theatres, with far more leg room. It retained its intimate atmosphere – the atmosphere in fact of a tent – untrammelled by the permanent material which has been used to define the original auditorium. That is one reason for its success.

Improvements have been carried out since then by the Pitlochry Festival Society, and the usual amenities of a more conventional theatre added as outbuildings, but the original idea remains intact and the Pitlochry Festival Theatre today is very much as John Stewart envisaged it.

Stewart died in 1957 and was succeeded by Kenneth Ireland, who confirms that the letter-box stage is almost as wide as that of Drury Lane Theatre and that every seat has three inches extra leg room. The back row of the auditorium is little more than forty feet from the stage. This ensures a remarkable degree of intimacy between the audience and the players. The theme of Kenneth Ireland's productions has been 'our stars, our productions' – and a Scottish welcome extended to every visitor. Front of house people wear dress kilts, and greet the public as they enter the theatre.

The success of the Festival Theatre is illustrated by the number of people who have visited it. In the first season the number was slightly less than 35,000, in 1963 it had risen to 60,000, in 1965 to 65,000. That is a remarkable record. It cannot be explained by the number of visitors to Pitlochry, which has varied comparatively little during the period. The reason must lie in the excellence of the dramatic fare which is offered by the festival. The aim is to provide a sensitive interpretation of worth-while plays, ancient and modern, the accent being on fine interpretation and direction rather than on period or authorship.

John Stewart had founded a theatre in Glasgow before he came to Pitlochry. His first festival production was of Maxwell Anderson's *Mary of Scotland*. The repertoire has been enlarged considerably since then; it is now possible to see six plays in a single week's stay in Pitlochry, including such masterpieces as *Murder in the Cathedral*, by T. S. Eliot; *The Amorous Prawn*, by Anthony Kimmins; *The King of Nowhere*, by James Bridie; *The Magistrate*, by Arthur Pinero; and *The Double Inconstancy*, by Marivaux. The international impact of the festival is exemplified by the fact that in one recent year the featured play was

Chekhov's *The Seagull*, produced by Jack Witikka of the Finnish National Theatre.

No one could demand a more varied choice. The Pitlochry festival season has recently been extended with performances beginning in April and ending in October. It has become so much part and parcel of the Scottish scene that visitors are surprised if they find the theatre closed. The success of this tentative adventure into Highland drama has never been fully explained, but there is not the slightest doubt that it is an important part of the cultural life of contemporary Scotland. The drama itself is supported by celebrity concerts on Sundays. Altogether Pitlochry is a remarkable achievement.

Full details of programmes can be obtained from the Secretary, Pitlochry Festival Society, Knockendarroch House, Pitlochry, Perthshire. Incidentally the Pitlochry Highland Games are held early in September, when the accent is on massed bands of pipers as well as on the normal programme of Highland games.

Renfrewshire

GLASGOW – Scottish Motor Exhibition

The forty-fifth Scottish Motor Exhibition, organized by the Scottish Motor Trade Association, was held in Kelvin Hall, Glasgow, in November 1965. It is a biennial event, held in the odd years, and is staged in the Kelvin Hall in November. It is a traders' show, not a manufacturers', its strongest point for visitors from outside Scotland being the commercial vehicles section. However, most makes of private cars are shown on the more than eighty stands devoted to private motoring. As in the case of the London Motor Show, the opening day and one other day, usually the following Wednesday, are special days on which a higher admission fee is charged to enable visitors to see the show at leisure without the distraction of the large crowds which are an inevitable feature of ordinary days.

Roxburghshire

JEDBURGH – The Jedburgh Games

The scene of an annual game between the Uppies, i.e. those born on the north side of the market cross, and the Doonies, i.e. those born on the south side of it. The game is held at Candlemas, 2nd February, and also on Fastern's E'en, the first Tuesday after the new moon after Candlemas.

> 'First comes Candlemas,
> Then the new moon,
> The first Tuesday after
> Is Fastern's E'en.'

The game is played with small leather balls through the streets of the town; the goals are points on the outskirts of the town arbitrarily determined. No doubt tradition is correct in ascribing the origin of the game to some battle between the English and Scots in which the victorious Scots played ball with the severed heads of slain Englishmen.

MELROSE – Melrose Festival

Situated between the picturesque Eildon Hills and the River Tweed, and well known for its seventeenth-century

Historic pageant at Melrose Abbey

'Up Helly Aa' by J. S. Walterson,
a Shetland art teacher whose
gouache painting portrays the
spirit of this festival

market cross which bears the arms of Scotland, as well as for the outstandingly beautiful ruined church of the Cistercian abbey of St Mary's, Melrose is the scene of a historic pageant starting near Midsummer's Day and lasting for three days (23rd–25th June in 1966). The underlying idea of the festival is to recall the historic heritage of Melrose on the sites on which the most important events in its history were enacted. These include the market cross, the suburb of Newstead where there was a pre-historic settlement, and where the masons of Melrose Abbey created the first masonic lodge in the British Commonwealth. Other places visited are Abbotsford, the home of Sir Walter Scott, and the abbey, where the most dramatic part of the pageant takes place.

Selkirkshire

HAWICK, SELKIRK – Common Ridings

These are two of the most colourful and important of the very many traditional ceremonies in the towns of the southern uplands. They owe their origin to the border warfare between England and Scotland in the later Middle Ages. Both commemorate great and tragic events in the story of the town concerned. In both cases the historic episode from which the ridings spring is the battle of Flodden, 9th September 1513, one of the most tragic episodes in Scottish history. King Henry VIII had married his brother's widow, Catharine of Aragon; this Spanish marriage made him an enemy of France. The Scots then, as for centuries before, were allies of France and were involved in what was virtually a war to the death with England. King James IV of Scotland, at the instance of the French king, personally led an army against England as a military diversion while the English King Henry was leading his troops in France. Queen Catharine, acting as regent, dispatched Thomas Howard, Earl of Surrey, with a strong army to meet the Scots. The two forces met at the foot of the Cheviot Hills at a place called Flodden Field, just a fortnight after the English under King Henry had routed the French at the battle of the Spurs. An old ballad gives the position of the two armies:

> The English line stretched east and west
> And southward were their faces set.
> The Scottish northward proudly pressed
> And manfully their foes they met.

Proud and manful the Scots may have been, but the Earl of Surrey placed his army between the Scottish army and their homeland. Without the supplies to advance south and unable to return by the way they had come, the Scots were hemmed in and utterly defeated. Only a handful of the Scottish army escaped slaughter, while King James IV

The Common Riding at Hawick

himself was found next day cut to pieces. Nine thousand Scotsmen were killed, perhaps more, including most of the nobles and the flower of the Scottish youth. Ballads and laments were composed almost without number. 'The Flowers of the Forest are all wede away.' The memory of Flodden is still with Scots people. That is why the Common Ridings of Hawick and Selkirk and some other places have such an important part in Scottish folklore.

At Hawick in 1514, just after the battle of Flodden, the young men – the Callants – defeated a company of English soldiers and captured their banner. This seemed an almost miraculous victory after the tragedy of Flodden. It is one which has been celebrated every year since then at the beginning of June by the Common Riding. It has been identified with the ceremony of riding the marches, or riding round the boundaries of the town – 'redding the marches', a custom dating from the Middle Ages, when it was often necessary to define the boundaries of a town which had been destroyed by fire after an English attack. A cornet (standard-bearer) leads the Callants round the boundaries of the town and the ceremony is followed by parades and band performances in the town centre.

At Selkirk the ceremony is also in commemoration of the time of Flodden, for this town suffered as badly as any other. According to tradition, all but one of the soldiers of the royal burgh were killed in defence of their king, the only survivor returning to the town with a captured English flag. Now the standard-bearer leads more than two hundred riders round the circuit of the town boundaries, and there is a ceremony in the market place commemorating the capture of the English standard. This festival also takes place in June.

There is a Common Riding also at Galashiels about the same time, and at Duns, Langholm and Lauder. The ceremony of riding the marches is carried on regularly in many towns of southern Scotland, including Dumfries, Lanark, Lockerbie, Peebles and Sanquhar. At Duns the ceremony is known as 'riding the bounds'.

Bo'ness Fair

This is an exception to the general rule in southern Scotland that celebrations are derived from the medieval practice of riding the marches or are in memory of a local victory at the time of Flodden. It is one of the most spectacular annual celebrations derived from the Act of Parliament of 1799, which relieved the miners of Bo'ness from their virtual slavery to the owners of the coal-pits. Bo'ness, or in its full form, Borrowstounness, lies about three miles north of Linlithgow. It is an industrial town and coal port on the line of the Roman wall of Antoninus, traces of which remain and are known as Grime's Dyke.

The Common Riding at Galashiels

The celebration in 1799 was a wholly spontaneous and genuine one. The miners in rough formation marched through the narrow streets to Kinneil House, the home of the Duke of Hamilton, who owned most of the pits surrounding the town. They were welcomed by the duke with whisky and food, as they were also at the home of Mr James Cadell, the other pit owner in the neighbourhood. So for the first time the owners and the pit men were united and the celebration or fair became an annual event, in which during the last decades of the nineteenth century other crafts joined, especially the potters, who have always represented an important part of Bo'ness craft tradition.

The modern festival took shape as each craft contributed to the traditional procession examples of its own work – sailing ships and china, miniature kilns and models of coal mines and miners at the pit face. Near the turn of the century the Bo'ness Fair acquired an unenviable reputation for the excessive drinking with which it was associated, but the police commissioners were persuaded to take part in the festivities on the undertaking that moderation would be observed. Since then the fair has provoked little or no criticism and children have been introduced into its programme by the election of a schoolchild as Fair Queen. The traditional element is still clearly evident, but the modern fair or festival consists mainly of colourful processions in which the Fair Queen plays a major part.

The Bo'ness Fair has been held every year this century except during the First and Second World Wars and during the depression years of 1921 to 1926. The miners are still the chief architects of the festival and are responsible for building the triumphal arches through which the queen passes in her procession through the town. Recently seven bands have taken part in the festival programme, playing as they march through the narrow streets of old Bo'ness.

The climax of the celebrations takes place in Glebe Park overlooking the River Forth, where a massed choir of up to three thousand children sings the songs which have been specially written for the event. The fair takes place in July at the beginning of the school holidays. The exact date of this and of the Common Ridings and the riding the marches ceremonies may be obtained from the Scottish Tourist Board, 2 Rutland Place, West End, Edinburgh 1.

Shetland

LERWICK – Up Helly Aa
The northern counties of Scotland and the islands were part of the dominion of the Norse kings until late in the Middle Ages. Sutherland means the 'south land', to distinguish it from the north land of the Orkneys and Caithness. The festival of Up Helly Aa is, as Arthur Robertson (who has done so much to maintain the tradition) says, 'the Shetlander's way of remembering with pride and admiration the way of life of his hardy ancestors, the Vikings. In Viking days the people of the north were in the early stages of their struggle towards civilization. Christianity was gaining ground, but the pagan gods still had a strong hold on the Vikings.'

Up Helly Aa is held in Lerwick, Shetland, on the last Tuesday in January (25th January in 1966). It is linked with the celebration of Yule, which was once accompanied by barbaric sacrificial rites. Up Helly Aa is indeed the final feast day in honour of the pagan god. Today this exciting

The burning of the boat during Up Helly Aa festival

festival is centred on a ceremonial procession of men in Viking dress who march beside a Viking galley in a magnificent torchlight procession to the town square. There the men gather round the ship, throw their torches into its hull and transform it into a fiery furnace, with repeated choruses of the Up Helly Aa song. The ship, a thirty-foot model, is burnt, but dancing and celebrations continue well into the night after the ceremony is over.

According to some accounts, the purpose of the festival is to welcome the return of the sun (the nights are very long in the Shetland Isles in winter) and is possibly a survival of sun worship.

Another possible explanation is that the ceremony represents the 'burning of the boats', an expression in use to this day, symbolizing the decision of these early settlers to stay in the new country in which they have landed without thought of returning to their homeland.

Stirlingshire

STIRLING – Stirling Festival
Historic Stirling, the bulwark of the north commanding the traditional route between the north and south, is dominated by its castle set on a precipitous rock, which has been fortified since the early Middle Ages and is still used as a garrison barracks. Here many Scottish kings held court and the castle changed hands many times in the wars between England and Scotland. Under the early Stuarts Stirling was a second capital and the castle was the sovereign's favourite palace from the time of James I to James VI. That is the historic setting of the Stirling Festival fortnight, held in mid or late May. It was founded in 1959 and has pursued a catholic policy, with concerts and recitals by artistes of international reputation covering a wide range of musical disciplines together with artistic and literary events of equally general appeal.

Most of the concerts are held in the Albert Hall, the art exhibitions in the Smith Art Gallery. The Scottish National Orchestra, the B.B.C. Scottish Orchestra and the Glasgow Theatre Ballet have been welcome visitors at several festivals. Regular features are a concert of popular Scottish music, a Gaelic concert featuring prize-winning amateur soloists and choirs, performances by members of the Scottish Community Drama Association and lectures by authors and poets such as Sir Compton Mackenzie and John Betjeman. Special exhibitions of painting and sculpture are staged in the art gallery and there is an exhibition of photography by the local camera club. Further details may be obtained from the Festival Co-ordinating Office, Municipal Buildings, Stirling.

Dancers in
Connemara costume at
the Galway Oyster Festival

Ireland

Ireland is a country particularly rich in Celtic legend and tradition. Its people, both in Northern Ireland and the Republic, are highly retentive of the folklore handed down to them from medieval times. It is not surprising, therefore, that a great number of festivals are held commemorating the saints and the ancient festivals of spring and harvest thanksgiving. There are, too, a number of historic events, such as the battle of the Boyne, which are marked by celebrations of a more or less traditional character. But Ireland has also kept pace with the modern trends in music, drama and the cinema; some of its cultural festivals have become truly international in scope and attract audiences from every part of Britain and many other countries.

Seaside Festivals in Northern Ireland

Almost every seaside resort in Northern Ireland – from Portstewart and Portrush facing the mouth of Lough Foyle round the coast of Antrim and Down to Bangor and Newcastle – has its special week or fortnight of gala and festival, full details of which can be obtained from the Northern Ireland Tourist Board in Royal Avenue, Belfast, or from the publicity officers of the towns concerned.

The Irish Folk Dance Festival at Bangor in June, the Carnlough Aquatic Festival Week, also in June, the Strangford Lough Regatta Week, and Carnival Week at Ballycastle in July are some which attract a large number of visitors.

One of very special interest is the Prawn Festival of Kilkeel, which has become associated with celebrations of the legendary Kingdom of Mourne. Kilkeel is the traditional capital of the kingdom, and a festival week, generally in June, has been held each year since the Second World War. On some occasions spectacular attractions have included a remarkably realistic 'raid' by Viking warriors, the historic enemies of the Mourne people a thousand years ago. More recently the accent has been on the Kilkeel fishing fleet, and pageantry has been associated with the success of the prawn fisheries, with programmes of traditional songs accompanied by Irish harps. The June festival provides an added reason for visiting one of the loveliest parts of Ireland, where 'the Mountains of Mourne sweep down to the sea' at a time when the hours of sunshine are long and the rainfall less than in other summer months.

Only a few miles from Kilkeel is the pony-trekking centre of Rostrevor and the large and better-known holiday resort of Newcastle under the slopes of Slieve Donard (2,796 ft), the highest mountain in Northern Ireland.

The Cities of Dublin and Cork

Dublin is the capital city of the Republic of Ireland. As such it is the very centre of Irish festival. Cork is the second largest city situated, as Spenser put it, 'on the spreading Lee that like an island fayre encloseth Cork with his divided flood'. It is a cosmopolitan yet still very Irish place, which had its origin in a monastery by the River Lee founded by St Finnbarr not later than the seventh century. It grew up rapidly as a trading centre, first with the Vikings, who appear to have lived peacefully side by side with the monastic settlement, and later with the Anglo-Normans. In the eighteenth century it achieved its greatest prosperity, when its glassware had an international reputation. There is abundant evidence of this prosperity in the really magnificent Georgian merchants' houses and public buildings.

Like Dublin, Cork shared in the cultural life of this period. The opera house, which was destroyed by fire a few years ago, was one of its chief musical and dramatic centres. It is appropriate that this great and interesting city should be the venue of two famous festivals.

Fishing Festivals

The whole of Ireland has fine fishing waters. That is as true of the Republic as it is of Northern Ireland. Everywhere, according to custom, coarse fishing is free, the charges for game fishing reasonable and sea fishing available with boatmen at almost every seaside resort. Brown trout make fine sport in practically every Irish lough and river and grow to exceptional size in many waters, including Lough Neagh and Lough Erne.

Fishing is one of the traditional occupations of Irish people, inevitably in view of the country's long indented coastline and the large variety of fish which can be caught in its rivers and loughs and off its coasts. There are angling competitions at practically every resort in Northern Ireland and the Republic. Some of the best known are the deep sea competition at Kinsale and the fly-fishing competition at Killaloe in May, the sea angling competition at Crosshaven and the trout-trolling competition at Killaloe in July, the open spear-fishing championships at Valentia and the shark-fishing competitions at Kinsale in August. Full details of these and many others can be obtained from the Irish Tourist Board. Information about the special facilities of sea angling at Kinsale can be obtained from the Angling Centre, Kinsale, Co. Cork.

Pilgrimage

Ireland was one of the cradles of Christianity. It suffered no devastating invasion by barbarian peoples after the fall of the Roman Empire. Even the Viking or Norse settlers who founded many towns in Ireland, as they did in England and France, were soon converted, though only after doing a great deal of damage to monastic life in the country districts. Through the length and breadth of the land there are a vast number of visible signs of early Christianity – the artistry of innumerable crosses, the early Christian oratories, the Round Towers which were the strongholds of the early monasteries, the more than 250 ruined abbeys and friaries. This long and virtually unbroken tradition of Christianity makes it natural that Ireland should possess some of the most important places of pilgrimage today, and that hundreds of thousands of people every year should take part in these Christian festivals. Here the spirit, if not the action, is as unselfconscious as when Chaucer described the pilgrims gathering at the Tabard Inn in Southwark on the way to the shrine of St Thomas at Canterbury.

Croagh Patrick, Knock and Lough Derg are national pilgrimages, but there are a great number of other holy places to which pilgrimages have been made by local people from time immemorial on a set day or days. These are known as 'patterns' rather than pilgrimages, or 'turus', which means journeys. The day appointed for the pilgrimage is normally the feast day of the saint associated with the spot, when local people gather together for devotional exercises and traditional prayers. Visitors from outside the neighbourhood are, however, always welcome at these patterns, and some have developed, if not into national pilgrimages, at least into festivals of far wider scope than was the case before the days of tourist travel and easier communication. Some places associated with patterns are of immense historic significance. Others are in regions of exceptional natural beauty. Included with the following festivals and events is a very brief selection from the hundreds of shrines.

Antrim

BELFAST – The Festival of Belfast
Belfast, the capital and administrative centre of Northern Ireland, has long been one of the chief centres of Irish cultural life. The Belfast Philharmonic Society has given concerts with guest artistes for many years, while the theatre has been well represented by the Group Theatre, which has kept alive the tradition of encouraging local talent, presenting many plays by Ulster playwrights, with a preference for those characterizing Ulster life, while the opera house has presented mostly plays from the London stage.

Recently a most important addition has been made to the artistic life of the country by the successful inception of a festival which was first held in 1963 with Sir Tyrone Guthrie as its patron, and Michael and Anthony Emmerson as its directors. This festival is centred on the Queen's University of Belfast and is generally held in November.

The Queen's University, one of the most distinctive buildings in a city famous for its Victorian architecture, was founded in 1845 and was designed in the Tudor style by Lanyon. It formed part of the Royal University, which included the Queen's Colleges at Galway and Cork, but was separately incorporated in 1909. It forms an attractive background to the greater part of the festival programmes. Much of the work to make the event a permanent part of Belfast life has been done by university staff.

The aim of the festival is to encourage interest in the widest possible range of music, drama and visual art, with special reference to the development of Irish talent, both in composition and performance. So much is compressed into little more than a fortnight that the authorities can boast with good reason that Friends of the Festival can be occupied with festive events from 11 a.m. until 3 a.m. every day. In a programme of a typical year, e.g. Festival '65, there were lectures by Irish writers every morning, films, music recitals and poetry readings at lunch time, and lectures on Irish history in the afternoon. The evenings are devoted to music, drama, ballet and opera, with late night programmes of music, films and revues. Folk song and jazz sessions take their place side by side with classical music.

It is difficult to summarize the enormous scope of the work presented. Festival '65 opened with a performance of Britten's *War Requiem* by the Ulster Singers and the

Studio Symphony Orchestra. On the last night the Grosvenor Choral Society gave the Fauré *Requiem*. One memorable concert was that in which the Radio Eireann Symphony Orchestra joined with the Belfast Philharmonic Society in a programme including the First and Ninth Symphonies of Beethoven. The City of Belfast Orchestra played a symphony by Raymond Warren specially commissioned by Festival '65.

Organ recitals were given by Allan Wicks, the organist of Canterbury Cathedral, and by Kamiel d'Hooghe of Bruges Cathedral. For contrast the Alex Welsh Band and the Ian Campbell Folk Group were two of the star attractions in the jazz and folk song section. The London Festival Ballet performed *Peer Gynt* and excerpts from *Swan Lake* and *The Sleeping Beauty*, while contemporary ballet was produced by the Belfast Modern Dance Group.

A number of exhibitions by Irish artists was also arranged in conjunction with lectures by Irish writers on literature and history. A new play by John Hamilton was performed, and the National Theatre was one of several distinguished visiting companies.

This festival certainly presents something for every taste, with forty classical concerts and recitals, eight folk song concerts, seven jazz concerts, fifteen feature films, five operas, five plays and eight ballets. Further details can be obtained from the Festival Publicity Manager, 40 Fitzwilliam Street, Belfast 9.

Other Belfast Events

Although a mainly industrial and commercial town, Belfast is also the centre of a most important and thriving agriculture. Industry and agriculture come together in the annual show and industrial exhibition staged by the Royal Ulster Agricultural Society in the last week of May. The society was founded nearly 150 years ago. The 1966 show is its ninety-eighth annual one. It is held at the society's permanent showground, Balmoral, within a few minutes' ride of the city centre. It is Northern Ireland's most important exhibition of livestock, implements and machinery. The programme includes many sporting events, including show jumping, and is designed to be of general rather than purely agricultural or industrial interest.

Full details may be obtained from the Secretary and Manager, The King's Hall, Balmoral, Belfast 9. The occasion of the Lord Mayor's Show towards the end of May, and that of the Battle of the Boyne Celebrations on 12th July (described overleaf), when historic pageants and demonstrations are presented are other times when the city has a special air of festival. Details of these and other events can be obtained from the Tourist Information Centre, 6 Royal Avenue, Belfast 1.

The prize-winning float in the Lord Mayor's Show at Belfast

One of the banners in the 12th July procession Battle of the Boyne Celebrations

Troops marching through the streets of Belfast during the Battle of the Boyne Celebrations.

The Battle of the Boyne Celebrations

The very words 'Battle of the Boyne' strike a chord in thousands of Ulstermen's hearts. They typify vindication of their defiance of a deposed king who attempted to quell them with the help of foreign armies. The celebrations of this event have become the most colourful annual festivals in Northern Ireland. To appreciate their significance it is necessary to know something of the history of the northern counties at the end of the seventeenth century.

With James II on the throne of England the whole country was racked by religious prejudices; the Protestants of Ulster never more bitter in their fear of the Roman Catholicism of the south. Their fear was probably real enough, for no support was likely to be forthcoming for a Protestant minority from a king who had Roman sympathies. In the last year of his reign James turned to the Irish Catholics and with the help of the Earl of Tyrconnell raised a force known as the Irish Guards. The raising of

the guards was the spark which fired the 'Glorious Revolution'. James fled to France, but made a final bid for the throne by making his base in Ireland, depending on Tyrconnell's guards and the help of troops and materials provided by the French King Louis XIV. It looked as if it would be an easy victory in Ireland, since the Earl of Tyrconnell had captured all the major Protestant strongholds in the north except Derry and Enniskillen. It assuredly would have been had not Derry refused to capitulate.

By then William of Orange was firmly on the throne of England and dealt with the situation with remarkable promptness. He landed at Carrickfergus late in June 1690 with an army of more than thirty thousand men, and met James with a mixed force of twenty-five thousand French and Irish troops at the line of the River Boyne on 1st July, inflicting a defeat which, although it was not decisive, proved the turning of the tide and led inevitably to the disruption of the Jacobean army and the release of Britain and Ireland from absolute monarchy. The battle of the Boyne took place on 1st July, but is celebrated on 12th July. That is because it was designed to commemorate also a far more decisive victory by the forces of William at Aughrim on the 12th, when the French general was killed and his army dispersed.

The celebrations have been organized by the Grand Orange Lodges, which were founded much later but have taken a large part in the social and political development of Northern Ireland and are still as strong as ever. Almost every village in Ulster has its festivities, and in the larger towns, especially in Belfast, Londonderry and Omagh, elaborate processions are staged and the day is made an occasion for historical pageants, concerts and carnivals.

A curious sidelight on the campaign, which ended with the battle of Aughrim, is that the regiments of the Irish Guards raised by Tyrconnell fled with the French troops to France and remained units of the French Army for nearly a century, only returning to service with the British Army in the time of George III after the French Revolution.

Londonderry

LONDONDERRY – Closing the Gates of Derry

This celebration, held on 18th December in the form of an historical pageant, stems from the relief of Derry during the same momentous period of Ulster's history as the battle of the Boyne. Londonderry, its garrison reinforced by numbers of Protestants who had fled behind its walls as other Protestant centres were overthrown by Tyrconnell's Irish army, was invested. The governor of the city, Colonel Lundy, was a Jacobite who would have surrendered without a fight. However, the people of Derry made short shrift of him, throwing him over the walls (according to tradition) and replacing him by a leader of their own choice, the Protestant Rev. George Walker.

But for the prompt action of thirteen apprentices, who have become famous in fiction as well as in history as 'the Apprentices of Derry', Tyrconnell's army might have entered the city unopposed. As the vanguard of the attacking force approached one of the gates which was open to receive them, these thirteen boys slammed and barred the gate, so thwarting Colonel Lundy's attempt to surrender the city. A state of total blockade lasted for 105 days and made this one of the most heroic and disastrous sieges in history. Thousands of the beleaguered garrison died of starvation or disease before the siege was lifted. Some accounts give the number as more than fifty per cent of the people within the walls.

The commander of the besieging army recognized the determination of the defenders and offered terms – far better terms than were usually given to towns surrendering in those circumstances. Yet when the terms were read to a mass meeting of the citizens there was an instantaneous cry of 'No surrender', which remains to this day the motto of the city. A boom had been thrown across the Foyle to prevent the entry of ships bringing food for the besieged, but on the 105th day the relief ship *Mountjoy* broke the boom and docked safely at the Foyle quay. The threat to Londonderry was not removed finally but the worst days of privation were over. The 18th December celebrations are primarily in honour of the thirteen apprentices and are organized by the Association of Apprentice Boys of Derry, the traditional highlight of the ceremonial being the burning of an effigy of the hated Colonel Lundy.

Amazingly the walls of Derry today are virtually intact, and one can walk round a large part of them, re-creating in the mind's eye the watches kept by the beleaguered garrison in those perilous days of the seventeenth century. In the vestibule of the cathedral there is the shell which contained General Hamilton's terms for capitulation and was hurled over the walls, and there is a commemorative tablet to Colonel Baker and Captain Browning, who led the military defence of the city, as well as fascinating documents concerning the siege in the chapter house.

Roaring Meg, a cannon which was used during the siege, stands on one of the seventeenth-century bastions near a tall column in honour of the Rev. Walker, ninety feet high and surmounted by a nineteenth-century statue of the cleric holding a Bible. One can see too the Ferryquay Gate, the entrance to the city closed by the thirteen apprentices. The Apprentice Boys Hall is a permanent memorial to their part in averting surrender.

KILKEEL – The Prawn Festival

This little festival started after the Second World War, as a festival week, culminating in a Viking raid, but soon became closely linked with the Kilkeel fishing fleet.

The programme is variable from year to year. The colour plate depicts King Neptune entering the harbour on board the fishing vessel which had been the winner of the Silver Prawn award. He was welcomed by King Archy I, the High King of Mourne, who presented him with the Freedom of the Kingdom. Like any two kings, they exchanged gifts while maidens played traditional songs on Irish harps. The Kilkeel festival, which happens around June, will bring you to the Kingdom of Mourne whose mountains 'sweep down to the sea'; a kingdom known as 'kindly Mourne', where, if you call at a cottage for a glass of water, they will give you a cup of milk, and where people still look up when an aeroplane flies overhead. Kilkeel is forty-five miles from Belfast, eighty miles from Dublin and has a few small hotels and boarding-houses. It offers a visitor some of the finest scenery in Ireland.

Full details may be obtained from the Kingdom of Mourne Development Association, Kilkeel, Co. Down.

Cork

CORK – International Choral Festival

The International Choral Festival is held in the second half of May and lasts for a week. It is a competitive choral festival which attracts entries from some of the leading choirs in many countries of the world.

International Film Festival

This is held in the second part of September. The tenth International Film Festival was held in 1965 and consolidated the growing reputation of one of the more recent but certainly not the more austere of the world's film festivals. It has often been criticized as coming too late in the season to receive entries of the most worth-while films which may already have received awards at other festivals. Experience has not justified the criticism. In general interest, if this can be judged by attendance, Cork festival compares with any.

The festival policy, apart from the showing and judging of films, is to be friendly in the Irish manner. Facilities are provided for all interested in films and in their making to meet producers, directors and stars. The accent at this, as at all other international festivals, is on the giving of awards to films which show exceptional techniques or direction or especially fine acting rather than to those which are necessarily box-office successes. Further details of this and the International Choral Festival may be obtained from the Irish Tourist Board, Dublin 2, Ireland.

LOUGH GOUGANE BARRA – Pattern

This lough, the source of the River Lee, is magnificently set in the midst of mountains which rise precipitously from its banks on three sides to a height of nearly two thousand feet. St Finnbarr, who drowned in the lough the one dragon which had escaped the destruction of noxious beasts by St Patrick, had his oratory on an island now linked with the shore by a causeway. Here a modern oratory has been built, and the journey to the holy site is on the Sunday after 25th September, the Feast of St Finnbarr.

Donegal

LOUGH DERG – Pilgrimage

Station Island, on Lough Derg, is one of Christendom's most important places of pilgrimage. This little island set in its lough among the thinly peopled moors of County Donegal is the scene of St Patrick's vision of purgatory. One of the legends associated with it is that the evil spirits which had been banished from Ireland by St Patrick took refuge in a cave on the island, but were driven thence by the saint's prayer. It is likely that this belief inspired Dante's *Divine Comedy*. The pilgrimage was well established by the middle of the twelfth century and probably began hundreds of years before that. In spite of many efforts to suppress it, it has continued without a break for the last eight hundred years, and during the later Middle Ages was counted one of the most important in Christendom. Then most who came to Lough Derg were from Europe, and long lists of pilgrims, many wealthy and politically significant figures, are preserved. It is a token of the high place which it held that Station Island appears on several maps of the sixteenth and seventeenth centuries as the focal point of Ireland.

Today the season during which pilgrims are welcomed extends from June to mid August. In these months visitors are numbered in hundreds of thousands and, though the majority are Irish, many also come from Great Britain and from countries farther afield. It is stressed that the nature of the pilgrimage is penitential, one of the most severe in all Christendom. A minimum of three days' residence on the island is commonly imposed and the programme includes fasting, continuous prayer and perambulation of the island. Thousands who share in the experience say that the reward is a complete spiritual renewal. Pilgrims individually or in parties can travel to the island any time during the season, driving to the lough side, leaving their car in the car park and completing the journey by a regular boat service. The first the pilgrim sees of Station Island is an utter surprise, for the buildings on it cover it so nearly completely that they appear to be floating on the water. The most prominent one is a church in the Byzantine

Station Island, Lough Derg

style of architecture. Inquiries must be made to the Reverend Prior, Lough Derg, Pettigo, County Donegal.

GLENCOLUMBKILLE – Pattern

Here was the principal monastery of St Columba (Columcille) and his disciples, in what is still one of the most remote places in Ireland, nestling under Glen Head, a promontory jutting out into the Atlantic, and near the magnificent precipice of Slieve League (1,972 ft), the highest cliff in Europe.

Pilgrims to Glencolumbkille visit the many links with the monastery, which was founded in the sixth century, including the House of St Columba, an oratory of rough-hewn stone, and several wayside crosses around the modern village. The official day of the pattern is the Sunday following the Feast of St Columba.

Dublin

DUBLIN – Festival Time

As a cultural centre Dublin stands in the same relation to the Republic as Belfast does to Northern Ireland. Its modern artistic tradition springs from the eighteenth century when much of the present city was built. Its Georgian atmosphere is indeed what gives Dublin its special appeal for many visitors – that and the unhurried tempo of life even in a city which is a thriving commercial centre with a growing number of industries.

Its most famous theatre, the Gate, is one of the halls of the Rotunda Assembly Rooms which were designed by the famous Georgian architect Cassels in 1750 and enlarged by Richard Johnson later in the century. The equally famous Abbey Theatre is the home of the Irish National Players. It has a history as long as that of the Gate, but unhappily the theatre in Abbey Street from which it takes its name was burnt down in 1951, when it was re-established in the Queen's Theatre. But all its associations are deeply rooted in the Georgian traditions of Abbey Street where the Custom House by James Gandon is the greatest masterpiece of Dublin's eighteenth-century architecture.

The Dublin Theatre Festival, usually held at the end of September, is the highlight of the Irish theatre calendar. The keystone of the festival policy is outstanding merit, whether that merit is Irish or not. One of its main features,

Jumping competition at the Dublin Horse Show

'Kilkeel Festival' by Barry Fantoni,
a London-born teacher at the Croydon
School of Art. On his first visit
to the Kingdom of Mourne he was
made an honorary subject by
general acclamation

however, is that it is a shop window for the work of modern Irish playwrights. The festival club is designed to bring together authors, players and the public, and has proved a remarkably successful innovation. Celebrity parties and midnight matinées are always featured.

The Dublin Grand Opera Season in the latter part of May at the Gaiety Theatre is a popular feature in the city's spring programme. The summer schools of University College and Trinity College in July have equally played for long a significant part in the city's cultural life. They are designed as vacation courses for all interested in Ireland from the political, social or artistic viewpoint, and apart from formal lectures and discussions include visits to concerts and theatre productions. Full details and programmes can be obtained from the Irish Tourist Board, Dublin 2, Ireland.

The Dublin Horse Show

This show, one of the chief social and sporting events of the year, is held in early August at Ballsbridge. It attracts regularly more than 100,000 people from many countries and in many years entries of more than a thousand horses. The finest of Ireland's bloodstock are entered for the show. One does not, however, need a professional interest to appreciate the attractions of this show of the Royal Dublin Society which, like so much else in Dublin, is of eighteenth-century foundation. There are military and civilian jumping contests on each of the five days. The principal event is the international team jumping contest for teams of four horses for the Aga Khan Challenge Trophy, and there are other international jumping events, children's jumping competitions and general competitions for civilians. The grand parade of prize-winning horses and ponies is a feature of the show. The auction sale of horses and ponies in the bloodstock paddock brings many buyers from all over the world. Musical programmes are given each day by army bands. Seats may be reserved either for the whole period of the show or on a daily basis. Full particulars and forms of application for reserved tickets may be obtained from the Royal Dublin Society, Ballsbridge, Dublin 4.

The Dublin Flower Show

The Royal Horticultural Society of Ireland's flower show is staged at Ballsbridge at the same time as the horse show and makes a wonderfully colourful and interesting display, for this is the most important flower show in a country justly famous for its horitulture.

Spring Show

The Dublin Spring Show and Industries Fair, held early in May, vies in interest and popularity with the August horse show. It too is staged by the Royal Dublin Society

All-Ireland senior football final at Croke Park

at Ballsbridge, and is in effect a shop window of Irish agriculture and industry. It features all types of farm animals, poultry and dairy produce. There is also a comprehensive display of trade exhibits featuring the mechanization which is revolutionizing Irish agriculture. For more general interest it presents a daily programme of horse-jumping events.

Gaelic Games

Dublin is the venue for the all-Ireland finals of the Gaelic Games. The Gaelic Athletic Association is responsible for the management of the three national games – hurling, football and handball. The last-named is a game for single opponents or pairs, but hurling and football are field spectator games of great interest. Their season lasts from early spring until Christmas and there are between three hundred and four hundred fixtures all over the country at most week-ends. The all-Ireland finals are both held at Croke Park, Dublin, the hurling final usually early in September, the football final near the end of September.

Hurling has been described as the fastest field game in the world. It is played with hurleys – ash blades about

hip high not at first glance unlike a hockey stick. The ball used is small and leather-covered and can be struck with the hurley either on the ground or in the air. It travels with great speed and is often difficult for players and spectators to follow.

Gaelic football has rules which differ largely both from those of Rugby football and of the Association game. Players may catch the ball and strike it with the hand deliberately as well as kick it. In other respects it is more akin to the Association game than to Rugby.

The days on which both finals are held are true festivals in Dublin. The crowds which gather have to be seen to be believed. Many come up from the country by excursion coach or train for a day out without much hope of seeing the game. This is Ireland at its most boisterous and memorable. But the crowd is at least as well behaved as an English cup final crowd. Dates of both matches, which vary slightly from year to year, may be obtained from any Irish Tourist Office.

Galway

GALWAY – Oyster Festival

This city is an important fishing port and also one of Ireland's finest angling centres, especially for salmon in the Galway River, a short stream which links Lough Corrib with the sea. It stages periodic coarse, game and sea fishing championships. It is a town of narrow quaint streets, especially near the harbour, where the fishermen's quarter is known as the Claddagh. The Feast of St John used to be the great festival of the Claddagh, but this has been celebrated in recent years only by the lighting of a bonfire. More recently the oyster fisheries of Galway Bay have become Galway's most celebrated sea industry, and the Oyster Festival, which is held in mid September, attracts an increasing number of visitors. A varied programme of events is arranged for a full-scale ten-day festival. These include a sea angling competition, a championship golf tournament, a contract bridge tournament, car trials, fashion shows, an elaborate pageant, ballad-singing and dancing exhibitions. The traditional part of the festival takes place on the final day, when the mayor welcomes Neptunia and her court, and the first oyster of the year is opened with due ceremony at Clarinbridge, with a tent lunch of sea food supplied to visitors. The day ends with a grand festival banquet. Further details may be obtained from the Irish Tourist Board, Dublin 2, Ireland.

Kerry

TRALEE – Festival of Kerry

The last days of August and the first days of September find Tralee, the capital of Kerry, in festival spirit. The

Queen Neptunia and her court at the Galway Oyster Festival

The Chairman of the Festival of Kerry presents a rose to the Dublin area Rose   *Photo: Tony O'Malley*

Kerry festival was founded as a point of contact for Kerry-men who had settled in other parts of the world. As more and more visitors have come to Ireland so the festival has become less local in its import. It has served to bring home to many people the fact that Tralee is a good centre for exploring the beautiful countryside of Kerry, and is within easy reach of the Lakes of Killarney and MacGillycuddy's Reeks and the fine sands of Ballybunion.

The festival includes the selection of the Rose of Tralee, the Festival Queen of the Year, a meeting at the nearby racecourse and a number of other sporting and social fixtures. The Folk Festival of Ireland featuring groups from many lands has proved a popular innovation.

The town is elaborately decorated with thousands of rosebuds donated by Irish and European rose growers. Twenty-foot-high heraldic pennants carry the crests of historic Kerry clans; thirty-five thousand multicoloured lights are switched on at dusk.

Louth

FAUGHART – Pattern
Faughart is probably the birthplace in the fifth century of St Brigid, the Patroness of Ireland. A shrine to the saint with a Lourdes grotto was opened in 1933 and contains a portion of the head of St Brigid. Faughart has become a much frequented place of pilgrimage on every day of the year, but the official date of the pattern is the first Sunday in July. There is a famous shrine and holy well sacred to

St Brigid (almost opposite the Tully Japanese Gardens) near Kildare, where the saint founded the first monastery in 490, and where in the church that has become Kildare Cathedral St Brigid's fire burned without a break from the early Middle Ages until the Reformation.

Mayo

WESTPORT – The Westport Festival
This sea angling festival, held for three days in the second half of June, is an exceptionally popular one, partly no doubt because of its friendly nature and well-organized programme, partly because of the beauty of the coast on which Westport is situated. Here on the shores of island-dotted Clew Bay, so full of islands that at a distance there seems to be more land than water, and surrounded by an imposing half-circle of mountains, Westport looks across the sea to the Curraun Peninsula and Achill Island. It is a little town with a number of small hotels and boarding-houses set around its handsome square and along the tree-fringed Mall which gives it a faintly continental air, with the Marquess of Sligo's Westport House, a Georgian mansion by Richard Cassels and James Wyatt, an additional centre of interest when it is open to the public between May and September.

As for the angling, in one year fishing teams and individual entries from twelve countries drew fourteen species of fish from the bay. An entry of 150 anglers is relatively disappointing, while in one recent year the total catch for

'Westport Festival' by J. C. Farrer,
who lives in Dublin and is a keen
angler himself

Pilgrims on the slopes of Croagh Patrick

three days was 13,302 lb. As so often, Thackeray's words in his *Irish Sketch Book*, nearly a century and a half ago, ring as true today as they did when they were written. 'If Westport were on the Mediterranean English travellers would flock to it by hundreds.' Full details of this festival may be obtained from the Sea Angling Festival Secretary, Westport, Co. Mayo.

CROAGH PATRICK – Pilgrimage

Croagh Patrick (2,510 ft), the Rick of St Patrick, is Ireland's holy mountain. It rises in isolation above Clew Bay in a graceful cone which once seen is never forgotten, a well-loved landmark all over the Plains of Mayo and as far away as Achill Island. A rough track winds round its shoulder to the summit plateau from a point on the Westport–Louisburgh road about six miles from Westport. On the summit there is a chapel, which in clear weather can be picked out with the naked eye from twenty miles away. Here St Patrick spent the forty days of Lent in the year 441 in prayer and fasting. According to ancient belief the saint banished every snake and every other noxious reptile from the land during his vigil. Certainly it is a scientific fact that today Ireland is one of the few countries without snakes of any kind.

The first pilgrimage to the holy mountain was in the Middle Ages. For more than a thousand years it has been one of the most frequented pilgrimages in the country, and with improved methods of transport has attracted more and more people until now nearly 100,000 make the ascent to the summit on the last Sunday in July. Traditionally the pilgrims walk barefooted, though in practice tradition

nowadays is not rigorously followed. Even so, many elderly people who make the journey take many hours to reach the summit, a hard climb for a robust walker. It is an unforgettable experience to take part in this pilgrimage. Many make the ascent during Saturday night or very early on Sunday morning, so that they are at the summit soon after sunrise. Priests celebrate a succession of masses and pilgrims carry out prescribed devotional exercises.

KNOCK – Pilgrimage

The pilgrimage to the Shrine of Our Lady at Knock is one of the most recent and also one of the most popular (if that is the right word) of the sacred festivals in the Irish calendar. Knock is a small village approximately six miles from Ballyhaunis, seven miles from Claremorris. It is set on high ground overlooking the rich pastoral country of the Plains of Mayo. Little was heard of it until the last decades of the nineteenth century. On 21st August 1879 an apparition of the Blessed Virgin lasting two hours at the gabled end of the church was witnessed by a number of people. Our Lady was seen clothed in white garments, supported by St Joseph and St John the Evangelist, with an altar on which there were a lamb and a cross. News of the vision spread rapidly and people began to flock to the scene in large numbers. Miraculous cures were vouched for and the journey to the shrine was soon recognized as a national pilgrimage.

The season lasts from the end of April until the end of October. In a recent year the number coming as pilgrims to the shrine has approached a quarter of a million. Individuals may and do make the pilgrimage on any day of the week, and there are organized pilgrimages every Sunday. Public devotions are held on Sundays, Thursdays

Pilgrimage to Knock

Visitors to the pattern at Our Lady's Island, Co. Wexford

and on all feast days of the Blessed Virgin. The village has been transformed. Throughout the summer it is thronged and the streets are lined with stalls selling rosaries and souvenirs. Details can be obtained from the Knock Shrine Bureau, 29 South Anne Street, Dublin.

Offaly

CLONMACNOISE – Pattern

The most important of Ireland's great monastic settlements was Clonmacnoise, with a famous cathedral founded by St Kieran in the sixth century. Today, though only ruins of the cathedral and several other churches together with two round towers survive beside the broad stream of the Shannon near Athlone, it remains one of the most sacred as well as interesting places in Ireland. The official pattern is on the Feast of St Kieran, 9th September. It is also celebrated on the following Sunday.

Wexford

WEXFORD – Opera Festival

This festival is held in the last week of October. Its setting is an ancient town which was founded by the Viking invaders in the ninth century and flourished until the middle of the seventeenth century, when during Cromwell's invasion it was taken by storm, its defenders put to the sword, its churches as well as its walls badly damaged. Yet Wexford retains one of its town gates, known as the

Westgate Tower, with a nineteenth-century church beside it on the site of the meeting between Anglo-Normans and Irish in 1169, when the first pact between the two nations was signed.

The standard of music and operatic performance at the festival has achieved a high reputation in the relatively short time since the festival was founded in 1951. Little-known operas are always included in the programmes. In a single festival Massenet's *Don Quichotte* and Mozart's *La Finta Giardiniera* were performed for the first time in Ireland, the former produced by Carl Ebert, of Glyndebourne fame. In addition musical programmes are staged with orchestral concerts, celebrity recitals and art exhibitions. A festival club serves the same purpose here as the similar one at the Dublin Theatre Festival. Fringe events include mumming performances, a hurling match, a barbecue, a late night revue and a festival ball. Further details and programmes may be obtained from the Opera Festival Secretary, Wexford, Co. Wexford.

OUR LADY'S ISLAND – Pattern

This is not strictly an island but rather a peninsula in the Island Lough, a narrow sea inlet or lagoon three miles long. It is the site of an early monastery, close to a Norman castle of which substantial fragments remain, including a 'leaning tower'. The pattern to Our Lady's Island, which invariably attracts very large crowds, is held on the Feast of the Assumption, 15th August.

The Festival Calendar 12

January

LONDON	Camping and Outdoor Life Exhibition, Olympia, first week
LONDON	International Boat Show, Earls Court, first fortnight
TWICKENHAM	University Rugby Football Match, first week
HAXEY	Haxey Hood Game, 6th
CHICHESTER	Plough Sunday Celebration, Sunday after Twelfth Night
EXETER	Plough Sunday Celebration, Sunday after Twelfth Night
BURY ST EDMUNDS	Cake and Ale Ceremony, Monday after Twelfth Night
BURGHEAD	Burning of the Clavie, 11th
CARHAMPTON	Wassailing the Trees, 17th
AYR	And elsewhere, Burns Nicht Celebrations, 25th
LERWICK, SHETLANDS	Up Helly Aa, last Tuesday of month
LONDON	King Charles I Commemoration, 30th

February

LONDON	Cruft's Dog Show, Olympia, early in month
ST IVES	Hurling the Silver Ball, Monday following first Sunday of month
ST COLUMB	Hurling the Silver Ball, Shrove Tuesday
SEDGEFIELD	Shrovetide Football, Shrove Tuesday
ASHBOURNE	Shrovetide Football, Shrove Tuesday
OLNEY	Pancake Race, Shrove Tuesday

March

LONDON	Ideal Home Exhibition, Olympia, throughout month
TICHBORNE	Dole Ceremony, 25th
WEMBLEY	All England Badminton Championships, last week
LONDON	Putney to Mortlake, Tideway Head of River Race, Saturday before next item
LONDON	Putney to Mortlake, University Boat Race, last Saturday, or first in April

April

LONDON	Westminster Abbey, Royal Maundy Presentations, Thursday before Easter
TISSINGTON	Well Dressing, Thursday before Easter
DUNSTABLE	Orange Rolling, Good Friday
BIDDENDEN	Dole, Easter Sunday
LONDON	Easter Parade, Battersea Park, Easter Sunday
HALLATON	Hare Pie Scramble, Easter Monday
PRESTON	Pace Egging, Easter Monday
MIDGLEY	Pace Egg Play, Easter Monday
STRATFORD-ON-AVON	Shakespeare's Birthday Celebrations, 23rd

HUNGERFORD	Hocktide Celebration, second Tuesday after Easter
STRATFORD-ON-AVON	Shakespeare Festival, second part of month
PITLOCHRY	Theatre Festival, second part of month
BOLTON	Music Festival, last weeks
BIRMINGHAM	Spring Festival, last fortnight
EDINBURGH	Royal Scottish Academy Exhibition, second part of month
SOUTHEND-ON-SEA	Spring Flower Festival, last week
WEMBLEY	F.A. Cup Final, Saturday at end of month or early May
BADMINTON	Horse Trials, dates vary

May

STRATFORD-ON-AVON	Shakespeare Festival, throughout month
PITLOCHRY	Theatre Festival, throughout month
LONDON	Royal Academy Summer Exhibition, throughout month
EDINBURGH	Royal Scottish Academy Exhibition, throughout month
BOLTON	Music Festival, first week
BEVERLEY	St John of Beverley Festival, first week
TILFORD	Festival of Music, first half of month
SAFFRON WALDEN	Festival, first half of month
OXFORD	May Morning Carols at Magdalen College, 1st
MINEHEAD	Hobby-horse Festival, May Day and following two days
PADSTOW	Hobby-horse Festival, May Day
GAWTHORNE	May Festival, first week
ABINGDON	St Mark's Fair, 3rd
HELSTON	Furry Dance, 8th
ELSTOW	Maypole Celebrations, first half of month
DUBLIN	Spring Show, first week
LONDON	Chelsea Flower Show, last week
SPALDING	Flower Parade, Saturday early in month
LONDON	White City, Oxford and Cambridge University Sports, early in month
WEMBLEY	Rugby League Cup Final, Saturday early in month
WINDSOR	Royal Horse Show, second week
ABBOTSBURY	Garland Day, 13th
BROMSGROVE	The Bromsgrove Festival, middle of month
LONDON	Chelsea, Spring Antiques Fair, first part of month
KENDAL	Lake District Festival, second half of month
STIRLING	Stirling Festival, second part of month
CORK	International Choral Festival, second half of month
DUBLIN	Grand Opera Season, last weeks
RYE	Scrambling for hot pennies, 23rd
LONDON	Westminster, start, Stock Exchange Walk, third Saturday
CHICHESTER	The Chichester Festival, last week
NORWICH AND NORFOLK	Triennial Festival, last week
ULSTER	Royal Ulster Show, Belfast, last week
HASTINGS	Blessing the Sea ceremony, 26th
CASTLETON	Garland Day, 29th
WISHFORD	Grovely Procession, 29th
WEMBLEY	Ice Skating Championships, last week
PORTREE	Skye Week, last week of month

June

STRATFORD-ON-AVON	Shakespeare Festival, throughout month
CHICHESTER	The Chichester Festival, throughout month
GLYNDEBOURNE	Festival Opera, throughout month

PITLOCHRY	Theatre Festival, throughout month
SELBY	The Selby Festival, triennially 1968, 1971 and so on
MONTROSE	Montrose Festival, first part of month
WALES	Urdd National Eisteddfod, first week
GARTHEWIN	Drama Festival, first part of month
LONDON	Royal Academy Summer Exhibition, throughout month
EDINBURGH	Royal Scottish Academy Exhibition, throughout month
CANTERBURY	Friends of the Cathedral Festival, date varies
PEEBLES	Beltane Festival, date varies
BROADSTAIRS	Dickens Festival, date varies
WYE	Stour Festival of Music and Painting, Kent, first week
HAWICK	Common Riding, first part of month
SELKIRK	Common Riding, first part of month
EPSOM	Derby Day, Wednesday early in month
HARPENDEN	Highland Gathering, first or second Saturday
CAERPHILLY	Arts Festival, Whit week
LICHFIELD	Greenhill Bower, Whit Monday
DUNMOW	Flitch Trial, Whit Monday
BIRDLIP HILL	Cheese Rolling, Whit Monday
CHIPPING CAMPDEN	Scuttlebrook Wake, Saturday after Whitsun
LONDON	White City, British Games, Whit Saturday and Monday
LONDON	Trooping the Colour, second Saturday
RICHMOND	Royal Horse Show, middle of month
BATH	Bath Festival, middle of month
WOLVERHAMPTON	Festival of Music, second part of month
DAWLISH	Arts Festival, last fortnight
READING	Summer Festival of the Arts, second part of month
ALDEBURGH	Festival of Music and Arts, second half of month
LLANDAFF	Llandaff Festival, second part of month
YORK	Festival of the Arts and Mystery Plays, last two weeks
CHESTER	Miracle Plays, last week, 1967, 1972
HARROGATE	Festival of Music, last week
SHEFFIELD	Sheffield Festival, last week
EDINBURGH	Royal Highland Show, second part of month
WIMBLEDON	All England Lawn Tennis Championships, last two weeks
ABINGDON	St Edmund's Fair, Saturday nearest to 20th
STONEHENGE	Midsummer Druid Festival, 24th
MELROSE	Melrose Festival, about Midsummer's Day
TIDESWELL	Well Dressing, last Saturday
BANGOR	Irish Folk Dance Festival, date varies
KILKEEL	Irish Prawn Festival, date varies
WESTPORT	Irish Sea Angling Festival, second half of month

July

STRATFORD-ON-AVON	Shakespeare Festival, throughout month
CHICHESTER	The Chichester Festival, throughout month
GLYNDEBOURNE	Festival Opera, throughout month
PITLOCHRY	Theatre Festival, throughout month
KESWICK	Theatre Festival, throughout month
NEATH	Craig-y-Nos Opera Festival, first part of month
LONDON	Royal Academy Summer Exhibition, throughout month
EDINBURGH	Royal Scottish Academy Exhibition, throughout month
CHELTENHAM	The Cheltenham Festival, first half of month
CHESTER	Miracle Plays, first week 1967, 1972

YORK	Minster Diocesan Musical Festival, first Saturday
LUDLOW	Summer Festival, first two weeks
ISLE OF MAN	Tynwald Ceremony, 5th
ISLE OF MAN	Peel Viking Festival, first week
BUXTON	Wells Dressing Ceremony, first part of month
BELPER	Well Dressing, first week
ROCHESTER	Admiralty Court, first Saturday
HENLEY	Royal Regatta, first week
LONDON	W.A.A.A. Championships, White City, first week
LONDON	A.A.A. Championships, White City, second week
EXETER	Lammas Fair, Tuesday before the third Wednesday
KINGSBRIDGE	July Fair, middle of month
BELFAST	Battle of the Boyne Celebrations, Londonderry and elsewhere, 12th
LLANGOLLEN	International Music Eisteddfod, second week
LONDON	The City of London Festival, middle of month
BEXHILL-ON-SEA	Festival of Music, second part of month
BROADSTAIRS	Festival of Music, second week
BUXTON	Festival of Music, middle of month
CAMBRIDGE	Cambridge Festival, last two weeks
HASLEMERE	Haslemere Festival, middle of month
CANTERBURY	King's Week Festival, third week
KING'S LYNN	Festival of Music and the Arts, last week
WINCHESTER	Southern Cathedrals Festival, also in turn at Salisbury and Chichester, last week
BLITHFIELD HALL	Shakespeare Festival, last week
BUILTH WELLS	Royal Welsh Agricultural Show, third week
LONDON	Royal International Horse Show, White City, latter part of month
LONDON	Royal Tournament, Earls Court, latter part of month
TWEEDMOUTH	The Tweedmouth Feast, third week
BO'NESS	Bo'ness Fair, last week
ST HELIER	Battle of Flowers, Jersey, last Thursday
WESTPORT	Croagh Patrick Pilgrimage, County Mayo, last Sunday
SIDMOUTH	Folk Festival, one week, last days of month and first days in August
HINTLESHAM	Summer Festival, last three weeks

August

STRATFORD-ON-AVON	Shakespeare Festival, throughout month
CHICHESTER	The Chichester Festival, throughout month
PITLOCHRY	Festival Theatre, throughout month
KESWICK	Theatre Festival, throughout month
LONDON	Royal Academy Summer Exhibition, first part of month
EDINBURGH	Royal Scottish Academy Exhibition, first week
WALES	Royal National Eisteddfod, various centres, first week
CANTERBURY	Cricket Week, first week
DUBLIN	Horse Show, first week
LONDON	Serpentine Regatta, first week
LONDON BRIDGE	Doggett's Coat and Badge Race, first of month or nearest convenient day
RIPON	Feast of St Wilfrid, first Saturday
HARROGATE	Festival of Arts and Science, middle of month
LONDON	International Sports Festival and Exhibition, Crystal Palace, middle of month
CARDIFF	Military Tattoo, middle of month
CILGERRAN	Coracle Week, middle of month
GRASMERE	Old English Games, middle of month
HYTHE	Venetian Festival, middle of month
INVERCAULD	Drama Festival, middle of month

EDINBURGH	International Festival, second part of month
EDINBURGH	International Film Festival, second part of month
EDINBURGH	Highland Games, third week
CRIEFF	Highland Games, third week
DUNOON	Cowal Highland Gathering, last week
STRATHDON	Lonach Highland Gathering, last week
DURHAM	Twentieth Century Festival, last week
EDINGTON	Music Festival, last week
TRALEE	Festival of Kerry, last week
PETERBOROUGH	Ponies of Britain Show, last week
SOUTHEND-ON-SEA	Illuminations, second part of month
MATLOCK BATH	Illuminations and Venetian Nights Festival, last week-end
BOURTON-ON-THE-WATER	Water Game, Bank Holiday

September

STRATFORD-ON-AVON	Shakespeare Festival, throughout month
CHICHESTER	The Chichester Festival, first week
PITLOCHRY	Theatre Festival, throughout month
KESWICK	Theatre Festival, throughout month
EDINBURGH	International Festival, first weeks
EDINBURGH	International Film Festival, first weeks
RICHMOND	Richmondshire Festival, Yorkshire, first part of month
WORCESTER	Three Choirs Festival, also in turn at Hereford and Gloucester, first week
BRAEMAR	Royal Highland Gathering, 5th
ABOYNE	Highland Games, first week
OBAN	Argyllshire Gathering, middle of month
PITLOCHRY	Highland Games, first half of month
ABBOTS BROMLEY	Horn Dance, Monday following Sunday after 4th
LICHFIELD	Sheriff's Ride, 8th
OXFORD	St Giles Fair, early in month
BARNSTAPLE	St Giles Fair, middle of month
WIDECOMBE	Fair, second Tuesday
WIRKSWORTH	Clipping the Church Ceremony, Sunday after 8th
BIRMINGHAM	Show, first week
BIRMINGHAM	Tattoo, second week
FARNBOROUGH	Flying Display, first full week
GALWAY	Oyster Festival, middle of month
ROCHESTER	Beating the Bounds of the Admiral's Jurisdiction, date varies
PAINSWICK	Clipping the Church Ceremony, Sunday nearest 19th
SCARBOROUGH	Cricket Festival, first part of month
WEMBLEY	Lawn Tennis Professional Indoor Championships, middle of month
BIGGIN HILL	Battle of Britain Day, 15th
LONG MELFORD	Festival of Music, middle of month
CORK	International Film Festival, second half of month
DUBLIN	Theatre Festival, last week
BLACKPOOL	Illuminations, throughout month
SOUTHEND-ON-SEA	Whitebait Festival, last week
SOUTHEND-ON-SEA	Illuminations, throughout month
MATLOCK BATH	Illuminations, throughout month
MATLOCK BATH	Venetian Nights Festival, each week-end
LONDON	International Caravan Exhibition, Earls Court, last week

October

STRATFORD-ON-AVON	Shakespeare Festival, throughout month

CHELTENHAM	Festival of Literature, first half of month
LITTLE MISSENDEN	Festival of Music and the Arts, first week
LLANGEFNI	National Drama Festival, first week
LONDON	Opening of the Law Courts, 1st
BLACKPOOL	Illuminations, throughout month
SOUTHEND-ON-SEA	Illuminations, first half of month
MATLOCK BATH	Illuminations and Venetian Nights Festival, first week-end
NOTTINGHAM	Goose Fair, first Thursday and two following days
STRATFORD-ON-AVON	Mop Fair, 12th
WARWICK	Mop Fair, 12th and following Saturdays
WEMBLEY	Horse of the Year Show, first half of month
LONDON	Autumn Antiques Fair, Chelsea, first part of month
SWANSEA	Festival of Music and the Arts, second week
STROUD	Festival, second part of month
BATH	Bach Festival, latter part of month 1970, 1975
HEXHAM ABBEY	Festival, last two weeks
WEXFORD	Opera Festival, last week
LONDON	International Motor Show, Earls Court, second part of month
COLCHESTER	Oyster Festival, 20th
LONDON	Trafalgar Day Celebrations, 21st and following Sunday

November

STRATFORD-ON-AVON	Shakespeare Festival, throughout month
BELFAST	The Festival of Belfast, during month
LONDON	State Opening of Parliament, first week
EDENBRIDGE	Guy Fawkes Celebrations, 5th
LEWES	Guy Fawkes Celebrations, 5th
RYE	Guy Fawkes Celebrations, 5th
LONDON	Veteran Car Commemorative Run to Brighton, first Sunday
LONDON	Lord Mayor's Show, Saturday after 9th
CAMBRIDGE	Poppy Day Rag, Saturday after 11th
LONDON	Festival of Remembrance, Saturday after 11th
LONDON	International Building Exhibition, Olympia, last two weeks

December

LONDONDERRY	Closing the Gates of Derry, 18th
BROADSTAIRS	Carol Festival, Sunday before Christmas
CAMBRIDGE	Festival of Carols in King's College Chapel, 24th
COVENTRY	Cathedral Carol Service, 24th
ANDOVER	Mumming Play, 24th, 25th and Boxing Day
MARSHFIELD	Mumming Play, Boxing Day
LONDON	St Paul's Cathedral and Trafalgar Square, New Year's Eve Celebrations, 31st
GLASGOW	Dundee, and elsewhere in Scotland, Hogmanay Celebrations, 31st
COMRIE	Torchlight Procession and Community Singing, Perthshire, 31st
STONEHAVEN	Swinging the Fireballs Ceremony, 31st
LONDON	Camping and Outdoor Life Exhibition, Olympia, last week